Essays in Honor of
William A. Paton

WILLIAM A. PATON

Essays in Honor of William A. Paton

Pioneer Accounting Theorist

Edited by
Stephen A. Zeff
Joel Demski
Nicholas Dopuch

Division of Research
Graduate School of Business Administration
The University of Michigan
Ann Arbor, Michigan

Library of Congress Cataloging in Publication Data
Main entry under title:

Essays in honor of William A. Paton.

  Bibliography: p.
  CONTENTS: Greer, H. C. Greer on Paton.—Devine,
C. T. Observations on internal controls.—Solomons,
D. The politicization of accounting.—Bierman, H.,
Jr. [etc.]
    1. Accounting—Addresses, essays, lectures.
2. Paton, William Andrew, 1889–   I. Paton,
William Andrew, 1889–   II. Zeff, Stephen A.
III. Demski, Joel S. IV. Dopuch, Nicholas.
HF5629.E68   657   78-27910
ISBN 0-87712-183-4

Contents

Contributors

STEPHEN A. ZEFF is Professor of Accounting at Rice University.

JOEL S. DEMSKI is Professor of Accounting at Stanford University.

NICHOLAS DOPUCH is Professor of Accounting at the University of Chicago.

HOWARD C. GREER is a retired corporate executive and a former member of the faculty of Ohio State University. He served as president of the American Accounting Association in 1932.

CARL T. DEVINE is Professor Emeritus of Accounting at Florida State University.

DAVID SOLOMONS is Arthur Young Professor of Accounting at the Wharton School of the University of Pennsylvania.

HAROLD BIERMAN, JR. is the Nicholas H. Noyes Professor of Business Administration at Cornell University.

MAURICE MOONITZ is Professor of Accounting at the University of California (Berkeley).

R. J. CHAMBERS is Professor of Accounting at the University of Sydney (Australia).

NORTON M. BEDFORD is Arthur Young Professor of Accounting at the University of Illinois at Urbana-Champaign.

GORDON SHILLINGLAW is Professor of Accounting at Columbia University.

R. LEE BRUMMET is Willard J. Graham Professor of Business Administration at the University of North Carolina at Chapel Hill.

Foreword

Many individuals, organizations, and institutions have benefited directly from William A. Paton's boundless energy, keen mind, and unlimited dedication and enthusiasm for accounting. Foremost among these are the University of Michigan's Graduate School of Business Administration, its accounting faculty, and now the Paton Center for Accounting Education and Research. But no less deserving of mention are his numerous friends outside the University of Michigan, former students, colleagues, and professional acquaintances. Accordingly, we at the University are indeed gratified to see him honored in this book of essays.

To the three editors and nine authors who have joined to make this tribute possible, we express deep appreciation. Truly, William A. Paton is a man of international renown, so respected and affectionately known throughout the academic and professional communities for his perceptive and enduring contributions to accounting theory and practice that all would do him honor.

With his colleagues, Professor Paton has left a legacy—and a trust—of excellence in teaching, research, and professional service to those of us now associated with the University of Michigan Accounting Faculty and the Paton Center. We acknowledge this legacy as a challenge to make our service worthy of his example.

DONALD H. SKADDEN
Chairman, Accounting Faculty and
first Director of the Paton Accounting Center

FLOYD A. BOND
Dean, Graduate School of Business Administration

June 1, 1978

Preface

Since the 1910s, William Andrew Paton has been a potent force in the accounting literature. In the welter of disputation over practices, rules, and conventions, Paton has consistently invoked economic reasoning to counter the heavy hand of accounting tradition. He has continually been concerned with the larger questions of valuation, the measurement of income, and the role of interest in accounting reckonings. To Paton, historical cost and accepted modes of allocation were not hallowed shrines. Unlike many writers, he has been interested not only in the technical content of accounting but also in the likely impact of its measurements and disclosures on the actions of management, investors, creditors, government, and indeed the general public.

Above all, Paton has been an unflagging advocate of the causes he believes to be just. Where Hatfield, the scholarly critic, might tease and taunt his colleagues in the spirit of lively and even playful debate, Paton has been forever serious in the pursuit of clearly perceived goals. When he feared that accounting measures were contributing to antibusiness sentiment following World War II, he launched a vigorous campaign against accounting procedures that gave rise to overstated profits and earning rates. When he believed that utility regulatory commissions were following unsound policies owing to their rigid adherence to "original cost," he set out in hot pursuit of the regulators.

In a doctrinaire literature, Paton refused to join the crowd. He has been an original thinker and an innovator, whose views are widely quoted by others. It is evident from the writings of Hatfield, Canning, Sweeney, Gilman, Vatter, Davidson, Moonitz, Devine, Chambers, Bierman, and others too numerous to mention, that

Paton's arguments as well as the example of his incessant questioning of accounting dogma have had a considerable impact on his colleagues and successors in the literature.

Paton has advocated accounting reforms long before they finally found their way into practice. One can recall his recommendation as early as 1916 that debt discount be deducted from the face amount of the long-term liability (and not shown as a deferred charge among the assets), a practice that finally came to be accepted in the United States in 1971. Also in 1971, the American accounting profession officially endorsed the practice of accounting on a fair value basis for the implicit interest on long-term contracts, a subject on which Paton had written as long ago as 1916. The practice of reducing gross revenue rather than charging "Bad Debt Expense" when allowing for estimated uncollectibles was recommended by Paton as early as 1922; even other textbook writers are today gradually accepting this dictum. Paton also was a pioneer of new terminology. The terms "Allowance for Depreciation" and "Allowance for Uncollectible Accounts" may be found in his textbooks as far back as 1918, when "Reserves" were seen everywhere else. In 1948 a committee of the American Institute of [Certified Public] Accountants recommended that the term "Reserve" no longer be used for valuation accounts.

Paton may not have been the first American to write textbooks that vigorously took issue with accepted accounting practice, but he has been probably the most celebrated and influential author of this genre of books. His succession of texts, beginning in 1916–18 with the heretical *Principles of Accounting* (co-authored with Russell A. Stevenson) and continuing with *Accounting* (1924), *Essentials of Accounting* (1938 and 1949), *Advanced Accounting* (1941), *Asset Accounting* (1952), and *Corporation Accounts and Statements* (1955), plus several that were co-authored in later years, were hardly prosaic primers on the rudiments of extant practice. They challenged the intellect and obliged teacher and student alike to define and redefine the role of accounting in economic society. Paton was sometimes criticized as a theorist who had little time for the "real world." Yet the manuals which accompanied most of his textbooks contained many problems and cases which were drawn from contracts, prospectuses, annual reports, court opinions, and newspaper accounts, thus setting a very practical stage on which to discuss and assess the implications of Paton's theories. He was among the first authors of American accounting textbooks to make extensive use of actual case materials.

Paton has won the widespread respect of his peers. He served as president in 1922 of the American Association of University Instructors in Accounting (forerunner of the American Accounting Association). He was one of three accounting academics (the others were A.C. Littleton and Roy B. Kester) who were named to the American Institute's Committee on Accounting Procedure in 1938, when that committee was first given authority to issue bulletins on accounting principles on behalf of the Institute. In 1940 he became the first academic to deliver the Dickinson Lecture in Accounting at the Harvard Graduate School of Business Administration. In 1944 he was one of the first three recipients of the Institute's Gold Medal for distinguished service to the accounting profession, and in 1950 he was among the first three individuals to be inducted into Ohio State University's Accounting Hall of Fame. Paton was the first academic to receive both of these accolades. In 1953 he was given the Alpha Kappa Psi Foundation's Accounting Award.

Paton was a founder and first editor of *The Accounting Review*. He was an author of the 1936 statement on accounting principles of the American Accounting Association, and in 1940 he and A.C. Littleton produced *An Introduction to Corporate Accounting Standards,* which has doubtless been the most influential treatment of accounting theory in the English language.

In 1947 Paton was one of approximately ten professors selected by the University of Michigan to hold the new rank of University Professor. Twenty-nine years later, the same university opened the William A. Paton Center for Accounting Education and Research building, which was financed by contributions from his many former students and other friends.

Now in his ninetieth year, Paton continues to write in the defense of free enterprise and sound accounting. We are pleased and honored to be joined by eight of our colleagues in saluting this extraordinary man. The essays in this volume have been written exclusively for this *Festschrift,* and we are grateful to each of the authors, to Howard C. Greer, and to the Division of Research at the University of Michigan Graduate School of Business Administration for making the publication possible. We thank Joseph M. Whelan for his assistance in compiling the comprehensive bibliography.

STEPHEN A. ZEFF

JOEL S. DEMSKI

NICHOLAS DOPUCH

July 1978

Greer on Paton

In the January 1965 issue of the *Accounting Review,* Howard C. Greer, a long-time friend of Paton's and himself a major contributor to the accounting literature, wrote an admiring review of *Paton on Accounting,* an anthology of Paton's articles and essays, edited by Herbert F. Taggart. With the permission of the American Accounting Association, we are pleased to reprint the review, as slightly amended for this occasion by Greer.

Examining this monumental compendium of Bill Paton's voluminous writings, I have been reminded of what happened, long years ago, to the brothers Scott, two distinguished members of the faculty of my Alma Mater, Northwestern University. John Scott was a renowned classical languages scholar; his brother, Walter Dill Scott, was a noted teacher of psychology, and later the university's long-time president.

As John Scott used to tell it: when the presidency became vacant, in the early twenties, the brothers agreed that one of the Scotts should be chosen for the job. It was decided that John would urge Walter's selection, and Walter would promote John's candidacy. "But it turned out," mourned John, "that Walter didn't have any influence—and I didn't get the job."

My experience has been similar. Years ago Bill Paton and I formed a mutual admiration society, the terms of which were that each of us would advertise the merits of the other's writings. I could suggest that the wider audience attained by his works implies my greater success as a promoter, though the relative merits of our literary efforts concededly may have played some part in the result. Anyhow, I'll stick to our bargain, and put in one more plug for my old friend, fully realizing that no living author needs it less!

Give heed, then, to this epic tome—the "Selected Writings" of the sage of Ann Arbor—a collection of some 46 articles from his busy pen. They are here republished in a handsome format, in chronological order, with illuminating editorial notes by Paton's long-time friend and

1

colleague, Herb Taggart (himself an author of distinction, whose discerning and humorous comments add much to the book).

The Paton articles span the years from 1917 to 1963, and run the gamut from an early-day exposition of the "Theory of the Double Entry System" to such esoteric topics as "Non-Application of Incremental Cost Principle to Postal Cost Accounting." Expectably, the majority of the material is from the files of *The Journal of Accountancy* (to which he was a faithful contributor), and THE ACCOUNTING REVIEW (of which he was founder and first editor), but his interests ranged widely, and we find him enlightening the readers of such diverse publications as the *Journal of Political Economy*, the *Public Utilities Fortnightly*, and the report of the Michigan Academy of Sciences.

The breadth of his audience-appeal is not surprising, for whatever else may be said of him, he is certainly the most *interesting* writer who has ever invaded the accounting field (with high rank in economic literature as well). The sharpness of his perceptions, the pungency of his observations, the clarity of his expositions combine to make him a fascinating commentator on any subject he may elect to discuss. And he has always had something valuable and thought-provoking to say; his lucid reasoning is forever delightful, even when one fails to share his conclusions.

In fact, one of Paton's greatest services to his profession has been his illumination of the many diverse facets of accounting theory and practice. It is at once the delight and despair of accountants to realize that most problems have several possible solutions, each useful and appropriate in its own context. Thus one may admire and applaud a reasoned conclusion, even though one's own experience and outlook suggest a different one. May a reviewer admit to differing with the author's conclusion on eight of 12 major issues presented, and still acknowledge a debt for a richer and fuller understanding of the subjects than would have been possible without his astute and imaginative analysis?

And so, whatever your beliefs, you should know what Paton has to say about recording appreciation in your accounts, figuring income charges in terms of replacement-cost value-expirations, and "equalizing" year-to-year income computations by varied accrual and write-off practices. And if you marvel at his scorn for the helpful last-in first-out principle of inventory valuation, you'll know that it extends likewise to the hallowed cost-or-market-whichever-lower philosophy. And you should identify him as the patron saint of the "one-step" net income computation, even if you share this reviewer's regret at his championing this dubious device.

Never mind, Bill—your admirers will forgive all in their gratitude for your stalwart and undeviating espousal of private enterprise, your cogent exposition of the indispensability of a free-price system, and your insistence on realism in measuring investment, capital, profits, and rates of return. And that paper you presented at the International Congress in 1962 (at the tender age of 73)—"Accounting and Utilization of Resources"—as a summation of economic realities and objectives, it's superb.

This book, however, is by no means limited to major issues and high-level economic philosophies. Paton can be measured and profound; he can also be topical, witty, and sardonic, as recent commentaries demonstrate.

Always quick to identify and deride fads and foibles, he can still turn a fast gun on exaggeration and sophistry. At an age when most of us are content to doze in the sun, he grabs the old muzzle-loader off the wall, rams in some shot, and blazes away at such targets as the "Deferred Income Misnomer," the "Cash-Flow Illusion," the neglect of overhead costs in price-figuring, and the like. Thus, if you're tempted to say something silly in some accounting publication, take heed of the old red-head skulking in the shrubbery—your temerity may fetch you a charge of buck-shot in the seat of the pants!

So you ought to have a copy of this enduring monument to the Great Educator, even if paying the $12.50 tab may deprive you of an evenir.g spent in a bar-room or at a girlie-show. If you are strong enough to heft a volume of 713 pages, plus introduction and bibliographies, try your muscle on this one.

And while so doing, let your enjoyment of Paton the author be enriched by some related appreciation of Paton the man. If you have not had the privilege of his acquaintance, you may still savor his warm and engaging personality, from the photo on the dust jacket (he's saying "Greer, you don't know what the hell you're talking about"), and from Herb Taggart's delightful biographical note, which prefaces the volume. You will be wholesomely reminded that obscure origin and straitened circumstances are no bar to achievement, and that success in life is not reserved for those who took their early nourishment from a silver spoon.

For Paton's eminence was the fruit of a career in the true Horatio Alger tradition. And if you are like those who once voiced doubt that Nazareth was a place out of which any good thing could come, you might reflect on what could reasonably be expected to emerge from the remote and meagerly endowed village of Calumet (pop. 1,959) where our hero began life. Or on what might result from an upbringing on a central Michigan farm, of the kind where whole families subsisted on cash incomes of $400 a year but no one was on relief.

Perhaps there's something special in the Michigan climate. The sleepy village of Montague (pop. 2,356), near which I once spent happy summers, eventually produced a Miss America, and a very charming one at that. Consider this a corollary of the fact that an isolated Copper Country ghost town inaugurated the career of the guy who to many of us will always be Mr. Accounting, for his enrichment of our knowledge, inspiration of our spirit, and gladdening of our dullest days.

HOWARD C. GREER

Lafayette, California

Observations on Internal Controls

Carl T. Devine

Overview

This essay begins with a lament over the lack of professional interest in the behavioral aspects of internal controls and reviews briefly some related literature in this area.[1] Accountants have not constructed indexes, designed measuring scales, or emphasized the psychological barriers that such controls are designed to induce. Attention is then directed to some decision models that might be appropriate for the initiator of a violation proposal and for those who are approached. The initiator is faced with probabilities of having his proposal rejected, and, if rejected, with further probabilities that rejection will or will not lead to disclosure. These possibilities are in addition to the usual chances of being successful in carrying out plans if the proposal is in fact accepted. Finally, some sort of bargaining model for sharing the expected gains is necessary unless the custodian's strategy is to steal and run and thus short-circuit the usual collusion requirement. The discussion then turns to the controller, who is faced with his own set of manipulatable variables, his own probability assessments, and his firm's cost-benefit situation.

1. For an interesting historical survey of early internal-control procedures see T. A. Lee, "The Historical Development of Internal Control from the Earliest Times to the End of the Seventeenth Century," *Journal of Accounting Research* (Spring 1971): 150–57.

While accountants have long assumed that the separation of functions and the necessity for collusion are important aspects of internal control, they have devoted little direct effort to assessing the relative effectiveness of barriers introduced by traditional internal controls. For example, how much is added to the strength of the deterrent by the introduction of a third party, e.g., an auditor, into the cycle? Does it matter if the participants are blue-collar or white-collar? Male or female? Rural or urban? Young or old? How effective is physical separation? Social distance? Common reference and peer groups? Is there more reluctance for bookkeepers to approach custodians than the reverse? What sorts of approaches are used to reduce the initiator's probability of rejection and the anticipated penalties associated with rejection?

The usual procedure, as most accountants know, is to select or construct an internal-control questionnaire. The audit supervisor often selects a standardized questionnaire and modifies it for the peculiarities of his specific engagement. Precisely how are the original questions selected and how are they evaluated? How can any questionnaire be constructed without some very specific organizational and behavioral assumptions? Presumably auditors identify a "representative" organization staffed with "normal" individuals whose reactions and attitudes are sufficiently homogeneous to be used as standards. Obviously there are some homogeneous features even in the primitive human condition, and it seems reasonable to assume that the degree of homogeneity may be modified by screening and indoctrination.

The typical audit supervisor selects a standardized questionnaire and modifies it to meet the peculiarities of his specific engagement. What peculiarities of a particular situation lead to what kinds of modifications? What subsequent observations serve as clues for change? The carping here is not with the assumption of some degree of homogeneity among members of an organization—such an assumption is inescapable. Nor is it implied that current professional procedures are necessarily bad. On the contrary, conventional wisdom has been filtered and modified until the resulting guidelines are applied with confidence and professional respect. The criticism at this point is that no shareable process of judgment formation has been disclosed and that the literature is almost entirely composed of *dicta* with little evidential support or systematic discussion.

Our purpose in this essay is to suggest a framework for investigating the internal control area. Accountants clearly hypothesize that sharing socially unacceptable goals is done with reluctance and that the necessity for approaching others with an invitation to participate in forbidden activity introduces an important barrier. An obvious professional task is to evaluate the relative strength of such barriers and to manipulate the avenues that are available for increasing their effectiveness. The suggested framework may be familiar to accountants, for it combines a traditional probabilistic view of rejection and disclosure with a cost-benefit evaluation of the consequences of success and failure. The conclusions are in terms of expected values with both probabilities and evaluations considered to be partially controllable by would-be embezzlers and by organizational bureaucrats.

Some Things We Know About Thieves

In spite of important work by Sorensen and others on the sociology of the profession,[2] it is ironical that we still know considerably more about professional thieves than we know about the behavior of accounting and custodial personnel.[3]

It is generally believed that the requirements of technical skill, status, consensus, differential association and organization are common to all professions including the activities of connivery and thievery. The skills of successful thieves take the form of planning and executing, providing for failure, and designing techniques to evaluate diverse alternatives. Status follows from skill, financial standing, connections, personal image, wide knowledge and general sophistication. The term thief among criminal elements is honorific. Consensus results from ability to work together, recognition of common enemies, adoption of a general *esprit de corps*, and acceptance of a common well-defined value system.

2. For example, James E. Sorensen, "Professional and Bureaucratic Organization in the Public Accounting Firm," *The Accounting Review* (July 1967): 553–65; and James E. Sorensen and Thomas L. Sorensen, "Comparison of 1965 and 1970 Organizational and Professional Profiles and Migration Plans of Large-Firm CPAs," in *Behavioral Experiments in Accounting*, Thomas J. Burns, ed. (Columbus: The Ohio State University, 1972), pp. 3–38.

3. The leading reference here is *The Professional Thief*, by Chic Conwell, annotated and interpreted by E.H. Sutherland (Chicago: University of Chicago Press, 1937). For a discussion of restricted role behavior to which only members of the confidence racket have access see D.W. Maurer, *The Big Con* (Indianapolis: Bobbs-Merrill, 1940). Numerous semi-popular books are available about stock manipulation, white-collar thievery, swindling, etc.

Differential association results from ability to define requirements of membership and to contact members of legitimate society in order to steal from them.[4] Thieves have organization in that they employ their own language, laws, history, traditions and customs. They establish specialized machinery for disposing of property and procuring defenses. It is good business for professional thieves and con men to shine their shoes, be pleasant company, and become engaging conversationalists.

Is the sociology of accounting—as a profession—as well defined? We have scarcely started the necessary investigations and consequently we simply do not know.

Some Items About Embezzlers

A study of embezzlers by Cressey is clearly one of the more useful studies in the behavioral foundations for accounting. Cressey wonders why "some persons in positions of financial trust violate it."[5] In the course of his inquiry Cressey emphasized the following conditions and variables.

> Trusted persons become trust violators when they conceive of themselves as having a financial problem which is non-shareable, are aware that this problem can be secretly resolved by the violation of the position of financial trust, and are able to apply to their conduct in that situation verbalizations which enable them to adjust their conception of themselves as users of the entrusted funds or property.[6]

Cressey's attempt to identify the determinants of such attitudes is not entirely satisfactory. Accountants, especially, may wonder whether he overemphasizes secret solutions and non-shareability of

4. With the typical sociologist's contempt for business (and politics), Sutherland points out that the intimacy is usually cold-blooded. "He [the thief] is like a salesman who attempts to understand a prospective customer only as a means of breaking down sales resistance." *Ibid.*, p. 277. Training in salesmanship deals exhaustively with different approaches and possible responses, and stresses the search for information under uncertainty. Even the broader social aspects of trust violation may be included. Unfortunately we accountants still know very little about the actual approaches used by parties in an internal control collusion so that they can better "understand" one another.

5. Donald R. Cressey, *Other People's Money* (Glencoe: The Free Press, 1953), p. 30; see also Cressey, "Embezzlers, The Trusted Thieves," *Fortune* (November 1957) and "Why Do Trusted People Commit Fraud? A Social-Psychological Study of Defalcators," *Journal of Accountancy* (November 1951).

6. *Ibid.*, p. 30 ff. Observe that if such problems are in fact unshareable, ordinary internal controls would not be effective.

experiences as key variables. Cressey feels that the shareability variable can be reduced to status, and, in something of an oversimplification, he relates status directly to financial conditions.[7] White-collar workers may find disclosure of gambling losses to be non-shareable but find disclosure of business losses entirely acceptable. (Needless to say other groups may find gambling losses highly shareable and appropriate for extensive conversation!) The tradition of being noble and going down with the ship may set up stresses and lead to violation as well as provide material for subsequent rationalization.[8]

With respect to ability to carry out violations, Cressey found lack of knowledge to be relatively unimportant. Television, motion pictures, radio, newspapers, gaudy paperbacks, often suggest feasible methods and possible defenses. The violators in his sample were already near the resources, could hardly fail to recognize available opportunities, and had little need for collusion. Thus the search for additional information for decision making under uncertainty was not an important part of Cressey's investigation. His subjects were almost entirely upper middle-class executives so that differences in their utility functions and value structures were not points for intensive study. Most violators were influenced by their peer-group morality, were "sorry" even before they were caught, and, when convicted, were reluctant to accept the role of common criminal.

About Auditors and Motivators

In view of obvious attempts by the auditing profession to establish an image of trustworthiness, sagacity, dependability, and fearless honesty, little seems to have been done to research either the positive or deterrent effects of an audit.[9] Churchill and Cooper have

7. A more careful association of status with peer-group influences and financial condition relative to group norms appears to be a more productive orientation for further research. Extreme loners, for example, may have few people with whom to share, may be less status conscious, and have weaker reference-group influences. He apparently assumes that loners are not likely to be in critical positions of trust.

8. The existentialist movement, to its credit, has undermined the persuasiveness of some once very effective rationalizations: It was only *natural!* After all I am a *human* being! I am a product of my *culture!* The *devil* made me do it! *Zeus* did it to me!

9. Raymond A. Bauer has been interested in the relation of belief to source credibility and has called attention to an unpublished dissertation by Murray Hilibrand (1964), *Source Credibility and the Persuasive Process.* See Raymond A. Bauer, "Applications of Behavioral Science," *Applied Science and Technological Process,* June 1967.

certainly made the most important empirical contribution.[10] Certain graduate students and industrial workers served as subjects, and accordingly the authors were reluctant to generalize widely. They found that the audit occurrence apparently exerted some influence even when not used in conjunction with an explicit reward-penalty system.[11] The direction of the influence was toward conformance with accepted accounting principles. Apparently most subjects assumed that the auditors would do what conventional wisdom assumes they will do—probe behind the documents to the associated events. Anticipation of future audits seemed to support traditional behavioral beliefs, and the threat of an audit had some effectiveness as a crude motivational club.

Consider now some more recent discussions of auditing and systems work in the area of internal controls. Until recently the former have been concerned primarily with statistical aspects of the problem, and to a large extent the latter have simply neglected the matter or have concentrated on broad control systems and computer-oriented controls. An initial breakthrough toward acceptance of auditing as a university endeavor came with the incorporation of modern statistical theory. Matters have greatly improved and full acceptability may now have arrived with an entire supplement of the *Journal of Accounting Research* devoted to *Studies in Statistical Methodology in Auditing* (1975).[12] A part of this supplement is concerned with

---

Reprinted in the Harvard University Graduate School of Business Administration Reprint Series. For more general research in this direction see Carl I. Hovland, A.A. Lumsdaine, and F.D. Sheffield, *Experiments on Mass Communication* (Princeton: Princeton University Press, 1949). For a useful summary and critique of Hovland and his various associates see A.R. Cohen, *Attitude Change and Social Influence* (New York: Basic Books, 1964).

10. N.C. Churchill and W.W. Cooper, *Effects of Auditing Records: Individual Accomplishment and Organization Objectives* (Pittsburgh: ONR Research Memorandum No. 98, Carnegie-Mellon Graduate School of Industrial Administration).

11. Further investigation of *implicit* reward-penalty perceptions might prove interesting. Specific fear of the system? Generalized anxiety? Unusually compliant citizenry? Desire to join the establishment?

12. The pioneer work is Lawrence Vance, *Scientific Method for Auditing* (Berkeley: University of California Press, 1947). The research was apparently done for his doctoral dissertation at Minnesota in 1942. Writers in the intervening period were, with few exceptions, concerned with statistical rather than behavioral applications; R. Gene Brown, "Objective Internal Control Evaluation," *Journal of Accountancy* (November 1962): 50–56; John A. Tracy, "Bayesian Statistical Methods in Auditing," *The*

internal controls and decision models that include cost-benefit analysis for determining whether further investigation is warranted. Normative decision theory may not be the final answer to all mankind's worries, but it is applicable to auditing and it promises substantial help to this branch of our troubled profession. Non-trivial decisions involve choices, choices involve values, and expected values require predictions. Auditing at all levels is concerned with alternative procedures and with the extent of detailed work to be done. These matters require predictions, value assessments, and cost-benefit computations.[13]

An encouraging development from this situation is the attraction of competent decision theorists to the problems of internal control. A further bonus may be in the form of meaningful research covering the precise interactions of internal controls and the amount of auditing to be done. The literature dealing with applications of Bayesian and stochastic processes is a tentative start in this direction, but mechanics alone are not going to solve these interaction problems. Our profession encounters such situations on a daily basis. Sooner or later someone must undertake the behavioral studies necessary for implementing these decisions and communicating the process to new members and to the financial world.

Accounting Review (January 1969): 90–98; James E. Sorensen, "Bayesian Analysis in Auditing," *The Accounting Review* (July 1969): 555–61; William R. Scott, *A Bayesian Approach to the Accounting Problems of Asset Valuation and Audit Size* (Ph.D. Dissertation, University of Chicago, 1972); John C. Corless, "Assessing Prior Distributions for Applying Bayesian Statistics in Auditing," *The Accounting Review* (July 1972): 555–66; Robert S. Kaplan, several articles, especially "A Stochastic Model for Auditing," *Journal of Accounting Research* (Spring 1973): 38–46; Seongjae Yu and John Neter, "A Stochastic Model of Internal Control Systems," (Working Paper, University of Illinois, December, 1973); Barry E. Cushing, "A Mathematical Approach to the Analysis and Design of Internal Control Systems," *The Accounting Review* (January 1974): 24–42; Robert H. Ashton, "An Experimental Study of Internal Control Judgments," *Journal of Accounting Research* (Spring 1974): 143–57; William L. Felix, Jr., "Evidence on Alternative Means of Assessing Prior Probability Distributions for Audit Decision Makers," *The Accounting Review* (October 1976): 800–7.

13. In this context see William R. Kinney, Jr., "A Decision-Theory Approach to the Sampling Problem in Auditing," *Journal of Accounting Research* (Spring 1975): 117–32, and "Decision Theory Aspects of Internal Control System Design Compliance and Substantive Tests," *Journal of Accounting Research,* Supplement 1975: 14–29.

Internal Controls—Employee View

Turn now to some attitudes and problems of individuals who are restricted by the effective operation of internal controls. To an important extent their problem is one of seeking information under conditions of uncertainty.[14] The approachor must be concerned with the probability that his invitation will be rejected. Moreover, if he is rejected, he must evaluate the chances of having his actions reported to authorities. If accepted, he must assess the further probabilities of apprehension after collusion. Such evaluations lead naturally to the assignment of values to possible outcomes and is related to appropriate reward-penalty systems. The approachee need not be concerned with rejection probabilities, but he does need to consider possibilities of being caught, and, if caught, of being punished. The point here is that many of these probabilities and conditional penalties may be modified by appropriate behaviors, preliminary screening, cautious approaches, and various buddy-forming devices.

Observe that custodians have access to the desired resources and are faced with problems different from those faced by clerical workers. For one thing, it is usually their assignment to circumvent the physical controls surrounding the resources. There is always some probability of lack of success in this activity, but the chance that clerical colluders will be drawn into any resulting penalty situations may be considerably less. If the custodian is a drifter or a loner, he may prefer to take his chances at circumventing the physical controls without help, and, if successful, simply abscond. In such cases he should assess the probabilities of his being able to change identity and keep clear of the hounds from bonding firms and policing agencies. The resulting expected values should then be compared with mathematical expectations from alternative courses of action.

There are obvious reasons why custodians may opt for collusion rather than for the steal-and-run policy. Tactics become especially important for the selection of alternative approaches, and considerable cost may be justified in seeking information about potential approachees. Additional information may decrease substantially the probability of rejection as well as the probability of being reported

---

14. Erving Goffman was among the early behavioral scientists to emphasize the necessity of searching for information about those with whom one must interact, the influence of the overall situation, the importance of physical regions, and the concept of Performance Teams. *The Presentation of Self in Everyday Life* (Garden City: Doubleday Anchor Books, 1959: 76ff).

if rejected. If rejected and not reported, the custodian may still retain the option to steal and run, while rejection and disclosure may end this opportunity. The steal-and-run option should be a lower-valued alternative not only because of possible future police action, but also because it virtually destroys the opportunity for continued embezzlement in the same organization. Keeping the option open for repeated violations without the necessity and danger of approaching other potentially hostile colluders and learning new physical safeguards may justify the cost of extensive search for additional information.

While the penalties for apprehension may be enormous, the absconder has one factor working for him. He does not have to share the spoils with his partners in collusion. If sharing becomes necessary, the process may be approximated by an ordinary two-party or three-party bargaining model with interesting complications. Clearly the bargaining and the probability of rejection and disclosure may not be independent, i.e., such probabilities may be influenced by the bargaining for the division of spoils.

For the above reasons we might advance a preliminary hypothesis that collusive inquiries will be initiated more frequently by clerical workers and directed toward custodians. We might speculate further that professionally trained custodians, say treasury personnel, will be more likely to reject and report invitations than custodians with less professional indoctrination, e.g., storeroom and toolcrib attendants. In addition the greater guilt sometimes associated with stealing money rather than other resources may tend to make cash controls more effective. Observe, however, that while cash may be more responsibly guarded due to such an attitude, currency can be disposed of more easily and with less probability of discovery.

To a potential initiator the population of possible approachees is certainly not homogeneous. Long sustained image construction may mean that auditors as a group are perceived as high-risk approachees, and it is possible that the training they receive on the job and in universities does increase the risk and make the group more homogeneous. Employees in the treasury may also view themselves as protectors of financial integrity and thus appear as high-risk targets. Without specific knowledge one wonders how systems designers actually design their control systems. What sorts of actions do colluding clerks make to reduce probabilities of detection by auditors? How often do internal auditors use their superior-inferior position to suggest proposals to clerks or directly to custodians? How do external auditors influence various groups and reinforce various barriers? What about invitations from middle and lower managers to subordinate employees?

A study of the techniques used by initiators to reduce probabilities of rejection and disclosure should prove to be useful. In spite of indoctrination and some measure of group discipline individual members are not homogeneous, and any thoughtful initiator should be able to reduce his risk by incurring some costs to identify those at the more cooperative tail of the distribution—the weak links. Once these members have been tentatively spotted, further costs to investigate techniques and methods appropriate for each case may be justified. The investigator may find well-developed buddy paths to potentially cooperative members in target groups. But how are such paths developed? Which directions do they run? What techniques are used to undermine organizational and professional loyalty? Do approaches develop by degrees so that retreat before final rejection remains possible? Does pretense of a joke lessen the probability of disclosure? What surrounding circumstances permit graceful exits?

Potential embezzlers should be aware of mechanical weak points in the general internal-control system and should be able to assess probabilities of success. Experienced clerical personnel are usually aware of undetected errors and shortages that have not been disclosed by previous audits and other control devices. Attitudes of superiors to such failings are normally noted. Meanwhile, custodians should have knowledge of existing physical controls and be able to appraise the probable success of circumventing them.

There should be a pooling of knowledge about the possibility of being ensnared by physical and internal devices after the collusive effort is under way. Gatekeepers and others may not remain persuaded, become victims of panic, or be swayed by pangs of conscience. Chance factors and unforeseen investigations are potential dangers. Changes in personnel, leaks from unskilled collaborators, undependable fences, and organization spies are further dangers. In general these factors are common to all approaches and are present regardless of the particular techniques used to circumvent specific internal controls. There may be, however, considerable interdependence, for not all colluders are equally skilled and existing physical controls certainly do influence the effectiveness of the internal controls. How shall we measure the importance of this interaction?

Consider for a moment cases in which approaches are made from clerical to custodial groups. Since clerical workers do not have direct access to the resources, the decision to abscond is not usually an original option or a possible retreat from rejection. It may therefore be omitted from their decision networks. Otherwise the procedures are likely to be similar. Different value systems and different abilities to assess probabilities may be involved. Buddy-path formation may have different characteristics and different techniques may be required. In each case, the initiator needs information to help him select potential collaborators, choose appropriate approaches, appraise probabilities, arrive at acceptable sharing formulas and assess payoffs generally. Further, the need for multiperiod knowledge is clear. Many situations require estimates of optimal amounts to be embezzled in each violation, the optimal frequency of violation, optimal timing of attempts, and possibilities for varying the methods to be employed. Moreover, the wise embezzler should develop alternate and sequential plans in case original schemes turn out to be unsuccessful. Some sort of leadership arrangements will need to be forged along with rules for assigning tasks and responsibilities. Means for incorporating new information as the process is implemented should be provided, and alternative defensive and offensive measures must be established when outcomes diverge from plans.

Suggestions for Decision Analysis

It is not difficult to construct a highly simplified decision tree for an initiator of an invitation to violate trust. The usual technique for applying such models is to assign probabilities for each branch and to assess conditional rewards and penalties for the resulting states. Presumably the line with the highest mathematical expectation—highest expected value—can be defined as the rational choice. The decision tree for an initiator from recordkeeping is similar except for the opportunity to abscond. A decision framework for the approachee does not involve the need for an initial proposal with probabilities of acceptance or rejection, but it should provide for the alternative of rejection with possible rewards for reporting the initiator.

From a behavioral viewpoint the problem facing possible participants may be viewed as a problem of information seeking and evaluating under uncertainty. Inquiry may be directed to the kinds of behavior that should be employed to procure the desired information at reasonable cost. More generally the problem can be structured as a balancing of cost and benefit assessments in a complicated interpersonal situation. At a more specific level research can be concentrated on efforts to change the probabilities of acceptance, detection, disclosure, etc., and to increasing the conditional rewards. To be useful, therefore, a decision framework or diagram must provide for *search* at each traditional decision point. The options are thus not simply two-way branches. The desirable (optimal) amount of search must be decided in terms of modifications of probabilities and conditional payoff assessments all along the line. The simultaneous interaction is obvious, and the need for severe simplification is clear.

In short a cost-benefit search should be made at each decision point in order to bring about acceptable probabilities and conditional rewards. For the initiator these search activities may be designed to bring about more favorable expectations in the following ways.

1. Decrease the probability of rejection, $P(R)$;
2. Decrease the probability of being turned in if rejected, $P(T)$, and for the case of interdependence, decrease $P(R \wedge T) = P(R) \cdot P(T/R) = P(T) \cdot P(R/T)$;
3. Decrease the probability of being discovered by auditors or other internal-control workers who are not in the collusive agreement, e.g., optimal timing, number of violations;
4. Decrease the probability of being caught by enforcement agencies, i.e., selecting competent colluders, discreet fences, effective escape methods;
5. Influence the reward-penalty system: decrease conditional penalties, and increase conditional rewards, e.g., finding optimal amounts for violations, finding ways to soften the penalties.

It is possible that the techniques of game theory are appropriate for analyzing problems of internal control. Clearly the division of rewards from successful collusion for both the approachor and the approachee depends in part on relative bargaining strength. After the fact, what one gains, the other loses so that the first appearance is that of a zero-sum game. In a more general context the zero-sum format does not seem to be appropriate, because if one colluder is caught, the others also lose to varying degrees. Thus the game has cooperative features along with the zero-sum aspects of the sharing model, and apparently there are at least two games to be given attention even for a single pair of participants.[15]

15. Those interested in related aspects of this problem might refer to C.B. McGuire and Roy Radner (editors), *Decision and Organization* (Amsterdam: North Holland, 1972), especially Radner's chapter, "Normative Theories of Organization: An Introduction." For an early, non-technical discussion of bargaining models generally see Lawrence E. Fouraker and Sidney Siegel, *Bargaining Behavior* (New York: McGraw-Hill Book Company, 1963).

Some further influences on the bargaining parties may deserve investigation. Does the initiator have a superior bargaining position because of his demonstrated daring, ingenuity or leadership qualities? Perhaps his position is inferior due to his vulnerability to rejection and disclosure. One might speculate that the custodian is usually in a superior position since he enjoys the option of absconding. Yet the clerical worker may be able to endure discovery with less serious consequences by creating the impression, if caught, of a mistake—a human error. It may be less difficult for the bookkeeper to explain his covering entries than for the custodian to explain the presence of organizational resources at his country estate. Bookkeepers, clerks, and auditors may be in an inferior position, for they usually do not have access to the resources and collusion is essential in order for them to embezzle at all.

Finally, one may wonder whether the positions of the controller (as a representative of the organization) and the colluders (as a coalition) form the basis for a zero-sum game. Even simple zero-sum games run into conceptual problems from differences in subjective utilities among participants, but the present situation is considerably worse. There is no reason to believe that the gain or loss to the colluders will be exactly offset by the loss or gain to the organization or to the particular corporate officers involved. The possibility of prison sentences, loss of prestige and employment are peculiar to the coalition members, and, while the monetary loss may be balanced by an equal monetary effect (except for fencing discounts, etc.), only by chance would the corporation enjoy measurable gains from an effective control system exactly equal to these intangible losses of a particular set of coalition members.

Controller's Viewpoint

The controller's decision process may be approached in a similar manner. In order to perform his functions the controller must be able to predict the behavior of those subject to his controls. A number of decisions and activities are usually available, and it is assumed that he will select alternatives on some sort of expected-value, cost-benefit basis. These activities may be summarized briefly.

1. Designing social factors to decrease the probabilities that the internal control personnel will get together and establish channels of rapport—age, sex and religious differences, social distances, status barriers;

To summarize these considerations, we offer the general speculation that the probabilities of being rejected and reported are related to the level of group indoctrination, to the homogeneity of group membership, to perceptions of rewards and penalties, and to the persuasive ability of initiators. Like potential embezzlers, auditors, system builders and controllers utilize a modified cost-benefit analysis with various degrees of control over many variables that influence employee behavior. Certain variables are manipulated in the context of internal controls to influence the actions of human beings whose own goals often differ from those of the host organization. In this situation, unlike the area of physical controls, the appropriate wisdom and knowledge is likely to come from psychologists, sociologists and various combinations such as social psychologists and organization theorists.

Some Possibilities for Research

In general terms the professional problem in this area is to assess the deterrent effect of all sorts of physical and group arrangements against all sorts of background variables and contrived modifications. Continuing discussions by our lawmakers over such topics as the effectiveness of capital punishment and harsh drug laws attest to the difficulties of forecasting the deterrent effects of rule-making. While the problem may be difficult to specify and impossible to measure, it arises in our profession and in our society every day,

---

after their countries are free. The outstanding work for a general view is George C. Homans, *The Human Group* (New York: Harcourt, Brace, 1950). Some useful extensions in organization theory may be found in James G. March and Herbert A. Simon, *Organizations* (New York: John Wiley & Sons, Inc., 1958).

Many psychologists have been concerned with roles, reference groups and personality factors. George H. Mead emphasized personality development in terms of signs that require adaptive responses from others and the importance of membership groups. (*Mind, Self and Society*, University of Chicago Press, 1934). Robert K. Merton made improvements in the concept of membership groups and earlier reference-group theory. Merton was also interested in objectives, legitimate and institutionalized means of attaining objectives. (*Social Theory and Social Structure*, Free Press, 1957). Leon Festinger has been a leader through his "urges" to compare beliefs, in order to be consistent with group attitudes, and to reduce dissonance. He also gave limited support to the hypothesis that smaller rewards *may* be more effective than larger ones. See *Conflict, Decision and Dissonance* (Stanford University Press, 1964). Earlier writings include Festinger and J.M. Carlsmith, "Cognitive Consequences of Forces Compliance," *Journal of Abnormal and Social Psychology* (1959): 203–10.

and every day it must somehow be met. Implicit solutions may not be optimal, but they obviously must be acceptable to some important segments of society.

In the specific field of internal controls there is an obvious lack of knowledge about the reluctance (deterrence) engendered by the necessity for collusion. The following summary is only suggestive.

1. Influences of pre-professional associations and groups—church membership, service clubs, parental attitudes, university course work;

2. Images of groups involved in internal-control circles—including the degrees of group homogeneity;

3. Interaction of physical deterrents and internal-control devices;

4. Influences of social distance and possible tradeoffs in various directions and at various levels;

5. Types of approaches used with variations from group to group;

6. Data on the directions invitations for violation of trust tend to take;

7. Sharing models used and relative bargaining strengths of each group under varying conditions;

8. Ways in which standardized questionnaires are constructed;

9. Mechanics for trade-offs of audit completeness and internal-control sufficiency;

10. Interpretation and modification of standardized questionnaires to meet particular situations.

Meaningful research in these areas is clearly difficult and may require the help of competent research professionals. Yet accountants are capable of carrying on some less demanding investigations along with many specialized inquiries within the profession. One less demanding technique is based on ordinary utility analysis with appropriate subjects being asked to adjust probabilities or conditional values. With a given reward for approaching some representative member of say the auditing group, the subject may be asked what reward would make him indifferent to approaching some typical member of another group in the internal-control circle. He is in effect asked to equate various expected values. Differences may then be used to construct measures of relative reluctance to approach members of each group involved. Intermediate and further steps may be designed to relate these differences to measures of rejection probabilities, turn-in probabilities, and perhaps probabilities of apprehension. Further questions may be designed to probe possible reasons for their judgments and to help isolate the determinants of their opinions. If the latter step is effective, the profession may get direction for planning both its control situations and its educational programs.

The obvious weakness in the above recommendation is that most proposals for trust violation undoubtedly travel from weak link to weak link rather than from average member to average member. It may be useful therefore to question subjects about their attitudes toward other members of their own internal-control groups. These questions may be designed primarily to evaluate the degree of homogeneity within groups. Thus a member of the bookkeeping group may be asked to consider a conditional reward and to think of the person in his own group whom he would be least (or most) reluctant to approach. Next he may be asked to place a relative figure on his reluctance to approach a group member selected at random. The purpose, of course, is to get some feel for the homogeneity of the group. Intergroup perceptions also require testing.

Probably the simplest approach is through a questionnaire designed to test differences in reluctance. A simple incremental approach might present unidentified individuals to the subject group. Subjects may then be asked to assess their own reluctance to deal with these individuals in matters of trust violation. After evaluating the responses the experimenter may offer additional information about the individuals, e.g., that they are auditors, cashiers, store clerks. Reevaluations may then be requested. Hopefully the evaluative differences will be influenced by the additional information. One advantage of this variation is that all sorts of background variables and attitudes may be appraised and relative values assigned.

Other characteristics of each individual may be relatively stable so that differences in responses may be associated with the additional role requirements of the position. Incidentally, possibilities for asking the subjects to consider all sorts of sequential bits of information about group stereotypes may prove to be useful. The ordering requirements imposed on the subjects for simple transformations of this kind should not prove to be too difficult or impossible.[19]

Some subjects may perform erratically due to the moral burden of involvement in even a hypothetical embezzlement. This burden may be more than they can accept and still be effective subjects. Such subjects may be excused, but perhaps they can be made into effective participants by simply stipulating that they approach the

19. These suggestions seem to be in line with the vague Braybrooke-Lindblom concept of "disjointed incrementalism." See *A Strategy of Decision* (New York: The Free Press, 1963), esp. Chapter 5.

situation as if they were already irrevocably committed to the required violation. A simple statement that the subject through no fault of his own has been subjected to an intolerable stress and that violation of trust is his only possible course of action may be effective. This stipulation should decrease uneasiness about revealing his individual character, and it should direct attention to the variable of concern—the relative reluctance and the relative strength of psychological barriers.

December 1976

The Politicization of Accounting

David Solomons

There was once a time, not so many years ago, when accounting could be thought of as an essentially nonpolitical subject. If it was not as far removed from politics as mathematics or astronomy were, it was at least no more political than psychology or surveying or computer technology or statistics. Even in those areas of accounting such as taxation, which might be thought to be most relevant to questions of public policy, practitioners were generally content to confine themselves to technical issues, without getting involved *as accountants* in the discussion of tax policy.

Today, to judge from current discussions of the standard-setting process, accounting can no longer be thought of as nonpolitical. The numbers that accountants report have, or at least are widely thought to have, a significant impact on economic behavior. Accounting rules therefore affect human behavior. Hence the process by which they are made is said to be political. It is then only a short step to the assertion that such rules are properly to be made in the political arena, by counting heads and deciding accounting issues by some voting mechanism.

There are several articulate spokesmen for this point of view. Dale Gerboth writes that

> a politicization of accounting rule-making [is] not only inevitable but just. In a society committed to democratic legitimization of authority, only politically responsive institutions have the right to command others to obey their rules.[1]

1. Dale L. Gerboth, "Research, Intuition and Politics in Accounting Inquiry," *Accounting Review* (July 1973), p. 481.

And in another passage from the same paper, Gerboth says:

> When a decision-making process depends for its success on public confidence, the critical issues are not technical; they are political . . . . In the face of conflict between competing interests, rationality as well as prudence lies not in seeking final answers but, rather, in compromise— essentially a political process.[2]

In the same vein, Charles Horngren writes:

> The setting of accounting standards is as much a product of political action as of flawless logic or empirical findings. Why? Because the setting of standards is a social decision. Standards place restrictions on behavior; therefore, they must be accepted by the affected parties. Acceptance may be forced or voluntary or some of both. In a democratic society, getting acceptance is an exceedingly complicated process that requires skillful marketing in a political arena.[3]

May and Sundem take a similar position:

> . . . in practice as well as in theory, the social welfare impact of accounting reports apparently is recognized. Therefore it is no surprise that the F[inancial] A[ccounting] S[tandards] B[oard] is a political body and, consequently, that the process of selecting an acceptable accounting alternative is a political process. If the social welfare impact of accounting policy decisions were ignored, the basis for the existence of a regulatory body would disappear. Therefore, the FASB must consider explicitly political (i.e., social welfare) aspects as well as accounting theory and research in its decisions.[4]

Other voices which call for an explicit recognition of the probable economic and social impact of a new accounting standard are not always easily distinguished from those who assert that political considerations should determine what the standard should be.[5] However, these two views should not be confused. I shall return to this point later.

The Structure Committee of the Financial Accounting Foundation grappled with the question of the political nature of the standard-setting task in their report on *The Structure of Establishing Financial Accounting Standards.* On the nature of the standard-setting process, they say:

2. *Ibid.,* p. 479.
3. Charles T. Horngren, "The Marketing of Accounting Standards," *Journal of Accountancy* (October 1973), p. 61.
4. Robert G. May and Gary L. Sundem, "Research for Accounting Policy: an Overview," *Accounting Review* (October 1976), p. 750.
5. John Buckley, in "FASB Impact Analysis," *Management Accounting* (April 1976), straddles this line most uncomfortably. His article has been thought to support politically slanted standards, though he nowhere explicitly says that he does.

The process of setting accounting standards can be described as democratic because like all rule-making bodies the Board's right to make rules depends ultimately on the consent of the ruled. But because standard setting requires some perspective it would not be appropriate to establish a standard based solely on a canvass of the constituents. Similarly, the process can be described as legislative because it must be deliberative and because all views must be heard. But the standard setters are expected to represent the entire constituency as a whole and not be representatives of a specific constituent group. The process can be described as political because there is an educational effort involved in getting a new standard accepted. But it is not political in the sense that an accommodation is required to get a statement issued.[6]

There is something here to please everyone. Yet the committee does finally come out on the side of the angels.

We have used the word constituency to indicate that the FASB is accountable to everyone who has an interest. We are not suggesting that the Board members are in place to represent them or that the standards must necessarily be based on a numerical consensus.[7]

That accounting influences human behavior, if only because it conveys information, is obvious enough, though research into the workings of "the efficient market" has cast doubt on some of the supposed results of accounting choices. There are, without question, political aspects of accounting. There are similarly political aspects of physics, which result in enormous expenditures on research into nuclear energy and weaponry. Geology, in its concern with the world's reserves of fossil fuels, obviously has political implications. Research into sickle cell anemia became a political question when the heavy incidence of this disease among black Americans came to light. There are very few areas of human knowledge which are devoid of political significance. But that does not mean that the processes by which knowledge is advanced or by which new applications are found for old knowledge are themselves political processes, in the sense in which that term is usually understood. Political motives for asking a question may be entirely appropriate. A politically motivated answer may or may not be appropriate. It obviously depends on the nature of the question.

It may be useful to look more carefully at the part which politics should and should not play in accounting standard setting. The future of the Financial Accounting Standards Board may depend on

6. *The Structure of Establishing Financial Accounting Standards,* (Financial Accounting Foundation, April 1977), p. 19.
   7. *Ibid.*

a better understanding of that issue. Indeed, the very credibility of accounting itself may be at stake.

Accounting and National Goals

The most extreme expression, so far as I am aware, of the view that political considerations should enter into the formulation of accounting standards—not merely into the choice of accounting questions to be studied, but also into the formulation of the standards themselves—is to be found in a lecture given in New York in November 1973 by Professor David F. Hawkins.[8] Hawkins noted that Congress and the executive branch of the federal government were

> becoming more and more aware of the behavioral aspects of corporate reporting and its macro economic implications. Increasingly, I believe, these policy makers will demand . . . that the decisions of those charged with determining what constitutes approved corporate reporting standards will lead to individual economic behavior that is consistent with the nation's macro economic objectives,. . .This awareness on the part of economic planners brings accounting standard setting into the realm of political economics.[9]

Events since 1973 have not shown any diminution of this awareness. The question is whether this trend is to be regarded as a threat to the integrity of accounting or as an opportunity for accountants, perhaps even an obligation, to cooperate with government in furthering its economic policy. Hawkins left us in no doubt where he stood in this matter.

> The [Financial Accounting Standards] Board's objectives must be responsive to many more considerations than accounting theory or our notions of economically useful data.[10]

And:

> Corporate reporting standards should result in data that are useful for economic decisions *provided that the standard is consistent with the national macro economic objectives and the economic programs designed to reach these goals.*[11]

8. "Financial Accounting, The Standards Board and Economic Development," one of the 1973–74 Emanuel Saxe Distinguished Lectures in Accounting (New York: Bernard M. Baruch College, C.U.N.Y., April 1975).
9. *Ibid.*, pp. 7–8.
10. *Ibid.*, p. 17.
11. *Ibid.*, pp. 9–10. Italics in the original.

As if that were not enough, he added that "because the Standards Board has the power to influence economic behavior it has an obligation to support the government's economic plans."[12]

In that last-quoted passage, the word "because" is noteworthy, implying as it does that the power to influence economic behavior always carries with it an obligation to support the government's plans. Even if the matter under discussion were, say, pricing policy or wage policy or some aspect of environmental protection, the assertion would be open to argument. In relation to accounting, where the end product is a system of *measurement*, the posture which Hawkins urges on the Standards Board could, I believe, threaten the integrity of financial reporting and deprive it of whatever credibility it now has.

There is no question as to the sensitiveness of some, indeed most, of the issues which have been or are now on the agenda of the FASB or its predecessors, and of course this stems from the fact that standards dealing with these issues have influenced or will influence behavior. One can only conclude that there is widespread skepticism about the "efficient market" hypothesis. Financial men are not at all indifferent to the accounting rules imposed on them by the Standards Board, but it is not the purpose of this paper to explore the nature of this concern.[13] For our purposes it will be enough to recognize that the FASB's constituents *think* it matters whether leases are capitalized or not, whether foreign currency transactions are accounted for by one method or another, whether contingencies are provided for by charges against income or by allowing retained earnings to accumulate. These questions do not affect the amount of information that is disclosed but simply the way in which these economic phenomena are reported; yet this fact does not make them less sensitive. Perhaps investors really are naive. Only on the basis of such an assumption (and on the assumption that no new information will be disclosed by a politically

12. *Ibid.*, p. 11.

13. Yet one cannot ignore the troublesome paradox posed by the numerous empirical studies which have shown "that the capital market does distinguish between [accounting] changes that appear to be reporting changes of no economic importance and those that appear to have substantive economic implications." (Nicholas J. Gonedes and Nicholas Dopuch, "Capital Market Equilibrium, Information Production and Selecting Accounting Techniques: Theoretical Framework and Review of Empirical Work," *Studies in Financial Accounting Objectives: 1974,* Supplement to vol. 12 of the *Journal of Accounting Research.*) If the market can "see through" accounting changes which result from changes in standards, why do they generate so much heat?

motivated standard) is the impact of politics on accounting standards worth discussing at all.

The Economic Impact of Accounting Standards

Few if any accounting standards are without some economic impact. The requirement that U.S. companies write off purchased goodwill is said to give an advantage to foreign companies in bidding for American businesses because, not being subject to the same accounting requirement, foreign firms can afford to offer a higher price. FASB Statement No. 2, which requires research and development to be expensed as incurred, has been said to constitute a threat to technological progress, especially for smaller companies which may be planning to seek access to the capital market and will therefore want to show good profits before doing so.[14] Many people believe that a ban on "full costing" by oil and gas companies and a requirement that "field" or "successful effort" costing alone be used will diminish investment to develop new sources of energy, especially by smaller companies.[15] FASB Statement No. 5 on *Accounting for Contingencies,* by greatly restricting the circumstances in which an estimated loss from a loss contingency can be accrued by a charge to income, is said to have caused American insurance companies to reinsure risks where they would previously have relied on self-insurance.

One of the most sensitive standards has been that dealing with foreign currency translation (Statement No. 8). Under the so-called temporal method mandated by the Standards Board, monetary assets and liabilities of a foreign subsidiary of a U.S. corporation have to be translated, for consolidation purposes, at the rate of exchange current at the balance sheet date. Assets which in accordance with GAAP are carried at cost or cost less depreciation have to be translated at the rate current at the time they were acquired. Exchange gains and losses, realized and unrealized, have to be brought into the income statement. For companies which formerly used a current-noncurrent classification, the important changes from their former practice lie in the treatment of inventories and of long-term

---

14. This argument led Hawkins in 1973, when the treatment of research and development was still on the FASB's agenda, to say, "I do not believe the Board can eliminate the alternative capitalization." *Ibid.,* p. 14. Events proved him wrong.

15. See the FASB's *Status Report* No. 55 (October 14, 1977) on congressional support for the retention of alternative treatments for oil and gas accounting.

debt. Inventories, as current assets, were formerly carried at the current rate and are now carried at the historical rate. Long-term debt, as a noncurrent liability, was formerly carried at the historical rate; now, as a monetary item, it is carried at the current rate. Moreover, unrealized translation gains, formerly kept out of the income statement, now have to be brought in. The result has been greatly to increase the volatility of the reported earnings of companies with important foreign operations. Criticism of Statement No. 8 has focused on this increased volatility rather than on whether the new rules result in a better or worse representation of financial performance.

Numerous other politically sensitive accounting issues could be cited; but none has received as much attention as accounting for inflation, for none has such widespread potential repercussions throughout the business world. Each method which has been proposed to replace or to modify our traditional methods would affect different companies differently, making some look more prosperous than they are under present methods, and others less prosperous. For example, current purchasing power adjustments to historical cost accounting (general price level accounting) tend to make utilities with heavy debt capital look better off; replacement cost accounting tends to make companies with a large investment in depreciable assets—steel companies, for example—look relatively less profitable. A system using exit values (e.g., continuously contemporary accounting or COCOA) would make firms using assets which are not readily salable look bad. Though the protracted arguments about the relative merits of these and other rival systems have not generally overtly recognized the vested interests which stand to gain or lose by the way the argument goes, the political implications of inflation accounting have probably done as much to hamper agreement on the direction of future moves as have the technical problems involved.

In some of these instances, notably those concerning contingency reserves and foreign currency translations, critics of the FASB are asserting that economic behavior, such as reinsurance or hedging, which would not have been rational under the old accounting rules becomes rational under the new ones. Such an assertion is difficult to defend, because the new rules have not changed the underlying cash flows or the risks attached to them. Only if significance is attached exclusively to "the bottom line," rather than to the present value of the enterprise, can the change in behavior be defended.

Measurement and Politics

The above examples will serve to illustrate some of the points of contact between accounting and politics. Many more could be cited. Indeed, because the need for standards arises mainly in areas where there is controversy, it is highly probable that in every case some will think the new treatment less favorable to them than the old, and there is constantly a temptation for such people to rush off to their legislative representatives to get the government to interfere. That sort of initiative represents the gravest threat on the horizon to the private control of standard setting.[16]

If we are looking for ways to achieve political ends by tinkering with methods of measurement, plenty of scope can be found outside the accounting field. Indeed, the danger has already been observed in other areas. For instance, the index of retail prices has a powerful effect on wage settlements in many industries. There is nothing absolute about a price index. The number obtained depends on the choice of base year, the items chosen for inclusion in the market basket, and the weights attached to the items in constructing the index. A statistician who agreed with Hawkins about the responsibilities of those concerned with measurement could easily construct an index which would damp down price changes—then take credit for aiding in the fight against inflation.[17]

When is a worker "unemployed"? How a government defines unemployment can have a powerful impact on monetary and fiscal policy in a society which has definite views on what is and is not an acceptable number of jobless citizens, for if 5 percent unemployment is accepted as "full employment" for policy purposes, a recorded level of 7 percent will be read as signaling the need for monetary expansion or lower taxes. The way in which unemployment is defined and measured therefore has a direct impact on economic policy. Would anyone seriously argue that the statistical

16. The letter dated October 6, 1977, addressed to the Chairman-designate of the FASB by Senator Proxmire and four Wisconsin congressmen, and reported in *Status Report* No. 55, October 14, 1977, is a case in point.

17. There is nothing far-fetched about this. In *The Final Days* (Avon Books, 1977, p. 177), Woodward and Bernstein state that "late in 1971, Nixon had summmoned the White House personnel chief, Fred Malek, to his office to discuss a 'Jewish cabal' in the Bureau of Labor Statistics. The 'cabal,' Nixon said, was tilting economic figures to make his administration look bad." Another example came to my notice when I was in Singapore in 1976. There the administration was accused of keeping the price index down by changing the grade of rice included in the index.

measure of unemployment should be rigged (or changed from time to time) to favor an expansionist policy or its opposite?

I have suggested elsewhere that the highway authorities could lower the average speed at which vehicles are driven, and thus reduce the accident rate, if they would have all speedometers consistently overstate speeds, so that drivers would think they were driving faster than they actually were.[18] Speedometers influence behavior. Why not influence it in a beneficent direction?

This last example will serve to lay bare the profound threat to accounting implicit in the propositions of Hawkins and others which have been referred to above. If it ever became accepted that accounting might be used to achieve ends other than purely measurement ends, then faith in it would be destroyed, just as faith in speedometers would be destroyed once people realized that they could be falsified to influence driving habits.[19]

The view that "because the Standards Board has the power to influence economic behavior, it has an obligation to support the government's economic plans" is, I believe, not only destructive of accounting, it is also infeasible.[20] Governments have a habit of changing their plans from year to year, and even from month to month. Are accounting standards to be changed with every change in the political climate? One has only to recall President Nixon's turnabout from a "no wage and price controls" stance to an espousal of rigorous controls in 1971–72, or President Ford's switch from proposals for tax increases to "whip inflation now" in favor of tax cuts to stimulate employment in 1974, to see how futile it is to talk about supporting the government's economic plans, or how impossible it would be for a Standards Board to keep up with the government.

The Importance of Neutrality

The mere fact that information has an effect on human behavior does not mean that it should not seek to be neutral as between different modes of behavior. Unless it is as neutral as the accountant can make it, one can hardly see how it can be relied on to guide behavior. As Chambers observes, "If the form of accounting is

18. David Solomons, Price Waterhouse lecture at Stanford University in 1972, "Financial Accounting Standards: Regulation or Self-Regulation?"

19. Support for this view is to be found in Arthur R. Wyatt's article, "The Economic Impact of Financial Accounting Standards," *Arthur Andersen Chronicle*, September 1977.

20. See note 13.

permitted to change with changes in policy, any attempt to scrutinize and to evaluate specific policies will be thwarted."[21]

Neutrality in accounting implies representational accuracy. Curiously, this quality has been little discussed, though others related to it have received more attention. The American Accounting Association's 1977 Committee on Concepts and Standards for External Financial Reports gets near the heart of the matter when they say:

> Users of financial information prefer that it have a high degree of reliability. Reliability is that quality which permits users of data to depend upon it with confidence as representative of what it purports to represent. But reliable information is not necessarily useful. It could, for example, be reliable but unrelated to the use at hand. Several relatively general terms are often used as synonyms for, or to cover parts of, the concept of reliability. Thus, verifiability, objectivity, lack of bias, neutrality, and accuracy all are related to reliability. Like relevance, reliability (above some minimal level) is a necessary but not a sufficient condition for usefulness of data.[22]

If "like relevance, reliability (above some minimal level) is a necessary but not a sufficient condition for usefulness of data," the two qualities together go far towards ensuring usefulness. Relevance comprehends subsidiary characteristics of information that one might list—such as timeliness. And the essential element in the reliability of information (at least for our present purpose) is that it shall as accurately as possible represent what it purports to represent.[23] This is what I mean by neutrality.

Neutrality, in the sense in which the term is used here, does not imply that no one gets hurt. It is true, as the American Accounting Association's 1977 Committee on the Social Consequences of Accounting Information says,

> Every policy choice *represents* a trade-off among differing individual preferences, and possibly among alternative consequences, regardless of whether the policy-makers see it that way or not. In this sense, accounting

21. Raymond J. Chambers, *Accounting, Evaluation and Economic Behavior*, (Englewood Cliffs, N.J.: Prentice-Hall, 1966), p. 326.

22. *Statement on Accounting Theory and Theory Acceptance* (Sarasota, Fla.: Committee on Concepts and Standards for External Financial Reports, American Accounting Association, 1977), p. 16.

23. This is close to Ijiri's statement that "in general, a system is said to be reliable if it works the way it is supposed to." (*The Foundations of Accounting Measurement*, Prentice-Hall, 1967, p. 137). But his more formal definition of reliability is couched more in terms of the predictive value of information, an aspect of the matter with which I am not here concerned.

policy choices can never be neutral. There is someone who is granted his preference, and someone who is not.[24]

The same thing could be said of the draft, when draft numbers were drawn by lot. Some people were chosen to serve while others escaped. The system was still, by and large, neutral in the sense that all males of draft age were equally likely to be selected.

Accounting as Financial Cartography

Information cannot be neutral—it cannot therefore be reliable—if it is selected or presented for the purpose of producing some chosen effect on human behavior. It is this quality of neutrality which makes a map reliable; and the essential nature of accounting, I believe, is cartographic. Accounting is financial map-making. The better the map, the more completely it represents the complex phenomena that are being mapped. *We do not judge a map by the behavioral effects it produces.* The distribution of natural wealth or rainfall shown on a map may lead to population shifts or changes in industrial location which the government may like or dislike. That should be no concern of the cartographer. We judge his map by how well it represents the facts. People can then react to it as they will.

Cartographers represent different facts in different ways and match the scale of their maps to their purpose. Every map represents a selection of a small portion of available data, for no map could show physical, political, demographic, climatic, geological, vegetational, and numerous other kinds of data and still be intelligible. The need to be selective in the data that one represents does not normally (though it could) rob the map of its neutrality.

Like the geographic features that cartographers map, different financial facts need to be represented in different ways, and different facts are needed for different purposes. It is perfectly proper for measurements to be selected with particular political ends in mind or to be adapted to a political end if users of the measurement know what is being done. For example, the government is entitled, for taxation purposes, to define taxable income in whatever way it considers suitable. It would be quite another matter if the government required accountants to use this definition for all purposes to which they might put an income number.

24. Committee Report, p. 24.

That maps, like financial statements, can mislead, even when completely accurate, is undeniable. John K. Wright, writing on the subjective element in maps, gave a good example:

> Assume, for example, that the frontier province of Pomeria, which formerly belonged to Sudia, was annexed by Nordia in the last war and that a recent census has shown that half of the population of Pomeria are Nordians and half Sudians. The Nordians are concentrated in the towns, the Sudians form the bulk of the rural population. On a detailed map of Pomeria in the Bulletin of the Sudian Geographical Society the areas where less than 10 percent of the total population is Sudian are left white and those where more than 90 percent is Sudian are shown in dark red, with intermediate gradations of lighter red to bring out intermediate percentages. Clearly most of the map would be red, giving an impression of a preponderant Sudian population.[25]

Wright did not use the phrase "creative cartography," but he might have applied it to many of the map features that he mentioned in his paper.

Cartographers sometimes map the unmappable. They use a term "isopleth" to mean "a line of assumed constant value." For example, a population isopleth is a line joining points having equal population densities. Of course, a point cannot have a population density. Yet we have no difficulty in accepting such a line as having representational value.

Some Contrary Views

Recently a different view of accounting from mine has been expressed, and it deserves comment here. Sometimes the difference in the weight to be given to economic impact in standard setting is merely a matter of emphasis. Sometimes it is more fundamental. Sometimes neutrality is dismissed on other grounds.

Probably no one argues that those who formulate accounting standards should do so with total unconcern for the economic consequences. Indeed, without some concern for such consequences, the problem areas which call for standards could not be selected. Presumably the economic consequences of not having a standard to deal with some particular problem directed attention to that area in the first place, just as early cartographers concerned themselves primarily with territory which had the greatest economic significance to their contemporaries. To require the Standards Board to report on the probable economic impact of a proposed standard when an

---

25. John K. Wright, "Map Makers are Human," *Geographical Review*, XXXII (October 1942), 530.

exposure draft is issued[26]—if it can be done, for the impact will often be unclear or ambiguous—is not at all objectionable, *so long as the standard is designed to bring about a better representation of the facts of a situation, with whatever behavioral results flow from that, and not to promote some preselected economic objective or mode of behavior.*

Some of those who would play down the value of neutrality in accounting standards do so because, they argue, the financial phenomena which accountants must report are not independent of the reporting methods which are selected. This view is expressed by the American Accounting Association's (AAA) 1977 Committee on the Social Consequences of Accounting Information, in the following passage from its report:

> The view that measurement merely involves representing or describing stocks and flows is a static view. It assumes that the stocks and flows are history, fixed forever, no matter how you measure them. But what about tomorrow's stocks and flows? They are governed by the business decisions of enterprises—decisions which might change depending upon how you choose to measure the stocks and flows. The traditional framework fails to take this interdependence of measurement and decisional behavior into consideration.[27]

Where human beings are the subjects of measurement, it is true that behavior and measurements are not independent of each other. But this does not make neutrality a less desirable quality of measurement in such cases. If one substitutes speedometers for accounting and driving behavior for stocks and flows in the AAA committee's statement above, one can see that as an argument against neutrality it is quite unconvincing. There is nothing static about the relation between the speed of a vehicle and the reading on the speedometer, and there is unquestionably feedback. The behavior of the driver is reflected on the dial, and what is on the dial affects the behavior of the driver. Speedometers still should register speed accurately and neutrally. The decision on how to react to the reading must be left to the driver.

A different criterion for the selection of approved accounting methods is put forward by Beaver and Dukes in a discussion of interperiod tax allocation.

> The method which produces earnings numbers having the highest association with security prices is the most consistent with the information

---

26. As recommended by Prem Prakash and Alfred Rappaport in "The Feedback Effects of Accounting," *Business Week*, January 12, 1976, p. 12.
27. Committee Report, p. 23.

that results in an efficient determination of security prices. Subject to [certain] qualifications, it is the method which ought to be reported.[28]

And having found that "deferral earnings are most consistent with the information set used in setting security prices," they conclude:

If one accepts market efficiency, the results suggest that the A[ccounting] P[olicy] B[oard] made the "correct" policy decision, in the sense that it requires a method which is most consistent with the information impounded in an efficient determination of security prices.[29]

Beaver and Dukes themselves point out that any inferences to be drawn from their evidence are "conditional upon the prediction models used to test the accounting measures. . . . Any findings are the joint result of prediction models and accounting methods, and only appropriately specified joint statements are warranted."[30] In other words the identification of the accounting method which is found to generate earnings numbers or cash flow numbers most closely associated with security prices depends on the way that "unexpected returns" are defined. The results of this analysis do not point unambiguously, therefore, towards a particular accounting method.

This could well explain why, left to themselves, companies do not all choose the same accounting methods. They do not all use the same prediction models, and therefore the accounting method that contains the most information for one company is not the one that contains the most information for another company. One moral might be that we do not need accounting standards at all, but rather that in an efficient market laissez-faire should prevail. A different conclusion about the Beaver and Dukes study is reached by Gonedes and Dopuch when they say that "under the contemporary institutional setting, capital market efficiency—taken by itself—does not imply that the prices of firms' ownership shares can be used in assessing the desirability of alternative information-production decisions."[31] In any case, whichever way the efficient market points us, it does not point us towards politically motivated accounting standards.

28. William H. Beaver and Roland E. Dukes, "Interperiod Tax Allocation, Earnings, Expectations and the Behavior of Security Prices," *Accounting Review*, April 1972, p. 321. They add, in a footnote, that "the criterion suggested above provides a simplified method for preference ordering of alternative measurement methods."
29. *Ibid.*, p. 331.
30. *Ibid.*, p. 332.
31. "Capital Market Equilibrium . . . , " p. 92.

Limitations of the Analogy with Cartography

There is a danger, with any analogy, of pushing it too far, and the analogy between accounting and cartography is no exception. Most maps represent external phenomena which have an independent existence of their own. The accountant is on safe ground only when he is doing the same thing as the cartographer—representing external phenomena, in his case cash flows, contractual rights, market values, and the like. Of course, cartographers have sometimes amused themselves by drawing maps of fictitious countries, like Erewhon or Atlantis, an activity which, too, has had its counterparts in accounting.

Whatever limitations representational accuracy may have in pointing us towards right accounting answers, it will at least sometimes enable us to detect a wrong answer. For instance, FASB Statement No. 2, which requires all research and development expenditures to be expensed as incurred, is bad cartography, because to represent the value of the continuing benefits of past research expenditures as zero will usually not accord with the facts of the situation, however expedient the treatment may be. Off-balance-sheet financing requires that certain unattractive features of the landscape be left off the map, so again the map is defective. The criterion for judging these rules is not the effect which they may or may not have on business behavior. It is the accuracy with which they reflect the facts of the situation.

Conclusion

It is not at all palatable for accountants to be forced to choose between appearing indifferent to national objectives or endangering the integrity of their measurement techniques. But if the future well-being of our discipline is what matters, the right choice should be easy to make. *It is our job—as accountants—to make the best maps we can. Others, or accountants acting in some other capacity, have the job of using those maps to steer the economy in the right direction.* If the distinction between these two tasks is lost sight of, we shall greatly diminish our capacity to serve society, and in the long run everybody must lose.

October 1977

The Feasibility and Desirability of Accounting Standards

Harold Bierman, Jr.

William A. Paton and A.C. Littleton start their classic monograph on accounting standards with this statement:

> The purpose of accounting is to furnish financial data concerning a business enterprise, compiled and presented to meet the needs of management, investors, and the public.

> A consistent framework of standards is needed to serve as a basis for judgment in constructing and interpreting financial statements.

> Accounting standards should be systematic and coherent, impartial and impersonal, and in harmony with observable, objective conditions.[1]

Later they explain their choice of terms.

> The term "standards" is used advisedly. "Principles" would generally suggest a universality and degree of permanence which cannot exist in a human-service institution such as accounting.[2]

These introductory statements act as a counterweight to a series of attacks that are currently being made on the suitability of establishing standards. For example, Demski writes:

> . . . generally speaking, we cannot rely on standards to provide a normative theory of accounting. No set of standards exists that will always rank alternatives in accordance with preferences and beliefs—no matter

Note: In calendar time it is over twenty years since I took my last course from Professor Paton. In real time it is a great deal less.

1. W.A. Paton and A.C. Littleton, *An Introduction to Corporate Accounting Standards* (Chicago: American Accounting Association, 1957), p. 1.

2. *Ibid.*, p. 4.

what these preferences and beliefs are, as long as they are consistent in admitting to the expected utility characterization.[3]

The Demski position is not completely inconsistent with that of Paton and Littleton if we recognize that Demski is attacking what Paton and Littleton define to be principles. It is clear that Paton and Littleton recognized the danger of indicating absolute preferences that were all-encompassing. Certainly their explanations for avoiding the word principles is not inconsistent with the spirit of Demski.[4]

The primary object of this paper is not to define explicit detailed standards for accounting, but rather to argue the feasibility and desirability of setting standards. Let us consider two approaches to setting standards.[5]

The most direct way to set standards is to take specific business transactions requiring accounting entries and recommend the exact manner in which these transactions will be recorded and presented. The *Accounting Research Bulletins* and the *Opinions of the Accounting Principles Board* of the American Institute of Certified Public Accountants—and now the "Financial Accounting Standards" of the Financial Accounting Standards Board as well—have all been prepared and presented in this spirit. The overall structure of accounting is not defined by these standards but rather is implied by the specific recommendations.

The difficulty with such an approach is that frequently the standards lack theoretical foundations and are aimed at being short-run solutions to long-run problems, offered for political reasons or as a compromise. One result is that many standards adopted one year are revised later and then revised again. This is the situation with the accounting standards that have been established for accounting-tax differences, the investment tax credit, and the accounting for leases. A second result is that solutions relating to different types of transactions may be contradictory despite basic similarities in the

3. Joel Demski, "General Impossibility of Normative Standards," *Accounting Review* (Oct. 1973), p. 721. Elsewhere (p. 720) he states: " . . . no set of standards exist that will single out the most preferred accounting alternative without specifically incorporating the individual's beliefs and preferences."

4. See also R.J. Chambers, "The Possibility of a Normative Accounting Standard," *Accounting Review* (July 1976), pp. 646–52, and Joel Demski, "An Economic Analysis of the Chambers' Normative Standard," *ibid.*, pp. 653–56.

5. In place of standard, words like framework, foundation, guidelines, rules, or conventions could be used. The use of the term standard is meant to imply somewhat more authority and no flexibility in choosing the method of accounting.

transactions. Finally, the solutions may well violate certain logical foundations of accounting which have been generally accepted by accounting theoreticians.

The last sentence above suggests a second approach to setting standards: defining a general set of operating guidelines that in turn can be used to evaluate the accounting for specific transactions. Paton and Littleton's monograph is consistent with this approach. Consider two possible standards: First, *Match revenues of a period and the expenses of earning these revenues to compute the income of a period.* Second, *Record transactions as if the firm is to continue operations unless there are specific reasons for assuming termination of operations.* These two standards are well known to all accountants. As an a priori judgment they seem to be a reasonable start toward constructing a basis for recording accounting transactions. Now consider Financial Accounting Standard (2) of the Financial Accounting Standards Board, which requires the expensing of all research and development expenditures. This is a conservative procedure in the sense that there is zero probability that research and development assets will be overstated: there will be no assets.[6] However, the choice of conservatism (not recording a risky asset as an asset) in preference to matching of revenues and expenses (the research and development costs give rise to a positive expected value) should be noted. The violence done to matching by Financial Accounting Standard (2) is a major departure from the logically consistent financial accounting that some of us would like to see.

The primary justification offered for expensing research and development (and thus abandoning matching) is that it ensures comparability among different firms. Unfortunately the comparability is to a great extent an illusion. There is little comparability between otherwise similar firms undertaking different amounts of research and development. On an ex-ante basis there is no reason for concluding that all research and development is worthless and should be expensed.

The Financial Accounting Standards Board started recommending accounting practices for such things as research and development without having established basic concepts. If matching is not a standard but conservatism is, then one can recommend the expensing of

---

6. In a previous paper Professor Roland E. Dukes and the present author commented in detail on this statement. The arguments of that paper are not reported here. H. Bierman, Jr. and Roland E. Dukes, "Accounting for Research and Development Costs," *Journal of Accountancy* (April, 1975), pp. 48–55.

research and development in the interest of advancing conservatism. The accounting for research and development is a good example of the dilemma facing accounting. If research and development is capitalized as an asset and systematically depreciated, we can conclude in some situations, after the fact, that the asset was overstated. If research and development is expensed, research assets will never be overstated. On the average, we can be certain that assets of firms engaging in research and development will have their assets understated. This certainty is based on the reasonable hypothesis, backed by empirical evidence, that the expected value of research and development is equal to or greater than its cost.

It has been argued that since some people can be harmed and others helped by the same type of error, there is no one correct method of accounting, and that the accountant should merely supply the basic information, such as the amount expended for research and development. In that case the calculation of financial position and income would be shifted to the user of the data. It is reasonable to recognize and to make clear the difficulty of accounting for certain types of transactions and the possibility that the values presented are estimates of random variables. It is not reasonable to argue that the accounting profession should not define standards that help the practicing accountant record these transactions.

Simple Counting Problems

If someone bets that one plus one equals three and you testify as an expert witness that one plus one equals two, at least one person will not be happy with your judgment. The question then becomes whether one and one can be said to equal two without regard to the uses of the information and the extent to which the parties using the information will be benefited or harmed.

In general we would say that one plus one equals two and would be willing to see our conclusion in print. In the above example, however, we are aware that one person benefits if a different answer is given. When we know the consequences of our response, therefore, we may find reasons for believing a different answer to be appropriate.

Most of us think, however, that an accountant should report the sum to be two, not three, since it is useful for society to know that one plus one always equals two. The standard here is simply that one should follow a specific counting rule regardless of what the person receiving the information might prefer for a specific purpose. We assume it helps society to know that one plus one equals two no matter what accountant does the measuring, and no matter how the result is going to be used.

An arbitrary conclusion (or hypothesis) exists that society is better off with an exact counting scheme than with situations where an unconventional result is presented because it might be more useful for one or more parties. The use of the counting procedure is exact and well defined; and although it may ignore the preferences of some individuals, it has long-run advantages that are considered more important than any short-run gains from a more flexible procedure.

According to the above example, we want a number system where the rules of addition are not affected by the preferences and utility functions of individuals, but one that still accomplishes certain objectives. As we move from a number system to a measurement system should there not be some rules (or standards) that we can agree are desirable and better than alternative rules, even though some individuals may be harmed by the application of such rules? Management might be happier if the accounting reports following a given set of rules did not reveal a downturn in income, but this is not a sufficient justification, in itself, for departing from accepted standards for an alternative set of rules.

In setting economic policy, such choices are made all the time. The same person can concede that interpersonal utility functions are not comparable, but at the same time he can strongly support or oppose a taxing law which implicitly assumes that the utility of one method of taxation is higher than the utility of another method. We can likewise conclude that one method of measurement, accounting, is superior to other methods.

Let us proceed from abstract examples and consider the accounting for readily marketable securities. Is it possible to agree that one measurement scheme is more desirable than another, leaving out tax considerations, regulatory policy, and any other legal peculiarities? Assume that the accountant is measuring financial position at the end of an accounting period. The choice is between cost, market, some mixture of the two (such as the lower of cost or market), or a direct estimate of the cash flows of the asset.

Having studied economic decision-making, we know that a sunk cost is not relevant for any decision. The cost of marketable securities is a sunk cost and thus not relevant. While we might use cost as an estimator of value in some situations, where value is not readily available, this action is not appropriate here since the market value is easily ascertained. One could argue in favor of using a risk-adjusted present value measure; but it is not necessary to estimate value by this technique, since the market value offers an objective measure of the market's evaluation of the future benefits adjusted both for time and risk. There is uncertainty, but the market price reflects the relevant risk considerations.

A priori there is a logical reason for using market value as the basis of measurement, assuming that these market values can be readily and cheaply obtained. The user of information based on market values of marketable securities will have better information for making decisions than one using cost or some mixture of cost and market. If a rational decision-maker is going to use the information to make a normal investment decision, and if presenting and obtaining additional information has a cost—if he has to make an outlay to obtain it—the decision-maker will want a market value measure if he behaves in a rational manner. (Remember that there are no taxes.) We do not have to know the decision-maker's utility function to reach this conclusion; the only requirements are rationality and a conventional decision. This does not mean that all users of the financial information will be happy with the use of market values.

A third party may benefit if the decision-maker has faulty information, preferring cost as the basis of reporting: for example, a current stockholder might be able to unload shares of stock to unwary purchasers if cost is used as the basis of reporting. In other instances, when the regulation of a firm might be based on the use of cost, the use of values which neglected regulatory considerations might cause confusion for investors.

For such reasons one or more users of the information might prefer the presentation that is more faulty from the point of view of conventional decision-making. Should these considerations affect the overall reporting procedure? A conclusion on how to present readily marketable securities, without taking a survey of preferences among the individuals using the reports, is possible only if one is willing to make assumptions about the objectives of accounting.

We can assume that the normal investor wants information about the market value of the securities held by an organization and the tax basis of the securities. Someone might also want to know the cost basis of the securities and the date of acquisition in order to evaluate the quality of managerial decisions. But we should be able to agree that cost information alone is not sufficient. We should be able to establish a reasonable standard for presenting information about marketable securities that includes market value measures.

One can assume that the objective is to supply information for conventional decision-making. If the use of values results in undesirable consequences for a regulated firm such as a bank, then perhaps the regulations should be changed. Furthermore accounting cannot be use to safeguard the interests of all investors, since the interests of some groups of investors will be directly opposed. For example, if the use of cost were to enable an investor to sell at a higher price, then an unsuspecting buyer is paying more than he would otherwise pay.

If the value information is readily available, even though the cost information is presented, it can be argued that the stock price of the firm will be set by an efficient market and the form of the accounting information is not important. This argument assumes that the market value information is readily available to enough investors to cause the market price to adjust in response to the value information. But in some situations the harm is done if only one buyer is taken in by the misleading accounting. For example, when one firm is acquiring a second firm which is privately owned, there is no market price. Rather the price is negotiated. If one bidder is faked out, this may be sufficient to set a price that is out of line with the facts of the situation.

An efficient market, by definition, readily digests and reflects publicly available information; but if the information is not readily available, the market is not likely to reflect it accurately. Suppose that a company has information about the value of land it possesses but that this information is not published. The market can only guess the value of the land. The company might indicate that it owns two million acres of timberland, but such a description is not a sufficient basis for evaluating the resources of the firm.

Measurement of Value

We have used the term value but have not defined it exactly. The word is somewhat ambiguous since it can have several meanings. First, we should recognize that the value of an asset is not necessarily measured by its cost, though the cost and value may happen to be equal. Three different measures of value are worth considering: the value in exchange, that is, either buying or selling the asset; the value in liquidation; and the value in use.

These three measures do not exhaust all the possibilities. For example, here we will consider value only from the point of view of the individual firm, but one could also consider it from the point of view of society or the economy.

The value in exchange, at the time of the acquisition, is equal to the cost of the asset. With the passage of time the value in exchange will not necessarily equal the replacement cost. If the asset is currently held, the owner might be more interested in what he could realize from its sale than what he would have to pay to replace it. The exchange value, if one is acquiring an asset, may not be identical to the exchange value if one is selling it, assuming that we are dealing with imperfect markets and there are implicit selling costs and discrimination by sellers and buyers.

Now let us consider the difference between the exchange value and the liquidation value. Liquidation value implies that the owner is forced to dispose of the asset within a given time. This pressure may require him to accept less than the exchange value in order to complete the sale within the time limit.

Finally, we must consider the value in use. Once a firm acquires an asset, the asset will have a value specifically associated with the firm that acquired it. For example, when a firm builds a plant, the plant may have one value to that firm, because of the firm's special skills, but another value if it were owned by a different firm lacking these skills. The amount that the asset could be sold for is less important than the value resulting from its prospective use by the firm.

Unfortunately there remain many unresolved problems in measuring values in use for assets and liabilities. Recognizing that uncertainty is present, rather than one value in use, we may have a probability distribution of outcomes. The actual value in use will depend on which state of nature takes place in the future. The present equivalent value, or risk-adjusted present value, depends on how the market measures and weights the different possible outcomes. This implies adjustments for time value, probabilities, and risk preferences. Also, value in use is not independent of the cost of replacing the asset since replacement cost sets a maximum limit on the asset's value.

Probability Distributions

Most accounting measures deal with economic resources to which some degree of utility attaches. In accounting, as in the physical or social sciences, the true or exactly correct measurement is seldom attainable. It may in fact be impossible to define. There is a likelihood that a measurement will coincide with the true state of nature, but it is more correct to speak of a probability distribution about the measure. A person can measure a table and say it is 6 feet long, but a more exact measure, perhaps with a different tool, may indicate 6.1 feet, or 6.15, or 6.158, and so on. We might find that the measure depends on temperature. Any of these measures, or an average of several measures, could be interpreted as a mean of a distribution, with the unknown true measure falling within a given interval. The "true" measure exists, but we do not know its value.

The word true is being used here in the same sense that Raiffa and Schlaiffer use it in the following passage.[7]

> . . . we shall be concerned with the logical analysis of choice among courses of action when (a) the consequences of any course of action will depend upon the "state of the world," (b) the true state is as yet unknown, but (c) it is possible at a cost to obtain additional information about the state.

We can rarely observe the true value; more generally we will have to estimate it. For example, J. Johnston makes this point in establishing the foundation of econometric solution to the problem of estimation:[8] "It may be that a variable Z is exactly related in a linear fashion to X by the relation $Z = \alpha + \beta X$, but errors of measurement obscure the true value Z, and instead of Z we observe $Y = Z + U$ where U denotes the measurement term."

The true measure in accounting may turn out to be a long description. For example, a firm might face a gamble when two possible outcomes occur at one period from now, as in the figure:

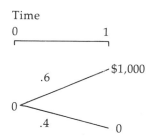

The figure gives us all the necessary basic information, but anyone faced with a large number of such choices might find some summary measures useful.

7. Howard Raiffa and Robert Schlaiffer, *Applied Statistical Decision Theory* (Boston: Division of Research, Graduate School of Business Administration, Harvard University, 1961), p. 3.

8. J. Johnston, *Econometric Methods* (New York: McGraw-Hill, 1960), pp. 6–7.

One summary measure is to compute the expected monetary value. This is $600. But the cash flows occur at time 1 and must be adjusted for timing. If the $1,000 cash flow is adjusted for time value, assuming that the discount rate is 10 percent, we obtain $909 for a present value and $545 for expected present value. It is still necessary to subtract an amount for the market's risk aversion. Reasonable persons might disagree on the amount of cash flows and their probabilities, the time value factor that is used, the deduction for risk aversion, and the sequence and method of calculation. But there should not be any disagreement on the desirability of developing the basic elements of the calculation, a summary measure of the risk-adjusted present value, as well as a full description of the nature of the asset.

It was suggested above that one could move the estimate of value away, on the average, from the unknown true value. This can be illustrated by considering the following biased measures for the example:

1. The use of $1,000, the maximum amount

2. The use of $0, the minimum amount

3. The use of $600, the expected value at time 1, without any time value adjustment

4. The use of $545, the expected present value, without any adjustment for risk preferences

In any particular situation one of the above may be better than a more sophisticated calculation. But in general all of the above measures have severe faults that introduce a bias away from a likely market value measure.

The accountant uses the unit of dollars to measure financial position at a given moment and income for a given period. Except in an artificially simple situation no one can measure either of these items exactly, but we can ordinarily tell when we are moving closer to the true measure or away from it. Assume that the true measure of total assets is A and that we are attempting to estimate A. We can measure a component of A in several ways and be reasonably certain that one of these ways will lead to a less biased measure of A than the others would yield. For example, we can count cash and consider that sum to be a component of A, or we can take the sum of cash and subtract $1 million in the interest of conservatism. The second procedure introduces a known bias and as a rule moves the estimate of total assets away from a true estimate of A. Thus, although one cannot expect to find the true measures of income and financial position—these terms are even difficult to define—we can move closer to the true measures instead of allowing known biases to exist.

The misconception held by some, that accountants should be able to present the one true measure, has hindered progress in the reporting of financial information. If accounting were limited to presenting the amount of cash in the bank, a true measurement might be attainable. But when the scope of accounting is broadened from the limited objective of measuring cash, the possibility of finding true measures or measures that are always correct disappears beyond reach. The goal should be to present useful financial information arrived at in a fair or reasonable manner.

Instead of fair, we could say objective—not in the conventional sense of the practicing accountant, but meaning relative freedom from the biases of specific individuals. It is reasonable to attempt to remove excessive biases of individuals and to reach common agreement, but such agreement should be what a reasonable person would conclude from the evidence. One should not expect that all reasonable persons would arrive at the same estimate, but rather that the estimates of a group of qualified, unbiased experts would not be too widely dispersed. Practicing accountants have preempted the term objective for a more narrow meaning than that suggested here.

Today the accountant presents information, and the knowledgeable reader knows that the reports are prepared in accordance with given rules. These rules restrict the differences between one accountant's results and those that another accountant might obtain; the dispersion of possible outcomes arising from hiring different accountants is thus relatively small, although by no means close to zero.

One must realize that measures of income or financial position are actually probability distributions. At best the accountant is presenting estimates and the true values (forever unknown) may be different. The physicist is willing to estimate the distances to stars in thousands of light years. There is no reason why accountants cannot apply the same sort of reasoned judgment to financial affairs.

More than One Method

The accounting profession has tended to search for one method of accounting that will fill all needs. Historically we have had the choices between cost-based accounting, value accounting, and price level accounting (price index applied to some items, common dollar, or some variation of replacement cost).

We should note that there are objective value measures for some assets, such as marketable securities, and where they are available and reliable these value measures should be used. For other assets, reliable value measures may be much more difficult, perhaps even impossible, to obtain. The value of specific assets may be so woven into the entire economic fabric of the corporation that if value were used to record the assets the accountant would have to value the firm. (He would then need to justify the value measure obtained, compared to the market value in total of the company's securities outstanding.)

In the presence of imperfect markets, uncertainty and long time horizons, and interrelationships of assets, the accountant may have to use original cost adjusted in some systematic fashion for wear and tear, that is, some depreciation procedure. But while we may be able to define reasonably the type of information which would be best for a rational decision-maker, it may not be feasible to supply that information.

The recommendation that cost may be a safe haven from a storm of uncertainty and complex relationships does not preclude a systematic adjustment for price level changes if the circumstances surrounding the decision require that type of adjustment. The accountant might even supply value estimators if reasonable bases for making the estimates are available.

For example, consider a stand of timber owned by a corporation. The cost of the seedlings thirty years earlier is obviously one bit of available information. But is that cost information more useful than a professional estimate of the current value, after the trees have grown for thirty years? A prospective purchaser of the firm would want an estimate of today's value of the timber and the land. A buyer of common stock deserves the same information.

Instead of timberland we could shift to a coal mine or an oil well. With such properties the costs of discovery or development are not likely to indicate the value of the resource. An investor in the securities of a corporation possessing such assets recorded at cost is handicapped in appraising the financial health and prospects of the corporation.

With respect to an oil company, we might not all agree on the best set of information, but could we agree that as a prospective investor we would be interested in these items?

1. The proven recoverable oil reserves and the types of oil
2. The location of the oil reserves
3. The costs of recovery and of getting the oil to market
4. The current price of the oil and the expected future prices
5. The rate at which the oil can be pumped
6. Any political or institutional factors, such as tax status, that might affect value

If this information were combined into one value measure we would no doubt differ on such estimates as future prices, time discount factors, risk adjustments, and the like. But we would easily agree that some measures for the listed items are needed by a rational investor. It will be more difficult to agree on the exact value of a summary measure of risk-adjusted present value.

Thus we should try to concur on the basic elements of information which a reader of a financial statement certainly needs, and then recognize that there is room for disagreement about the refinements of presentation.

We may still be willing to accept some generalizations as standards. The following statements might help to establish such standards:

1. Revenues should be recognized when earned.
2. When reliable value measures are available, they should be used.
3. When cash flows are to be received or disbursed in the future, the time value of money should be taken into consideration using the best estimators of interest rates.
4. Depreciation expense accounting should be a systematic method of allocating the cost of an asset to expense over the life of the asset, taking into consideration value decreases when justification exists for estimating such decreases.

The above statements are not presented as absolutely correct or all-inclusive standards, but rather as candidates for consideration. Others could be suggested. The establishment of a set of standard guidelines is useful, however, as a basis for accounting procedures for specific transactions.

Are there any standards affecting accounting that we can accept universally? Let us consider the time value of money. Most accountants would agree, one hopes, that in the normal commercial world, with its opportunities to lend and borrow funds, a dollar received today is worth more than the dollar received one year from today.

If the basic concept of time value of money is accepted, then accounting transactions should take note of interest costs. For example, a building that will cost $10 million if payment is made at time 0 may cost $12 million if payment is made two years later, when the building is ready for occupancy. What is the cost of the building? Does the cost depend on whether the payment is $10 million at time 0 or $12 million at time 2? Would it help to know that the firm can borrow or lend at an interest rate of 10 percent? Would you want to know whether the building was financed with debt or common stock?

However one answers the above questions, it is clearly incorrect to record the building at a cost of $10 million if the payment happens to be made at time 0 and $12 million if the payment happens to be made at time 2. This situation illustrates the ever-present and unresolved problem of interest during construction. Some firms recognize interest and some do not, a practice suggesting that the presence or absence of interest is a function of the specific corporation for whom the accounting is being done. Accounting should acknowledge the universality of interest (time value of money) and then decide how it should be treated in situations where there are interest costs.

General standards can never be expected to solve all accounting problems. There will always be specific situations that require analysis peculiar to the circumstances. For example, one of the major deficiencies of current reporting practices is the failure to consolidate the financial affairs of a parent and its captive finance company. The captive finance company carries the receivables of the parent (financed with a large percentage of debt), but this separate entity is not consolidated since it is a "different type of business." A standard is needed to define more exactly those corporations which are not to be consolidated.

Conclusions

We sometimes tend to think of accounting as entailing unique difficulties of measurement. Its problems are common to other disciplines, an example being the relatively easy problem of measuring the maximum life span of a person. One can give a facile answer based on recorded history, but consider the following statement by William Feller:[9]

9. William Feller, *An Introduction to Probability Theory and Its Applications* (London: John Wiley & Sons, Inc., 1950), pp. 7–8.

It is impossible to measure the life span of an atom or a person without some error, but for theoretical purposes it is expedient to imagine that these quantities are exact numbers. . . . Is there a maximal age beyond which life is impossible, or is any age conceivable?. . .Moreover, if we were seriously to discard the possibility of living 1000 years, we should have to accept the existence of a maximum age, and the assumption that it should be possible to live x years and impossible to live x years and two seconds is as unappealing as the idea of unlimited life.

In the same spirit that Feller is willing to accept the probability that a person might live to be a thousand years old, we should be willing to estimate the financial position and income of a business firm.

Henry Morgeneau has written that measurement cannot be "exempt from analysis; for if it were, every measurement would require to be simply accepted as a protocol of truth, and one should never ask which of two conflicting measurements is correct, or preferable."[10]

The accounting profession cannot consider the basic questions of measurement to be exempt from analysis. Present accounting practices of measurement are not "protocols of truth." We must understand the nature and problems of measurement if the practice of accounting is to realize its full potential in reporting financial information. Not all accountants are entirely in agreement, and accounting conventions are constantly changing. The accountant is charged with reporting financial affairs in an uncertain world. Inevitably there is controversy about the methods of accounting and about the actual measures presented. This controversy is welcome. One's profession is much more interesting when it is dynamic, ever changing, and challenging than when it is stagnant.

The relevant question facing accountants is whether a set of intuitively appealing, logically consistent standards can be established on an a priori basis. Or is it necessary to determine the utility of the alternatives and choose the alternative with the highest measurable utility? If we insist on the latter course we must conclude that the setting of standards is not feasible. If on the other hand we recognize that we must choose between different measurements despite the incompleteness of our information, and that the solutions we reach will not necessarily be the best in all respects, we can then make these choices with good conscience.

---

10. Henry Morgeneau, "Philosophical Problems Concerning the Meaning of Measurement on Physics," in C.W. Churchman and P. Ratoosh (eds.), *Measurement, Definitions, and Theories* (New York: John Wiley & Sons, Inc., 1959).

Accounting is not a science, subject to the same exact rules as counting. On the other hand, accounting should not be without a well-defined structure.

Accounting is the art of measuring and communicating financial information about economic events in accordance with reasonably well-defined conventions that are intuitively appealing. Once we agree that the tasks of measuring the financial position and income of a period with perfect accuracy are impossible, we can proceed with improving the state of the art.

June 1976

Accounting for Investments in Debt Securities

Maurice Moonitz

This study of accounting for investments in debt securities treats a part of the broader topic of accounting for intercorporate investments and is a companion to a recent study of intercorporate investment in shares of capital stock.[1] The discussion here is conceived as an aid to decision-makers in the field of accounting. Accordingly it starts from the conventional practices of the day, subjects them to close scrutiny, considers the alternative use of the consistent use of market values, and makes a few recommendations.

Nature of an Investment

Investments in equities (capital stock and rights to acquire capital stock) and in debt instruments clearly qualify as assets of the investor. They are economic resources that are sought after, or valued, because they embody the right to or expectation of future cash receipts; those rights and expectations are protected in varying degrees by contractual and statutory provisions, enforceable if necessary in a court of law. In brief, investments possess the usual desired attributes of assets.

Investments differ, however, in one important respect from other items classed as assets. Always in form and frequently in substance they represent an interest in someone else's operations. Their value

---

1. Reed K. Storey and Maurice Moonitz, *Market Value Methods for Intercorporate Investments in Stock.* Accounting Research Monograph No. 2 (New York: American Institute of CPAs, 1976).

depends in large measure on the extent to which the issuers of the securities manage their operations. The owner-investor can do little except, given a well-organized securities market, decide to hold, to buy (invest), or to sell (disinvest). An obvious exception to this statement is the parent-subsidiary relationship: in such cases the securities that represent the legal tie between parent and subsidiary do not appear in the consolidated financial statements that are prepared to reflect the economic substance of the activities conducted within the controlled group.

The management of an economic entity has direct control over its assets other than investments. The costs and benefits of managing those other assets flow directly to the entity, not indirectly as is the case with investments generally. The skills needed to manage the two groups of assets are somewhat different. To manage a factory requires skills in designing and operating factory facilities, for example, or procuring raw materials, recruiting and training a labor force, and marketing the product. To manage a portfolio of securities requires some skill in assessing the quality of business operations and estimating the effect of securities-market forces on particular investments. In large measure a skilled factory manager looks inward, a skilled portfolio manager outward.

These considerations suggest that financial reporting could reflect this basic difference among the assets. For example, a statement of financial position could group the investments together under a single caption separate and apart from the assets devoted to the other activities of the entity. An income statement could report the results of investment activities (for example, dividends, interest, capital gains and losses) in one place or section, distinct and apart from the results of other activities; and a statement of the flow of funds could be handled similarly.

Difference between Equity and Debt Securities

Equity securities are open ended. Ownership of these entitles investors to participate in the results accruing to the class of security held, according to the priorities and formulas contained in the contracts with the issuers. If results are poor, investors in equity securities stand to gain little, if anything, and may lose part or even all of their investment. If results are good, they stand to gain much. This characteristic is evident, for example, in the prevalent rule that dividends on such securities do not inure to the benefit of investors until they are earned *and* declared by the directors of the issuer. No financial return is guaranteed to investors until earnings emerge and dividends are declared. Other evidence of open-endedness is the absence, in most cases, of a maturity date. There is no guarantee that investors will ever get their money back. In such a situation the equity and the market price of an investment are more important than its historical cost in assessing its significance.

Debt securities are typically closed, rather than open ended. By contract, ownership entitles an investor in debt securities to a stipulated return, regardless of the results accruing to the issuer (debtor) as an entity. As long as the issuers have the wherewithal to pay, investors in debt securities are entitled to their interest and principal. But they have no claim to anything more. Debt securities have an absolute priority over equity securities. Interest accrues on the debt as a function of time, whether earned by the issuer or not. Debt securities also ordinarily have a fixed maturity date, at which time the remaining principal (or other amount unpaid under the debt contract) must be paid by the issuer to the investors. As a result of these attributes, the equity of debt securities in the operations of the debtor has no special or distinctive meaning. Cost and market are the figures of importance in assessing the significance of this type of investment.

The distinction drawn above presumes the existence of two separate classes of securities: equity and debt. In the world of finance the two classes do exist and are of considerable importance. But in addition some securities are designed to combine features of both: for example, convertible debentures and income bonds. There are also some debt instruments, such as low-grade bonds, issued by companies that no longer have the unchallenged capacity to pay according to contract terms. In that case the low-grade bond behaves in many respects like an equity investment.

The present study does not consider securities that combine debt and equity characteristics, as those are described above, the motive being to focus attention on the important cases in which issuers of debt securities do in fact live up to their commitments. By this device we can isolate the effects of market forces on the value of the debt instrument and analyze the consequences for accounting.

In the case of a debt security the terms of the contract assume great importance. The contract spells out the amounts of money to be paid by the issuer to the investors and the dates on which those amounts will move. At the date the investment is made the market rate of interest serves as a discount factor to equate the promises just described with the market price. After that date the market price fluctuates in response to two factors.

The first is the degree of doubt that emerges regarding the ability of issuers to keep their promises. As that doubt increases, the market value of the investment will ordinarily fall. Since this factor derives from forces confined to the issuer, and not to the market generally, we will not analyze it here but merely note its existence. Our attention will instead be devoted to the case in which a change in market price, if any, is attributable to the second factor, the market rate of interest.

When the market rate of interest drops, the discounted (present) value of the fixed set of promises contained in a debt instrument increases. It takes more money today to bring forth the fixed promises of the debt instrument. When the market rate increases, the discounted (present) value declines. It takes less money today to bring forth the same stream of cash receipts.

If investors hold debt securities to maturity, they will recover their initial dollar investment (principal), regardless of changes in the market rate of interest, because at maturity any debt instrument is worth its face value. If, for example, the market rate of interest has been increasing, the market value of the debt security will decline at first but then rise again to face value as the maturity date approaches.

Many investors do not, of course, hold debt securities until maturity but sell them instead to other investors. If so, the first investors stand to gain or lose from changes in the market rate of interest, since that rate in turn helps determine the market price of the security. Their proceeds from the sale will be more, or less, than the cost of their investments.

Here is another way of looking at the difference between holding a debt security until maturity and selling it prior to that time. As long as investors hold debt securities, they will receive the amounts promised in the contract and will therefore earn the market rate expressed or implied (the effective rate) in the price paid at date of investment, regardless of fluctuations in market price. This may be termed the contractual gain. The contractual gain may always be realized (unless insolvency or bankruptcy of the issuer occurs) merely by holding the investment to maturity.

At the same time, if the market price does in fact rise or fall, investors can realize an additional gain or loss by selling the investments. This we may term a holding gain (loss), also frequently referred to as a capital gain (loss). The market price of a debt security may then be described as the algebraic sum of its cost (amortized cost if premium or discount is present) and the holding gain (loss). The holding gain (loss) becomes explicit (realized) to the seller if investors do in fact sell. It is implicit (unrealized) if they do in fact hold. But the opportunity to realize the holding gain is lost if the investment is held to maturity.

Two related issues then emerge in accounting for these investments: when to recognize and report the realized (explicit) holding gains (losses); and when to recognize and report the unrealized (implicit) holding gains (losses).

Analysis of Change in Market Rate of Interest

In order to pinpoint the assertions made in the preceding section and to provide a vehicle for further discussion, we present a detailed analysis of the behavior of an investment in a debt instrument during a rise in interest rates. Specifically we examine the behavior of a $1,000 bond with a ten-year maturity, issued with a 4 percent coupon in a 4 percent market, the bond being therefore initially issued at par or face amount. In this way we avoid the complications of the amortization of premium or discount and instead assume effectively that we are dealing with direct placement.

We chose to avoid the presence initially of a premium or a discount because they are not essential elements of any debt contract. Premium and discount emerge as technical market devices to equate a coupon (contractual) rate with a market or effective rate that is lower (premium) or higher (discount) than the coupon rate. Premium or discount can always be avoided by stating the contractual rate at the market rate, as is done in the case of direct placements.

During the ten years of the bond's life the market rate of interest is at 4 percent for two periods; then it rises to 5 percent for two more periods and finally levels off at 6 percent. As a result of the behavior of the market rate of interest, the market value of the 4 percent bond drops to a low of $916 at the end of the fifth period then rises slowly to $1,000 at maturity, the end of the tenth period. All of this is summarized in the first three columns of Table 1.

The money flows are there displayed for two cases. In case A, the investor holds the 4 percent bond to maturity. In case B, the investor switches from the 4 percent bond to a 6 percent issue at the end of the fifth period by selling the 4 percent bond and investing the proceeds in a 6 percent issue. The details are shown in the last two columns of Table 1.

Table 1

BEHAVIOR OF INVESTMENT IN A $1,000 BOND DURING A RISE IN INTEREST RATES

Date	Market Rate of Interest (Percentage)	Market Price of $1,000,* 10-year, 4% Bond*	Particulars	Case A Hold 4% Bond to Maturity	Case B Sell at t_5 and Reinvest in 6% Bond
t_0	4	$1,000	Invest $1,000 in 4% bond	$(1,000)	$(1,000)
t_1	4	1,000	First coupon (4% of $1,000)	40	40
t_2	4	1,000	Second coupon	40	40
t_3	5	942	Third coupon	40	40
t_4	5	949	Fourth coupon	40	40
t_5	6	916	Fifth coupon	40	40
			Sell 4% bond	—	916
			Invest in 6% bond	—	(916)
t_6	6	931	Sixth coupon (4% bond)	40	
			First coupon (6% bond = 6% × $916)		55
t_7	6	947	Seventh coupon (4% bond)	40	
			Second coupon (6% bond)		55
t_8	6	963	Eighth coupon (4% bond)	40	
			Third coupon (6% bond)		55
t_9	6	981	Ninth coupon (4% bond)	40	
			Fourth coupon (6% bond)		55
t_{10}	6	1,000	Tenth coupon (4% bond)	40	
			Fifth coupon (6% bond)		55
			Redeem bonds—Face amount	1,000	916
			Gain for ten-year period	$ 400	$ 391

*Market price is calculated net of the coupon falling due on the respective dates. The formula for market price is:

$$\$1,000 \times \frac{1}{(1 + i)^n} + \$40 \times \frac{1 - \dfrac{1}{(1 + i)^n}}{i}$$

where i is the market rate of interest at the valuation date, and n is the number of periods from the valuation date to maturity. The first term in the bond formula above is the market value of the principal, the single sum of $1,000 due at maturity. The second term is the market value of the coupons, which constitute an ordinary annuity of $40 per period for n periods.

Case A—The Bond Is Held to Maturity

Under conventional accounting for commercial and industrial companies, the investment in the $1,000, 4 percent, ten-year bond is carried at $1,000 throughout the life of the bond. Each year one coupon of $40 matures and is collected. The same amount is reported as interest earned. The financial statements therefore report a steady 4 percent rate of return on this particular investment. This rate is squarely in line with the rate contracted for when the investor lent $1,000 to the issuer against a set of promises to pay $40 per year for ten years, plus $1,000 in a lump sum at the end of the tenth year.

As far as the formal financial statements are concerned, conventional accounting conceals the drop, and subsequent rise, in the market price of this bond. Where material, this drop would no doubt be disclosed either by parenthetical notation in the balance sheet or by other notes to the financial statements. The failure to recognize the implicit holding loss (and subsequent gain) is therefore not too serious as far as the asset side of the balance sheet is concerned. Readers can substitute the disclosed market price for the historical cost figure, if they so wish. But what the statements do not disclose is the fact that investments of the type represented by this bond are earning 5 percent for part of the ten-year period and 6 percent for another part. This type of information cannot be gleaned from formal financial statements, parenthetical disclosures, or notes. It is information external to the financial reports. Thus the fact is not disclosed that the investor committed funds to a 4 percent contract, when the funds could have been earning 5 percent and 6 percent on the same kind of investment for a large part of the ten-year period.

If the type of conventional accounting just described is modified to incorporate the changing market price of this bond in the formal accounts, a loss of $58 will be reported at the end of the third period, when the market rate of interest rises from 4 percent to 5 percent. (This loss of $58 will be offset in large part by interest income of $40 from the third coupon.) The financial statements for the fourth and fifth years will then report a rate of return of 5 percent from this investment. The 5 percent is represented by the sum of the $40 coupon plus appreciation in market price, divided by the market price of the bond at the beginning of the period. Thus for the fourth period, total income from the investment equals the $40 coupon, plus a $7 increase in market. And $47 is 5 percent of the market price of $942 at the beginning of that period.

Another loss of $33 is reported at the beginning of the sixth year, reflecting the rise in the market rate of interest from 5 percent to 6 percent. The financial reports will reflect a 6 percent rate of return for the last five periods, a rate calculated by taking the sum of the coupon ($40) and the appreciation in market price during each period and dividing that sum by the market price at the beginning of the same period. Accordingly the incorporation of market prices in the formal accounts not only has the advantage of reporting the current realizable value of the investment. It also shows the loss from holding a 4 percent (contract rate) investment in a 5 percent and 6 percent market.

Incidentally, at maturity the $1,000 invested in the bond is freed, regardless of the method of accounting pursued. At that time investors can shift their money to 6 percent debt and enjoy a $60 return each year, or they can elect to get out of debt securities and use the money in some other way.

Case B—The Holder Chooses to Reinvest

In this case we assume a swap or switchover at the end of the fifth period, ignoring transaction costs. At that time the holding loss of $84 becomes explicit (realized) and is recognized under conventional accounting procedures. The $1,000, 4 percent bond is sold for its market price of $916. The proceeds of $916 are immediately reinvested in a 6 percent coupon bond. The drop in price resulting from holding a 4 percent coupon bond in a 5 percent and 6 percent market becomes manifest and cannot be ignored.

As in case A, conventional accounting would report a 4 percent return ($40 coupon each year on an asset carried at $1,000) during the first five years, even though the market rate of interest rose to 5 percent at the end of the third year and the market price of the bond dropped accordingly. Conventional accounting then reports the loss of $84, an investment in a new bond of $916, and a return of 6 percent for the last five years of the ten-year period. The return of 6 percent is represented by the coupon of $55 on the new bond. For the last five years, the financial statements are squarely in accord with the realities of the market because the market rate of interest remains unchanged. At maturity, with the end of the tenth year, the investors receive the last coupon of $55 and principal of $916. They can then reinvest the proceeds of $916 in another 6 percent debt security, thereby continuing to receive $55 per year on the coupons, or they can decide to invest in some other direction altogether.

If conventional accounting is modified to incorporate the changes in market price, the financial statements will report a $58 holding loss at the end of the third period, a $7 holding gain for the fourth period, and a $33 holding loss at the end of the fifth period. These three amounts net out to $84, the loss recognized at the time of the switchover by conventional accounting. In each of the ten years the financial statements will report a rate of return on the investment equal to the market rate in effect during that period. The rate of return for any period in which the market rate of interest does not change is calculated by taking the algebraic sum of the coupon for that period plus, or minus, the change in market price during the period, and dividing that sum by the market price of the bond at the beginning of that period.

Comparison of the Two Cases

We are now in a position to make some comparisons and raise a question or two about the exchange of a 4 percent coupon bond for a 6 percent coupon bond in a 6 percent market. Table 1 shows that the net gain for the entire ten-year period from investing in a 4 percent coupon bond and holding it to maturity is $400. The net gain for the same period from switching in midstream is $391, or $9 less than if the investor had stood pat.

The shortfall of $9 in net cash inflow in case B compared with case A results from the earlier receipt of cash in the last five years for case B. Case B yields cash from coupons of $55 each year of the last five; case A yields $40. If the yearly excess of $15 were invested promptly at 6 percent, it would amount to $84 at the end of the tenth year:

$15 × 5.6371 = $84.

(5.6371 is the amount to which an ordinary annuity of one per period will grow in five periods at 6 percent, compounded once per period.)

The resultant amount of $84 is $9 more than the deposits of $75. It is also exactly the amount of the loss that was recognized at the time of the sale of the old 4 percent bond at the end of the fifth period and the immediate reinvestment of the proceeds in the new 6 percent bond.

The important conclusion from these technical considerations is that the swap created no income for the ten years taken as a whole. It merely rearranged the cash movements, moving the coupon payments forward in time. This rearrangement, however, occurs at the cost of a reduced terminal value—in the case before us, a reduction of $84. The fundamental question is this: where is the gain that we hear so much about from bond swaps or switchovers?

The only way in which the reinvestment in case B can be made to seem more profitable is to focus exclusively on the cash receipts from coupons and to ignore the changes in market price, even the one realized explicitly in the sale of the 4 percent bond at the end of the fifth period. We are fully aware that a rearrangement of cash movements may be of advantage to certain investors. They are the best judges of the pattern of receipts and outlays that they want. But that pattern involves working capital management, not the calculation of periodic profits or losses from operations. In ordinary accounting terms we once again confront a confusion in many discussions between the kinds of data that are to be included in an income statement, broadly conceived, and the kinds to be included in a statement of source and application of funds.

The preceding analysis also points up a type of locked-in effect for investments in debt securities. If investors elect to stay with debt securities of the type already held, and if interest rates rise, they can shift to a security carrying the current market rate of interest, but only at the cost of taking a loss on principal. In formal language, they can only exchange one set of fixed promises—their original holdings as in case A above—for another set of fixed promises with the *equivalent (discounted) value*. This is illustrated in detail in case B.

If they want to stay in debt securities, investors should hold on to their investments until maturity. At that time they get $1,000 and can reinvest in a 6 percent bond, as in our example above, and enjoy a $60 per annum return from that point on. Referring again to case B, they could take the extra $15 from each coupon during the last five years, reinvest it at 6 percent, the current market rate, and get back the $84 lost at the date of the switchover. But this is equivalent to considering just $40 of each coupon during the last five years as earned, the result investors get if they stand pat on the original 4 percent coupon investment.

Investors have another option. They can elect to get out of debt securities altogether. For example, assume that in case B investors expect equity securities to yield more than the 6 percent rate prevailing in the market for debt. They will then be better off to sell the 4 percent bond and reinvest the proceeds in a nondebt security.

A further point implied by the preceding analysis is that the historical-cost basis of carrying an investment in debt securities leaves the way open for income management by investors. If market rates of interest drop, the market value of the holdings will increase; but the increase will not be recognized until and unless the investors choose to sell. If market rates rise, the holdings drop in market value; but again, the change will not be recognized until the owners choose to sell. A thoroughgoing market-price basis will make it impossible for investors to manage reported income in this manner. Furthermore it opens the way to the use of realizable profit or loss as the preferred method of measuring the results of investment activity.

One other important observation is in order. In a sense the loss from a rise in interest rates, implicit or explicit, is timeless. It does not accrue, as we ordinarily use that term. It results from a change in discount factor, from 4 percent in our example to 5 percent, and then to 6 percent. In ordinary accounting terms, it clearly qualifies as an extraordinary item, even as a prior period adjustment in retained earnings. This kind of loss—or gain, if interest rates drop—is different from the gain we showed above, for example, in the market price of the 4 percent bond during the last five years. The gain in that case came about because the future cash receipts, especially the large principal payment at the end of the tenth year, moved one period closer, *but with no change in the market rate of interest used as a discount factor.* We should have no difficulty in agreeing upon the nature of a rise in market price from this cause, even though we may disagree on the precise time at which it should be recognized in the formal financial statements. Market appreciation and declination resulting from changing interest rates, however, are of a different type. In the accounts they should not be combined or classed with the results of operations directly attributable to the passage of time.

Bond Swaps of Public Employees' Retirement Systems

Highlighting some of the points made above are the problems encountered by certain public employees' retirement systems (PERS) or pension funds. Two types of events related to our discussion occur in the management and operation of these funds.

1. A PERS sells its low-coupon, tax-exempt municipal and state bonds and invests the proceeds in higher-coupon corporate bonds. For the ordinary investor the yield from these corporate bonds is fully taxable under existing provisions of the U.S. Internal Revenue

Code. But the PERS itself is exempt from U.S. income tax. As a result, the swap is clearly advantageous. It is only possible because the rules governing these retirement systems permit them to invest in high-grade corporate bonds.

This type of swap should create no special accounting problems. For example, a PERS invests $1,000 in a 4 percent tax-exempt municipal bond, principal amount, $1,000. It sells this bond for $1,000 and invests the proceeds in a 7 percent corporate bond, paying par for the new bond. The swap itself gives rise to no gain or loss on the books of the PERS. Its income rises from $40 to $70 per year, without the loss of principal we encountered in case B. Such arbitrage is possible in this instance because the markets for the two classes of bonds are distinct—the market for tax exempts being characterized by relatively low coupon rates, and the one for taxable corporates being characterized by relatively high coupon rates. A PERS is in a position to move between these two markets without affecting its tax-exempt status. It is therefore in a position to register a real gain by making a substantive change in its investment pattern.

2. A PERS sells its low-coupon bonds and invests the proceeds in higher-coupon bonds *of the same class* (for example, high-grade corporate bonds) in order to increase its cash flow. In this case the PERS may object to recording the loss on the sale of the old bond as realized all in one year. Instead the PERS proposes to defer the loss and amortize it over the remaining life of the new issue. But to defer the loss contradicts the known facts of this case. The loss is the cumulative result of the changes in interest rates that have occurred since the initial investment in the bonds. It belongs to the past. The latest date for it to be reflected in income or retained earnings is the date of the swap.

As we can see, this is precisely the kind of swap analyzed at some length in case B. The analysis there is applicable here. In brief, the so-called gain from increased cash flow is offset by the loss on the sale of the old bond. On balance, for the life of the two issues taken together, no gain or loss emerges.

As long as a PERS is required by law or regulation to follow generally accepted accounting principles it should account for its operations as though it were a profit-seeking investor. As a policy matter, a special exemption for such entities might be acceptable, but not the pretense that their bond transactions are somehow different from other investors' bond transactions, and therefore that the accounting principle applied to them is different from the one applied to investors generally. Different principles for different purposes lead to confusion and chaos. The path should rather be toward narrowing the area of differences in accounting.

Determination of the Market Rate of Interest

The previous discussion assumes that we know or can readily determine the market rate of interest applicable to an investment in a debt security. As a practical matter, market rates vary for different kinds of securities, so that a constellation of rates seems to exist rather than a single rate applicable to a broad class. The selection of the rate to be used as a discount factor then becomes of some importance if the debt security is not listed, and therefore no quoted market value is available. In that case, the market rate to be used as a discount factor has to be estimated.

The Accounting Principles Board (APB) issued *Opinion* No. 21, "Interest on Receivables and Payables" in August 1971. That *Opinion* is not directly concerned with bonds or the other forms of long-term debt that we have been discussing. Instead it is concerned primarily with so-called non-interest-bearing debt instruments and those carrying rates of interest on their face so low as to be entirely unrealistic. In those cases the APB requires the calculation of a realistic present value of the receivable or payable by the use of an interest rate as a discount factor. The discussion in *Opinion* No. 21 of the ways to select an appropriate rate of interest is what should be helpful in resolving the problems with which we are concerned.

Realized Gains, Unrealized Gains, and Market Values

The central point of this section is that attempts to combine profits measured by realization with profits measured by changes in market values in a single calculation of net income will at best confuse and at worst mislead.[2]

If historical cost and its twin, realization by sale, are to be the basis of accounting for investments in debt securities, then changes in market price should not affect the calculation of net income or the totals shown in the balance sheet for assets, liabilities, and owners' equity. Market values of securities held at balance-sheet date can be

---

2. The discussion in this section draws heavily upon Chapters 4 and 5 of Storey and Moonitz, *Market Value Methods*.

disclosed parenthetically or by note, but they should not otherwise enter into the financial statements.

If market values are to be the basis of accounting, then realized gains (the difference between acquisition cost and proceeds from sale) should not be included as an element of net income. Cost basis of securities still held can be disclosed parenthetically or by note in the balance sheet; the difference between acquisition cost and sales proceeds can be shown parenthetically or by note in the statement of source and application of funds, but it too should not enter into the financial statements reporting the results of operations.

To convey the reasons underlying the conclusions just stated, we need some symbols. Capital letters represent items that could appear in financial statements—balance sheets, income statements, statements of retained earnings, and funds statements. Lower-case letters identify the particular securities involved:

M is the market value of securities held.

C is the cost of securities acquired, held, or sold.

P are the proceeds (cash received) from the sale of securities.

G is the gain or loss under the market-value method, exclusive of interest income on the debt instruments.

R is the gain or loss under the cost method, exclusive of interest income.

b designates securities held at the beginning of the period.

e designates securities held at the end of the period.

a designates securities acquired during the period.

s designates securities sold during the period.

G is an interesting element. It consists of changes in the market values of four mutually exclusive classes of securities. We therefore create four subdivisions of G:

Gw denotes the change, from the beginning of the period to its end, in the market value of securities held throughout the period.

Gx denotes the change, from acquisition to sale, in the market value of securities bought and sold within the period.

Gy denotes the change during the period in the market value of securities held at the beginning of the period but sold within the period.

Gz denotes the change in the market value of securities bought within the period and still held at its end.

We now set forth the differences between the cost and market-value methods:

Market Value		Cost
$Mb + Ca + G - Ps = Me$	Balance sheet	$Cb + Ca - Cs = Ce$
$G = Gw + Gx + Gy + Gz$	Income statement	$R = Ps - Cs$
$Ps - Ca = F$	Funds statement	$Ps - Ca = F$

Note: F is the net inflow or outflow of funds from investments in debt securities.

This tabulation indicates that the funds statement is the only one that contains identical data under both methods. The neutrality of the funds statement toward alternative valuation formulas is one of its greatest strengths and should be built on. The proper place to show what was received and what was spent is the funds statement, not the income statement. The income statement is the proper place to show the results of operations, measured by accrual accounting as accurately and with as much sophistication as is attainable at any particular moment.

The formulas for the income statement indicate that G and R are incompatible concepts and measures. Gx, the gain or loss on securities bought and sold in this period, is an element in R; but no other part of gain or loss under the market-value method is found in the gain or loss under the cost method.

What then of the proposals to report realized and unrealized gains and losses in the financial statements? To complete the analysis, we need additional symbols:

U denotes the unrealized gain or loss in our holdings of securities.

Ub denotes the unrealized gain or loss at the beginning of the period,
$$Ub = Mb - Cb.$$

Ue denotes the unrealized gain or loss at the end of the period,
$$Ue = Me - Ce.$$

A basic arithmetic relationship now emerges: $Ub + G - R = Ue$. In terms of a credit-balance account for unrealized gain, this relationship describes how that account changes—the balance unrealized at the beginning of the period, plus the increase in the market value of all securities held at any time during this period, less the amount of gain realized on those securities sold in this period equals the balance unrealized at the end of the period. A simple rearrangement of the symbols reveals a useful shortcut: $G = (Ue - Ub) + R$.

This form of the arithmetic relationship indicates that we do not have to calculate the change in market value during the period for each of the four elements of G, namely, Gw, Gx, Gy, and Gz. Instead we merely have to value the portfolio at the beginning and end of the period, take the difference $(Ue - Ub)$, and add the realized gain from sales during the period in order to get the total amount of G. This is a useful work-sheet technique, but hardly a solid basis for reporting these elements in the financial statements. The central point is that G and R are incompatible and noncomparable magnitudes for conventional accounting periods of a year or less.

If we include realized gains and the change in unrealized gains in the same income statement —that is, if we add together R and $(Ue - Ub)$—we get G, the gain under a pure market-value basis. Why then bother to separate G into two incompatible elements? In that case both the balance sheet and the income statement are, in principle, on a pure market-value basis. The market-value method should therefore be used consistently throughout the financial reporting system.

If we exclude unrealized gains from the calculation of income and from owners' equity, we have a spurious type of market-value method. The income statement is on a historical-cost basis, and so is the balance sheet; but the balance sheet looks as though it is on the market-value basis. A more straightforward approach is to stay with the historical-cost basis in the formal financial statements, and to disclose market value of the securities parenthetically or by note.

Inclusion of both realized and unrealized elements, so labeled, in the same set of financial statements is sometimes defended as a transitional device, a means of smoothing the shift from accounting on a historical-cost basis to the use of a market-value (or other current value) basis. The motive is commendable; but the technique, as we have seen, is logically faulty and risks confusing or misleading the reader of the financial statements. It would be more straightforward first to calculate net income on a market-value basis and transfer it to retained earnings, after which management as a precautionary or conservative step could earmark a portion of retained earnings as restricted.

This procedure makes a clear separation between the measurement problem, reflected principally in an income statement calculated on the basis of the most up-to-date information available, and the policy decision as to the proper disposition of the reported net income. To the fullest extent possible, we should resist the incorporation of management's policies and biases into the steps we take to measure financial position and results of operations. To be most useful, accounting measurements need to be neutral toward the competing and sometimes conflicting interests of the various groups that have a legitimate interest in the affairs of the accounting entity.

September 1976

The Hard Core of Accounting

R.J. Chambers

Through the work of William Andrew Paton there runs a strand of confident assurance of the essential serviceability of accounting. Its function is indispensable in the conduct of economic affairs; it needs neither exaggeration, nor bombast, nor apologetics. In that confidence Paton has striven as a painstaking craftsman so that accounting would come to serve the financial community as widely and as well as human intellect can make it. He has always been aware of blemishes in the art and in its theoretical foundations; his characteristic reaction has been to seek out the principle at issue and to explore afresh the source or cause of an apparent difficulty or dilemma. It seems beyond doubt that, if his successors had followed up more of his many suggestions, the present state of accounting and accounting theory might have been happier than it appears to be.

The last two decades have witnessed a growing uneasiness about the possibility of developing firm and well-founded accounting principles. Rules and principles which once were asserted confidently are now hedged about with a plethora of provisos, qualifications, and exceptions. There is perfervid talk about problems, issues, and questions but no corresponding drive to solve, resolve, or answer them.

There are signs of a belief that accounting problems cannot be solved by intellectual effort but must be tackled by the procedures of quasi-political compromise. But the belief is defeatist—and otiose. For, if we must make compromises, we should need to know what is being sacrificed for what; we need some notions of what is ideal.

We are told frequently that accounting is a man-made device, and that its doctrines and rules can never be as precise as those of the sciences. But this is mere excuse, and false in substance. The body of knowledge popularly described as "science" is also man made. It is under constant examination and reconstruction. As for its precision, it is precise only at the level of principles; at the level of technological application it is no more precise or exact than human skill and judgment can make it.

We are told that there are no fundamental truths which underlie and which could give firm shape to the practice of accounting. But this is only quibbling. Artisans who have no knowledge of fundamental truths have pursued their work with great skill, simply by observing carefully the outcome of their work and accepting the discipline that the characteristics of their materials impose.

We are told that there is no singular concept of income, that no single method of general purpose accounting is "best," and that rules and practices must remain matters of judgment. This is mischievous. Judgment is an element of all technical arts. But if we have no firm idea of what is serviceable in a given setting, we have no way of determining whether a particular judgment is good or bad, and hence reliable or unreliable.

Such misconceptions as these threaten to make accounting like clay in the hands of an artless potter; or, to change the simile, like a clump of tumbleweed, blown about by every shift in the economic and political breeze. This may not have mattered when accounts were largely a matter of private concern. But now, to a much greater degree than fifty years ago, financial statements and the information they contain are used in a multiplicity of settings in which conflicts of interest arise. These conflicts turn on the disposal of money and money's worth. It is the concern of accounting with money and money's worth (or, generally, with dated money equivalents) which prompts the title of this paper—"The Hard Core of Accounting." For if accounting deals with flows and holdings of money and money's worth, its rules and processes must be disciplined by what can legitimately be said from time to time about those flows and holdings, and by the use which can properly be made of what is said.

The Variety of Financial Calculations

The forms and uses of financial calculations, statements, and reports are numerous and varied. Expositions of accounting commonly deal at length with their individual contents or components, treating each class of statement to a considerable degree in isolation from the others. We shall deal with all statements here as systematically related or relatable, for that is the way they are used in the reasoned conduct of financial affairs. For reasons which will become apparent we will adopt a temporal classification.

There are *past factual calculations,* describing the financial consequences of actions and events up to specified past dates. For present purposes, "past dates" will refer to all dates other than those defining the most recent period and balancing date. An income account will be taken to represent the aggregate change in the amount of net assets during the period ended on any such date. The sources, varieties, or subclasses of revenues and charges against revenues may be specified. But in essence the account is an aggregative account, explaining the change in the net wealth or net assets of a firm. A balance sheet will be taken to represent the financial position of the firm at a stated date. That position is indicated by subaggregates of assets and equities of different kinds. Because different kinds of assets and equities subject the firm to different risks or obligations and put it in a position to gain from different kinds of operation or events, judgments of the past and of the future turn on the composition of assets and equities from time to time. Successive balance sheets represent the shifts in the composition of assets and equities during the periods they enclose.

There are *contemporary factual calculations.* For present purposes "contemporary factual" will relate to statements covering the immediately past period and the latest balancing date. To take a fine point, these statements are past factual, for all factual positions and results are discovered after the event. But since the most recent statements have a more direct bearing on judgments about future actions than more remote statements, it is useful to classify them separately.

The components or contents of all retrospective financial statements, past factual and contemporary factual, are determinate in principle. The actions have been taken; the events have occurred; their financial consequences within a past period up to a stated date are or have been observable. Those consequences are independently testable.

There are *exploratory calculations* regarding the possible outcomes of alternative future courses of action. The most widely acknowledged form of exploratory calculation is the calculation of present values or discounted cash flows. A present value is an aggregative figure, in the same general fashion that an income figure is aggregative. It is the discounted expected consequence of the use in a specific way of a complex of assets. But just as an income statement represents only one aspect of the consequences of past actions and events, so does a present value calculation represent only one aspect of contemplated actions and events. Other aspects are represented in exploratory calculations of periodical incomes and financial positions. These are no less necessary than present value calculations, for any choice from among alternative courses of action will turn, in part, on the actual timing of net receipts (for that bears on dividend paying and other similar prospects) and on the expected future compositions of assets and equities. There will, of course, be adequate exploratory calculations in respect of each alternative course of action available at the time of any choice of actions.

Into these exploratory calculations will enter the purchase prices of new assets, the expected selling prices of present assets, and the replacement prices of substitute assets if replacement is one of the possible future actions. Commonly there are more ways than one of doing a given technical job, each entailing potentially different outlays and inflows. The only purchase price or replacement price which becomes of consequence to the firm is that for the chosen course of action; and it becomes of consequence only at the time of choice. Only for that purpose (and consequently for budgets embracing that choice) are replacement prices pertinent.

There are *anticipatory calculations* in respect of the outcome of a selected course of future action. These are embodied in budget statements of operations, income, and resultant financial position, representing the changes in the amount of net assets and in the composition of assets and equities that are expected to flow from a selected complex of actions. In principle a budgetary calculation will be one of the sets of exploratory calculations mentioned above, though in practice it may be more elaborate. The function of budget statements is to give direction and guidance to the activities of the firm, and to provide a point of reference for any revision of operations or expectations in the light of experiences during the course of the budget period.

There are also *auxiliary calculations* in respect of particular facets of the operations of business firms, calculations or product costs, process costs, sectional costs, and so on. These may be retrospective, exploratory, or anticipatory.

The Linkages of Past, Present, and Future

The past, which is the subject of retrospective calculations, is fixed, unalterable. Whatever can be known about the facts of the past can be known at the end of each successive period. Certainly it cannot be known whether some action taken in the past, but not completely consummated at any present date, will turn out in the future as was intended or expected. But the progress made up to any present date is discoverable; and when it is discovered one can then decide whether to continue with any such action or to abandon it, in the light of past progress and the currently expected outcome. (The originally expected outcome is no longer relevant, for the circumstances of the firm are no longer what they were when the action was taken.)

Exploratory and anticipatory calculations are distinctively different from retrospective calculations. The firm does not face a known or determinate "state of nature." Neither the firm's future environment nor its own operations in that environment can be considered fixed and determinate. The future is "to be made." Every action of the firm and every interaction of it with firms and other persons will influence its results and position in ways unknown at the time of calculation. All calculations relating to the future are imaginative constructions. Under these unstructured conditions, there is nothing firm which would provide a basis for assigning probabilities to possible outcomes.

The base point of these imaginative constructions of the future is a known present: for, first, no calculation about the future can be made without knowing the means available for the operations contemplated; and, second, no future position can be preferred to a present position without knowing that present position. All other components of exploratory and anticipatory calculations are expectations or guesswork. They may be founded, in part, on known past trends and currently known facts; but in principle they are hypothetical or heuristic. Of course, in selecting these hypothetical components, the imaginations of managers and their aides are not foot-loose and fancy-free. In the most general terms, they are constrained by the financial position at the time, and they are constrained by the wish or preference to be better off or in some better position at a future time.

Further, although temporally different magnitudes must be derived by different processes, the objects or properties of which they are magnitudes must be conceptually similar. "Income," for example, must refer to the same kind of thing in the term "attained income" as it does in "expected income." The income we strive for is the income we expect to spend, or use otherwise, if we attain it. If "expected income" and "attained income" did not refer to a common and particular notion of income, there would be no sense in comparing one with the other; no sense in saying, for example, that a firm's income was better than expected. The same applies to all other notions which have a past manifestation and are the subject of a future expectation. There are thus not different concepts of past and future magnitudes; there are simply differently dated quantifications of the same concept. This terminological linkage is essential to a coherent discussion of the coherent progression of thoughtfully managed enterprises of any kind.

These generalizations may be illustrated by reference to a specific type of problem situation. Suppose a firm's debt to equity ratio has been rising (*past* factual knowledge). Suppose the ratio has now reached a point where, under an existing bond indenture or other contract, the firm has little reserve borrowing power (*present* factual knowledge). And suppose it has in contemplation a *future* course of action requiring more cash than is expected to be available in the ordinary course of business:

1. The firm may make a new issue of shares, simultaneously reducing its debt to equity ratio and providing the required cash. Whether it will decide to do this will depend on its *past* rates of return and dividend record, its expected *future* returns from all sources, and its *present* knowledge of the state of the security investment market.

2. Or the firm may vary its present asset holdings, disposing of some to acquire the requisite cash. To consider this will entail a set of calculations of the *(future)* exploratory type, based on the *present* position and knowledge of the *past*, for each of the assets or combinations of assets it seems feasible to realize, and for the contemplated action and any auxiliary actions made possible or necessary by the sale of present assets. The present values, and the consequential results and positions, of all feasible variants would be compared.

3. Or the firm may vary its present policies to make available the requisite cash. It may reduce credit given, or the inventory levels it holds, or the dividends it plans to pay.

In appraising these possibilities the firm will make use of *past* and *present* knowledge and make judgments about the *future* reactions to or consequences of the variations considered.

In any such exercise, the products of calculations relating to the past, present, and future are all engaged, each in its own way. There are many such "actions in contemplation": the retirement of debt and the settlement of other obligations; expansion or reduction in the scale of business; variations in wage and salary levels and in labor usage; claims for governmental aid or bounties; reactions to changes in exchange rates in respect of foreign purchases; sales of investments; and so on. In every case use will be made of some combination of past and present information and future expectations. Since the processes of accommodating the firm to the numerous and varied shifts of circumstance that it may encounter are well-nigh continuous, its accounting system must stand ready, continuously, to supply information pertinent to all possible problem situations. That information, we shall hold, will necessarily represent stocks and flows of money and money's worth.

Money and Money's Worth

Every shift in the circumstances of a firm and every possible response has a money-quantifiable or financial aspect. Each, of course, has other aspects; and decisions must be made in the light of all aspects of the actions in contemplation. Each aspect must therefore be assessed severally before a judgment is made or a preferred course of action determined—"all things considered."

Physical, commercial, technical, economic, and financial aspects are separately conceivable, each in its own terms or its own appropriate "language." But it is not possible to discuss or describe any one of them in the language of another. Physical characteristics of assets are not described in monetary terms or financial aspects in physical terms. There is no determinate and invariant relationship between technical or physical features and the financial features of assets. Given the price of a five-horsepower motor there is no way of deriving from it the price of one-horsepower of "service potential"; given the price of a five-passenger automobile, there is no way of deriving from it the price of "one-passenger service," or "ten-passenger service." However, the traditional calculation of depreciation charges and depreciated asset values, being based on expected output or service life or service potential (all of them nonfinancial notions), presumes that there is such a relationship. This long-standing solecism has persisted in financial accounting, in lieu of the direct discovery, by reference to market prices, of the periodical financial magnitudes of depreciation and asset values. It has yet to be recognized that there is no such thing as a physico-financial magnitude, or a physico-financial income statement and balance sheet.

To return to money. Money flows in, money flows out, and money balances are held from time to time. The survival of every firm depends on its continued ability to command money receipts and to pay money out for goods and services, wages and salaries, rates and taxes, interest and dividends, and the retirement of debt. The importance of stocks and flows of money is undeniable. The traditional financial statements, however, include accruals and valuation adjustments which are not the amounts or consequences of money flows. The emergence of the so-called funds statement or cash flow statement is token recognition of the interest of users of financial statements in money amounts and money flows. The whole of the recent emphasis on the use of accounts for the prediction of cash flows evidences at least a ventral apprehension of the pertinence of money amounts and flows. Present value or "discounted cash flow" calculations seem also to command support on the ground that the arbitrary "cost allocations" made in traditional accounting are avoided. We shall argue, however, that these are partial and unintegrated responses to a basic deficiency of financial accounting.

The liquidation or conversion to cash of nonmonetary assets, inventories in particular, is the principal way in which firms acquire the means of meeting day-to-day obligations and adapting their operations to their circumstances. But cash holdings are precautionary, not profit making. Cash which is surplus to shortly expected requirements is invested in other forms; and at any time cash holdings are but a small proportion of the total asset holdings of a firm. The firm's "cash position" thus represents only a small part of its aggregate financial position. Changes in the money's worth (market resale prices) of noncash assets also affect the firm's financial position and results; and their magnitudes are just as relevant to internal and external judgments about the firm as are movements in cash holdings.

The traditional accounting process does not accrue these changes as they occur. And because the funds statement is, in principle, a derivative of the income account and balance sheet, it can do no better. Taking the three statements together, their users remain uninformed about such accrued changes in the money's worth of noncash assets as are disregarded, for whatever reason, in the accounting process. But *all* vendible assets are potentially convertible to cash; they represent accessible cash to the extent of their resale prices at any time. They are "as good as cash" to that extent, for all financial calculations. The amounts by which they are represented, even when they do not represent money's worth or money equivalents, are included in calculations of asset-backing and debt coverage and rates of return; that is, these assets are treated as if they were as good as money. If the income account and balance sheet were so designed that they represented the consequences of all shifts in money and the money's worth of other assets and in money obligations, the case for an auxiliary funds statement would collapse.

A further argument against the funds statement shows how tenuous is the belief in the usefulness of financial statements as indicators of prospective cash flows to investors and others. There is no necessary relationship between aggregate cash flows and any other financial aggregate. The management of the composition of assets is opportunistic. Funds which are surplus to the ordinary trading functions of a firm will be laid out in the most promising form of expansion, renovation, or other investment. There is no way of knowing in advance what opportunities will open up or close, what changes in governmental, commercial, or fiscal policies will influence the availability of and the demand for cash, or even what pressures on the part of competition and factor suppliers will affect the inflows and outflows from ordinary trading functions. If, as we have said, the future is yet to be made, there is no way in which any factual financial information published at a given date can yield outsiders a reliable indication of prospective cash flows. But it can be expected that dated financial information will indicate the *financial potential* of a firm at that date, the amount of money and money's worth which it commands at that date. This aggregate is intelligible and usable; and reference to it may enable outside users of financial statements to estimate at least the impact of external events as they occur.

Present Value Calculations

Present value calculations, or discounted cash flow calculations, are typically internal to the firm. Under our earlier classification they are exploratory, not anticipatory. Their products do not enter into budgets, although their component (undiscounted) figures for a selected course of action may do so, and thus may yield an indication of expected cash inflows and outflows. But the products of present value calculations serve a different function. They are used in the course of choosing, by people who are aware of (or can be aware of) the hypothetical or imaginative elements of their components, and can therefore fairly judge between alternative prospective projects.

By intention, present value calculations exclude the traditional provisions, such as depreciation charges, on the ground that these do not represent real outflows of money. Money outflows are deemed to occur at the date of purchase of the durables necessary to any project; and inflows from disposal of these assets are deemed to occur at the terminal date. In effect the outflow is treated as a sunk cost and the assets as having no recurrent periodical financial significance.

But we have contended that money inflows and outflows are no different in effect from changes in the money equivalents of non-monetary assets. The object of trading is an increment in wealth, not merely increments in cash. It follows that the test of alternative proposals is the discounted changes in wealth or money's worth from each proposal.

The use of present value calculations for commercial projects is derived from their use in purely financial settings. And those settings provide additional justification for the view we have just expressed. First, in all compounding and discounting calculations it is assumed that the accumulated sum at the end of one period is the sum invested in the next. It does not have to be received in cash; it is simply accrued, since it is "as good as" a receipt in cash. Second, the typical finance textbook represents the rate of return on a security investment by a formula of the style, $R = (D + \Delta P)/P$, where R is the rate of return, D is the dividend paid in a period, P is the price paid for it or its price at the beginning of a period, and ΔP is the change during the period in the price of the security. Here also the change in the money equivalent of the security enters into the calculation, for it is "as good as" cash. If an exploratory calculation of present value is made for a succession of future periods, the return for each period would properly include the increment or decrement in the "cash value" or money equivalent of the investment in each period; otherwise the result will not represent the effect of the temporal pattern of net flows.

The formal consequences of making present value calculations in the traditional way and in the manner suggested by the preceding argument may be illustrated by a simple example.

Suppose that one of the projects being considered by a firm at a certain time entails the purchase of a machine at the end of year 0, its use for five years, and its disposal at the end of the fifth year. Suppose that all other expected receipts and payments occurred at the ends of the years. Take the discount rate as 10 percent per annum. The traditional calculation is as follows:

Present Value—Cash Flows Only (traditional calculation)

Year	0	1	2	3	4	5
Revenues	$	$400	$600	$600	$600	$600
Purchase (sale) of machine	−1,000					200
Operating expenses		−200	−300	−300	−300	−300
Net cash inflow	−1,000	200	300	300	300	500
Present values of inflows	$−1,000	$182	$248	$225	$205	$310
Net present value of project	$ 170					

This calculation implies an immediate decline in wealth of $1,000 at the outset and a "rediscovery" of $200 on sale of the machine. But if that decline were not immediate—that is to say, if the firm expected residual money equivalents of the machine at the end of each year—the traditional calculation would not represent the flows of wealth in a temporally correct manner.

Suppose then that the expected money equivalents (resale prices) of the machine at the ends of the years were those indicated in the following revised or all-inclusive calculation, and that in all other respects the data were the same. The calculation would be as follows:

Present Value—Money Equivalent (M.E.) Flows (inclusive calculation)

Year	0	1	2	3	4	5
Closing M.E. of machine	$	$500	$400	$300	$200	$200
Opening M.E. of machine	1,000		500	400	300	200
Net M.E. inflow, (a)−(b)	−1,000	500	−100	−100	−100	-
Revenues		400	600	600	600	600
Operating expenses		−200	−300	−300	−300	−300
Total M.E. inflow, (c)+(d)−(e)	−1,000	700	200	200	200	300
Present values of inflows	$−1,000	$636	$165	$150	$137	$186
Net present value of project	$274					

This inclusive calculation represents that, for example, at the end of the first year the firm expects to hold an asset which is "as good as cash" to the extent of $500. An equivalent amount becomes an outlay, or outflow, in the second year, as in line (b). The closing cash value, resale price, or money equivalent, of the asset in each period is just as properly an offset to the outlays of the period as the $200 cash receipt on sale of the machine is an offset at the end of the project.

The textbook treatment of present value calculations makes a point of the different timing or dating of expected receipts; early receipts are discounted less heavily than later receipts. But it disregards the timing of expected diminutions in the money's worth of holdings, whereas these are no less significant than the timing of receipts in choosing between projects.

Standing by itself, a present value of a project has no more significance than as a calculation of a hypothetical outcome of hypothetical events. Both of the above calculations are identical in this respect. Present values do *not* represent the market values or market prices of projects, except in the case of perfect foreknowledge of the outcomes of projects, and this is not possible for purchases and sales of goods and services. But given that the decision-maker, or the calculator in a decision-making setting, knows the hypotheses on which the calculations are made, the present values of alternative projects may legitimately be compared.

The above calculations are made in respect of a given project which is expected to result in an aggregate net inflow of $600 over the five years. But we may put the two sets of figures in a decision-making setting by taking them as inclusive calculations for two distinct projects, T and R respectively, expected to yield the same net money equivalent inflows. In this case the T-machine is assumed to be a nonvendible durable over the five-year period, whereas the R-machine is vendible throughout the five-year period (or the R project is some other project making no use of a machine but otherwise having the same inflows and outflows and vendible asset balances as the R example).

Now, clearly, R is more advantageous than T; for under T there is no way of easing the adaptation of the firm to a change in technology or a fall in demand for the machine's products, whereas under R the money equivalent of the machine could, at any appropriate time, be redeployed in such circumstances. The advantage shows up in the net present values (taking them as "inclusive calculations" for different projects), namely $PV(T) = \$170$ and $PV(R) = \$274$. If, on the other hand, the present values of the two projects had been calculated in the traditional manner (that is, for cash flows only), both projects would appear to have the same present value; there would be no quantified difference between them, although there is a commonsense and practical difference. The decision-maker would have no quantified basis for discriminating between them. That the "inclusive calculation" provides such an explicit, quantified basis for choosing between the projects is the first advantage it has over the traditional calculation.

A second advantage lies in the possibility of integrating the calculations and their results with other calculations. The periodical net cash inflows used in traditional present value calculations are not relatable to the gross gain of the firm from any chosen project involving a vendible durable. Under the inclusive calculation, however, the periodical net money equivalent inflows are estimates of the periodical gains from the project. The component figures could be entered in the exploratory financial statements mentioned earlier, and in the budget statements for any chosen project; in the latter case they would also serve as the basis for subsequent reviews of the progress of the project. The present value calculation and the budgetary calculation would relate to the same elements and consequences of the project. The result would be considerable economies of cerebration on the part of managers who make use of the products of the several kinds of calculation; for instead of having mentally to relate discounted cash flows, periodical expected net cash flows, and periodical expected (all-inclusive) gains from projects, they would be dealing with increments which were all of one kind—all-inclusive increments in money-quantified wealth.

One additional excursion, into the quantification of profit, will provide some further indications of the possibility of integrating the varied kinds of calculations we have considered.

Profit

It has long been held that income is the resultant of matching some quantum of charges, determined largely by judgments, with the amount of periodical gross revenue. The balance sheet is, on this view, a statement of the balances remaining after clearing those charges and revenues from the accounts. The income account and the balance sheet are formally articulated. But the rules which influence the judgments have been found to yield results which, in some settings and in some senses, are unrealistic. There have consequently been proposals to use different quantification rules for the two statements, and hence to abandon their articulation. Indeed, there have been proposals to abandon the aggregation of balance sheet items, prompted by recognition of the fallacy of adding quantities of different kinds. These proposals for disarticulation and disaggregation can only lead to chaos. They seem designed to preserve the traditional rules rather than to force their rationalization or modification in the interest of systematic and realistic accounting.

Let assets be defined as severable goods, and let them be represented by their money amounts or money equivalents. Let equities be defined as the money-quantified equitable rights in the assets. Let liabilities be defined as equities ranking for settlement ahead of ownership equities. The residual amount of ownership equities may be described as net assets. Let income be defined as the periodical increment in net assets. The definitional linking of these central ideas—their articulation, if you will—is more than a formality. A system which expresses the stated relations enables the effects of actual or expected changes in the magnitude of one category to be traced through to its effects on other categories. If judgments are used in deriving some income account magnitudes, or if the records are incomplete in any respect, deficiencies may be found by cross-checking with the independently discovered magnitudes of assets. Income will not simply be the outcome of whatever judgments and calculations are made; for it must agree with and be the equivalent of the ascertained increment in net assets. Income will not simply be "what income is calculated to be"; it will correspond with a real, observable increment in the money amount of net assets.

The integral relationship between assets, equities, and income was adumbrated in Paton's *Accounting Theory* (1922). It is also central to continuously contemporary accounting (CoCoA). But some have found its implications in the latter case difficult to accept in relation to durable assets and work in progress. Under CoCoA, durables would be written down periodically to their money equivalents, nonvendible durables to zero at the outset. Work in progress which is not vendible in its balance date state would also have a zero value. There would be corresponding charges, in some cases heavy charges, in the income account or against some other residual equity account. Critics of these consequences of the rules of CoCoA contend that this is "hard doctrine" yielding "unrealistic" figures. But is it?

Consider again the hypothetical figures in the previous section on present value calculations. An asset was to be acquired for $1,000, the whole of which, under traditional present value calculations, is implicitly deemed to be sunk, gone, no longer accessible. Whether or not the asset, when acquired, turns out to be vendible or nonvendible, the common accounting treatment of it would be to charge off a fraction of the amount, based on judgments of service life and depreciation pattern. There is an obvious inconsistency in the modes of calculation. Certainly a present value calculation is exploratory, and an account of events after their occurrence is, in principle, past factual. But both concern the same set of events. There can be no reason for choosing according to one financial criterion (cash flows) and calculating the consequences of the choice according to another (cash flows less periodical valuation adjustments); for the object of choosing is to procure a desired financial consequence, and the function of accounting is to report on an achieved financial consequence. Retrospective diagnosis is futile unless "consequence" has reference to the same thing that it refers to in exploratory calculations. Those who endorse the traditional form of present value calculation, therefore, cannot legitimately or consistently object to the rapid writing down of some durables which CoCoA entails.

Nor can they object to the "dropping out" of a valuation of non-vendible work in progress and its restoration when it acquires vendible status, as under CoCoA. For that is exactly what is done in the traditional present value calculation. The cash outlay is treated as instantaneous dropout; the cash inflow expected from sale of the asset appears when the asset is expected to be liquidated. Subject only to the difference that CoCoA deals with money equivalents, its treatment of work in progress follows the same pattern as the traditional present value calculation.

But there is more substantial ground for integral calculation than mere consistency of information-processing. Income is expected to be a genuine increment in assets which is divisible, at least by those who expect dividends. Income before tax is expected to represent a genuine increment against which taxes may be levied. Income is taken by parties to wage and price negotiations as a genuine increment in assets, indicative of what may be divided up differently in the future from what was done in the past. Retained income is considered as an increment to the borrowing base of a firm and as an increment providing for growth or the redeployment of assets. The matter is put in a nutshell in the letter of transmittal by the Chairman of the Securities and Exchange Commission of the staff report on the financial collapse of the Penn Central Company (1972):

> It is essential that the end result of applying accounting principles be a realistic reflection of the true situation of the company on which a report is prepared. Here, there was no adequate presentation of the fundamental reality that reported income was not of a character to make a contribution to the pressing debt maturities or liquidity needs of Penn Central, nor was it of the sort that might reasonably be expected to be evidence of

continuing earning power. Income is clearly expected to be "real," represented by money's worth.

The only way of being assured that this is its nature is by making its calculation integral with a balance sheet representing assets and equities in terms of money and money's worth.

Towards Integral Calculation

Our object has been to indicate the specific purposes to which specific financial calculations and magnitudes are relevant, and to suggest that the whole range of past, present, and future calculations should follow a common systematic pattern. The integrating element in this pattern is the use of dated money equivalents (including money amounts). The dominant importance of money equivalents lies in their pertinence to the processes of exchange which are the means of securing the survival, adaptation, and growth of firms.

In the general case, the products of past factual, contemporary factual, and exploratory calculations converge on the occasion of evaluating and choosing; and anticipatory calculations represent the expected consequences of choices made. If these temporally sequential calculations embody a homogeneous class of appropriately dated magnitudes, analysis of the past and preparation for the future may be reasonably and coherently done. But only confusion and inefficiency can be expected if any temporally identified calculation or statement embraces components of a different temporal class. For if users of the statements are aware of anachronisms, besides trying to absorb what the statements say, they must make their own mental reservations and adjustments as their deliberations proceed—a prodigious task considering the variety of substantive and temporally different quantities related to judgment. Or if users are ignorant of the anachronisms or logical incompatibilities of the statements, they will simply make inapt appraisals and judgments.

Statements of the past say nothing about the future. Statements of expectation say nothing about the past. In particular the use of present values (even of the "inclusive" variety) in any dated statement of financial position is inapt, for it represents a multiperiod expectation reduced to a point valuation. Though it is one means of discriminating between possible courses of action, in no way does it represent a factual element of a dated financial position. The use of replacement prices in any past or contemporary statement of financial position is also inapt. They may be elements in any exploratory or anticipatory calculation, but that is their sole use. The long-standing and growing tolerance for these magnitudes in statements of financial position is symptomatic of a confused and anachronistic view of the functions of different temporal classes of information.

Ideally accounting would deal systematically and consistently with stocks and flows of money and money's worth—in representations of financial states and results, and in all exploratory calculations and budgetary statements. To calculate asset values, financial positions, incomes, discounted cash flow valuations, and other financial magnitudes according to different rules is to esteem the chaotic more highly than the systematic, the divergent more highly than the convergent, the vagrant more highly than the disciplined, the unintegrated or disintegrated more highly than the articulated—in thought and in action.

There *is* a hard core of accounting. The money equivalents of assets and equities are material in all judgments of financial consequences and prospects. No system other than accounting deals with them. But if the idea of a hard core is rejected, and every magnitude in financial statements or calculations is determined uniquely according to its own item-specific rule, accounting will not be the monitor of status and progress in the aggregate that we expect it to be.

The study and teaching of accounting processes, present value calculations, and budgeting as separate techniques is perhaps inevitable, if expertise and expert knowledge are to be developed. But unless they are also seen as integrated, necessarily related elements in the whole continuous process of administration and decision-making, each of them may be pressed severally into a shape and style inconsistent with its specific function and inconsistent with the related functions of them all. The result will abort all attempts to conduct business affairs with economy and clarity of thought.

The range of matters which have commanded Paton's attention, and the analytical skill which he has directed to their exploration and elucidation, evidence his devotion to a belief in the disciplinary power of reliable knowledge in the conduct of business affairs. In tandem has been a belief in the versatility and essentiality of the accounting framework, suitably refined, as a means of systematizing the indications of financial progress and prospects on which efficient administration and informed investment depend. One could hope that one's own exercises might appear to be in like direction, with like respect for intellectual tidiness and practical pertinence.

January 1977

Paton on the Effects of Changing Prices on Accounting 1916–55

Stephen A. Zeff

From 1916, when he first contributed to the accounting literature, to 1955, when he published the last major textbook of which he was sole author, William A. Paton wrote frequently and with feeling on the vexing subject of the impact on accounting of changing prices. His writings have been widely quoted by both academics and practitioners, and one may confidently conclude that Paton was among the most influential American writers on accounting in this period.

Unfortunately the accounting literature in the English language contains very few historical studies showing how the thought of major contributors has evolved. For this reason, it may not be generally noticed when important normative writers alter their theoretical constructs or, in the light of particular economic and political conditions, introduce variables which affect their conclusions and policy recommendations. That Paton has done so in his writings on the impact of changing prices on accounting is my belief, and in this essay I propose to examine his contributions over a period of four decades in order to test this hypothesis.

More than most accounting writers, Paton has been acutely sensitive to shifting currents in the socioeconomic context in which accounting is performed. Over the period of this study, Paton seemed to accommodate his vision of accounting to his changing perceptions of the economic, legal, and political forces in the accounting environment.

It is no surprise that in the first significant period of his writings,

Note: I am grateful to Harold Bierman, Jr., William W. Cooper, Maurice Moonitz, William A. Paton, Jr., Edward Stamp, Herbert F. Taggart, and Roman L. Weil for their useful comments on an earlier draft, but the responsibility for errors is solely mine.

1917–18, Paton emerged as an idealist. Accounting writers are inclined to cite his 1918 textbook, *Principles of Accounting*, which he wrote with Russell A. Stevenson, as his most uncompromising challenge to accounting orthodoxy. And it was. But beginning in the 1920s, and continuing to the end of the 1930s, Paton gradually retreated from his enthusiastic and optimistic advocacy of 1917–18, as preoccupations over the post-World War I inflation, companies' questionable revaluation practices during the 1920s and early 1930s, the economic stagnation of the Depression, and the growing influence of the law in business operation collectively persuaded Paton to become more circumspect and constrained in his avowal of accounting reform. By the early 1940s, his penchant for innovation again became evident, and he began to employ his effective debating style to gain support for his measures among the accounting and legal authorities to whom deviation from precedent and convention was anathema. Following World War II, the accelerating pace of inflation, coupled with the persistent attacks on business and the free enterprise system, rekindled Paton's fire and enthusiasm of 1917–18, this time to persuade accountants, the Securities and Exchange Commission, Congress, and federal wage tribunals that corporate profits were being vastly overstated.

Paton was profoundly influenced by Sweeney's "stabilized accounting," and he frequently cited Sweeney's opus *Stabilized Accounting* in articles and speeches.[1] While he never preferred "stabilized accounting" to the booking of replacement costs, he regularly recommended that reckonings on a "common-dollar" basis be provided in supplementary disclosures. His enthusiasm for including unrealized appreciation in net income faded entirely in the 1920s and 1930s, and during these same two decades he showed growing reluctance even to reflect replacement costs formally in the accounts and financial statements. By the early 1940s, he had devised several techniques—the upward quasi-reorganization, the "compromise procedure" for supplementing plant costs and depreciation on a replacement cost basis without altering reported income, and the revaluation of assets upon the reacquisition of a corporation's own shares at a cost different from their book value—by which current costs or values might gain admission to the accounts and financial statements. Following the war, his advocacy of these and other reforms (including "common-dollar" accounting) assumed an intensity not before seen in his writings.

---

1. Henry W. Sweeney, *Stabilized Accounting* (New York: Harper & Bros., 1936).

This historical essay is organized on chronological lines, and at various stages the evolution of Paton's thought is explicitly examined. It is not my objective to argue with Paton, but instead to endeavor to understand and explain the development of his writings on this controversial subject. A more ambitious study would have included extensive references to the contemporaneous writings of other authors, both in the United States and in other countries. A complete examination of Paton's contribution to the literature would require the development of these links with the works of other writers, but the reader will appreciate that even my more limited undertaking is a large assignment. It is to be hoped that future studies will supply the missing dimension and that we might finally have a definitive study of Paton's impact on the literature of changing prices and accounting.

PRINCIPLES OF ACCOUNTING (1916)

The years 1916–18 were, following an uncertain start, the years of Unbridled Advocacy, since they produced Paton's most enthusiastic avowal of current-cost accounting. Idealism governed. Paton was a graduate student in economics at the University of Michigan when he and Russell A. Stevenson collaborated on a textbook entitled *Principles of Accounting.* The book appeared in three versions, published in 1916, 1917, and 1918. The 1917 and 1918 versions are not designated as second and third editions, although the titles are identical. Of the three versions, the one published in 1918 is by far the best known—indeed, few citations to its predecessors may be found in the literature. The successive versions grew steadily from 222 pages to 373 and finally 685 pages, reflecting, among other things, the authors' expansiveness and increasing conviction of the rightness of their controversial conclusions.

The 1916 version of *Principles of Accounting,* containing Paton's first published utterances on accounting measurement, bespeaks a degree of irresolution, as if the authors had not fully grasped their conception of accounting. While they endorse the principle of booking appreciation in the accounts, they hedge on its specific application. Paton and Stevenson emphasize that "accounting is concerned with the value representation of things," not with physical facts.[2]

2. William A. Paton and Russell A. Stevenson, *Principles of Accounting* (Ann Arbor: [no publisher], 1916), pp. 14, 101.

They add,

> The accounts should always show the present value of the property being used by an enterprise in producing its product, if accounting statistics are to furnish the entrepreneur with the information which shall enable him to make rational use of the economic resources at his disposal.[3]

The authors' underlying philosophy is taken from Wesley C. Mitchell's *Business Cycles:*[4]

> Prices render possible the rational direction of economic activity by accounting, for accounting is based upon the principle of representing all the heterogeneous commodities, services, and rights with which a business enterprise is concerned in terms of money price.

Their general principle is stated as follows: "The accounts, if they are to be scientifically accurate, should record *all* [value] changes, and immediately. That is, the accounts should be as sensitive as possible to all price and value changes."[5] It is nowhere stated, however, that revenues, or even net income, might in principle be credited for appreciation. Paton and Stevenson leave the inference that credits in respect of appreciation should be made to Surplus (a term which, in those days, implied an amalgam composed of the excess of total stockholders' equity over legal capital). When land appreciation is discussed, the authors worry over "a tendency to credit these increases to current revenue in lean years, which is illegitimate." "Increases in land value," they conclude, "should not be used [to] inflate current income, but should be credited to accumulated surplus." An equivocal qualification is added: "If, however, increases in land value are conservative estimates, and are not used to juggle the current Income sheet, there is no valid reason for keeping such items out of the accounts."[6] In the best light, the authors' discussion of the impact on net income of recorded appreciation is sketchy and incomplete.

To what extent should appreciation be recorded at all—as a practical matter? For merchandise, raw materials, etc., which move quickly through enterprise, it is not "expedient" to keep a continu-

---

3. *Ibid.,* p. 101. Although the authors do not define "present value," it is understood to mean any soundly based contemporary price or valuation.

4. Wesley C. Mitchell, *Business Cycles,* as quoted in Paton and Stevenson, *Principles of Accounting* (1916), pp. 31–32.

5. Paton and Stevenson, *Principles of Accounting* (1916), p. 103.

6. *Ibid.,* p. 105. Out of the accounts, or out of the Income sheet? The passage is unclear.

ing accounting record of changing prices. Only when "market prices fall or rise considerably or a long interval is involved," should market prices be entered in the accounts. A lower-of-cost-or-market solution is rejected as "unreasonable." For securities, "the reasonable course is to use cost prices unless market prices are widely divergent and for a long period, in which case securities should be valued at the market."

The authors' preoccupation with railroad property (numerous examples are chosen from this industry) evidently prompts a judgment that appreciation on land is the principal concern. Permanent changes in the value of buildings and machinery are asserted to be decreases more often than not, and any actual appreciation in such properties is said to be ordinarily offset by depreciation. Only land is left, and even here the authors are troubled by the booking of "unwarranted estimates."

The authors' 1916 position, therefore, is to recommend that the accounts continually reflect price and value changes; as a practical matter, however, valuations of land are open to suspicion, any appreciation in buildings and land is "normally more than offset by depreciation," and short-term assets should be kept at cost unless the price changes are pronounced over a long period.

"The Theory of Accounts" (1917)

By 1917 Paton, writing alone, achieves a clearer integration of his theory and policy recommendations. In his doctoral dissertation, "The Theory of Accounts," Paton unqualifiedly endorses the booking of appreciation as part of "net revenue" (a term he often used between 1917 and 1924 in place of net income).[7] He continues to espouse the accounting recognition of appreciation, but with the same exceptions for merchandise, raw materials, and securities, in virtually the identical language, as in the 1916 edition of *Principles of Accounting*. But the credit in respect of currently accrued appreciation is to be made to "net revenue."[8] He adds that "if an item of appreciation covers several accounting periods before it is recognized in the accounts [it] should be credited, not to net revenue,

7. William A. Paton, "The Theory of Accounts," unpublished doctoral dissertation, University of Michigan, 1917. The preface is dated May 1, 1917, and the manuscript extends to 144 pages, double-spaced, including bibliography.
8. *Ibid.*, pp. 119–20, 126–27.

but to surplus." The argument that a "net revenue" which includes appreciation might obscure the results of "actual operation" is met by the recommendation of a two-tier income statement, which would contain the calculation of "net revenue from operation, so-called, and total net revenue as well."[9] Paton shrewdly observes that conventional net income already includes a speculative price change, as, for example, when products purchased in a falling market are sold in a rising market. But his proposal would include unrealized effects as well.

In the dissertation, Paton repeats the idealistic conceptual statements about appreciation from the 1916 version of *Principles,* but he no longer harbors doubts about the practical implementation. In characteristic Paton debating style, he confidently dismisses the standard objections to booking appreciation and including appreciation in net income. As to the argument that appreciation is too subjective an estimate to appear in the accounts, Paton glibly replies, "As a matter of fact the appreciation of fixed property can be more accurately estimated than the depreciation." To those (such as Paton and Stevenson, in the 1916 version of *Principles*) who might be concerned about possible manipulation by management of appreciation estimates, the Paton of 1917 responds, "It is no more likely that illegitimate use will be made of appreciation than of depreciation."[10] In dealing with "that long-exploded notion that profits must be available in liquid assets in order to be considered as profits," Paton contends that stockholders can sell some shares and thus realize on the enhanced value of their equity interests whether "net revenue" is available in liquid form or not. Moreover, a dividend could be paid in respect of appreciation on fixed assets by borrowing "on short-term notes or otherwise." He concludes with the firm opinion that "all decreases in the values of assets constitute expense, and all increases represent revenue." "The net revenue figure for the accounting period," he adds, "is not accurately discovered until *all* these changes have been taken into consideration."[11] A stronger endorsement of current-value accounting could hardly be imagined.

The object of accounting is succinctly expressed: "From the standpoint of either the private enterprise or of the industrial community the accounts should answer the question: what economic resources

9. *Ibid.,* pp. 126–27.
10. *Ibid.,* p. 125.
11. *Ibid.,* pp. 128–29.

are being devoted to this or that particular end?"[12] Accounting is seen as an essential element in the free enterprise system, so as "to make effective the direction of economic activity by the system of market prices." Paton suggests that the severity of business cycles may be diminished by an accounting that reflects current price trends.[13] Perhaps the factor that led Paton to alter his position on the inclusion of appreciation in "net revenue" was a concern for the temporal impact on creditors and stockholders of "net revenue" measures that ignore appreciation. He notes that "the personnel of the owners is usually changing from day to day due to the ease with which securities can be transferred from one person to another."

> Thus [he continues] if an error in stating net revenue is made in one period it is probable that the rights of some of the individuals whose equities have been misstated cannot be restored by the correction of the error in a later period, because these rights are then in other hands. . . . The income bondholder, for example, has a right to income only when net revenue exists. . . . In the modern enterprise the constant shifting of the investors and the variety of property-rights as regards the aspects of ownership render imperative the *accurate* determination of [net revenue].[14]

The exigencies of a fluid market for equity interests, therefore, argue for current valuation in the accounts notwithstanding the absence of distributable funds corresponding to increments in net income. According to Paton of 1917, the prompt reflection of appreciation in the prices of equity shares was of paramount importance.

In the dissertation, Paton's meaning of the term "appreciation" is not always clear. At one point, it is described as "present value." A footnote explains that present value "may be based upon liquidating value, cost of reproduction, or going value to the specific enterprise. The cost of reproduction basis is the most significant—certainly in competitive enterprise."[15] A few pages later Paton also seems to include in appreciation the changes in the general level of prices, although this suggestion may have been developed mainly for the benefit of the Interstate Commerce Commission, whose property accounting rules were frequently the object of Patonian disdain.

12. *Ibid.*, p. 118.
13. *Ibid.*, pp. 6–8.
14. *Ibid.*, pp. 14–16.
15. *Ibid.*, p. 117.

PRINCIPLES OF ACCOUNTING (1917)

In their second version of *Principles of Accounting*, Paton and Stevenson include a seven-page section on "Appreciation and Depreciation," which is taken almost verbatim from Paton's dissertation.[16] Appreciation is to be credited to "net revenue," and all of the standard arguments (save one) against the booking of appreciation and the inclusion of appreciation in net income are rejected with the same aplomb as in the dissertation.[17] Two arguments in the dissertation, however, are omitted from the book. Nowhere in the book is Paton's argument against the view "that profits must be available in liquid assets in order to be considered as profits." His suggestions that short-term borrowings can be used to pay dividends and that stockholders can realize on the appreciation by selling off some of their stockholdings are not to be found in the book.

Also omitted from *Principles* is Paton's closing judgment in the dissertation that "all decreases in the values of assets constitute expense, and all increases represent revenue."[18] It is possible that these omitted items were too controversial for Stevenson's taste. But in other respects, the 1917 edition of *Principles* is entirely faithful to the contents of Paton's dissertation.

PRINCIPLES OF ACCOUNTING (1918)

In the third version of *Principles*, the substance of the authors' position on appreciation is unchanged from 1917, although their discussion is more expansive and confidently expressed than before.[19] That Paton was evidently the principal author of the well-known Chapter XX, "The Basis for Revaluation," is confirmed by his article published in the same year, "The Significance and Treatment of Appreciation in the Accounts," which closely corresponds to the chapter in *Principles*.[20]

16. William A. Paton and Russell A. Stevenson, *Principles of Accounting* (Ann Arbor: George Wahr, 1917).

17. *Ibid.*, pp. 213–19.

18. Paton, "Theory of Accounts," pp. 128–29.

19. William Andrew Paton and Russell Alger Stevenson, *Principles of Accounting* (New York: Macmillan Co., 1918).

20. William A. Paton, "The Significance and Treatment of Appreciation in the Accounts," in G.H. Coons, ed., *Twentieth Annual Report of the Michigan Academy of Science*, 1918, pp. 35–49. Reprinted in Herbert F. Taggart, ed., *Paton on Accounting* (Ann Arbor: Bureau of Business Research, University of Michigan, 1964), pp. 21–35; and in Stephen A. Zeff, ed., *Asset Appreciation, Business Income and Price-Level Accounting: 1918–1935* (New York: Arno Press, 1976), second article.

For the first time, Paton and Stevenson distinguish clearly between the booking of appreciation based on changes in replacement cost and the "illegitimate practice of forecasting profits in the accounts."[21] They write:

> To use selling prices in taking inventories—in other words to capitalize the services of the firm before those services are performed—is to anticipate profits. To recognize changing capital costs and equity changes due to the appreciation of working or fixed assets is an entirely different thing.[22]

The authors argue that an efficient management must be cognizant of replacement cost—that is, "the present significances of all assets as nearly as these facts may be ascertained"—in order to achieve "a wise utilization of available resources." But is it necessary that these figures appear in the actual accounts? Yes, reply Paton and Stevenson, "since it is generally admitted that it is an important function of the financial accounts to furnish information which will assist the management in making rational decisions regarding the employment of the investor's capital." In 1940, Paton retreated from this view, contending that management could be supplied with this information without disturbing the accounts. But in 1917, Paton and Stevenson claimed that "it is the function of the accounts to show economic facts."[23]

The authors cite Middleditch's path-breaking 1918 article when discussing the possibility of explicitly showing "changes in the significance of the money unit in the accounts."[24] They believe that such changes should not be displayed in the accounts, supporting their conclusion as follows:

> It has been argued thus far that costs of replacement should form the basis for the revaluation of assets for accounting purposes; and actual sacrifice and cost of replacement are not likely to coincide. The change in the value of the dollar reflects *general* price changes. But it is not values in general but *specific* values which the accounts should show.

In later years, Paton continued to avow that specific price changes, not the effects of general price trends, should be used if any modifications were to be made in the accounts or in the body of the financial statements.

21. Paton and Stevenson, *Principles of Accounting* (1918), p. 242.
22. *Ibid.*, p. 464.
23. *Ibid.*, pp. 456–57, 459 n.
24. *Ibid.*, p. 461. Livingston Middleditch, Jr., "Should Accounts Reflect the Changing Value of the Dollar?" *Journal of Accountancy* (Feb. 1918), pp. 114–20.

Most of the objections raised in the 1917 dissertation against the booking of appreciation and its inclusion in net income are again unqualifiedly rejected in this version of *Principles*. Even the argument that "profits must be available in liquid assets in order to be considered as profits," on which the 1917 version of *Principles* was silent, is rehearsed here, and the authors dismiss it with the same disdain displayed by Paton in his dissertation.[25]

Paton and Stevenson mention a new objection to the recording of appreciation: "that such a practice savors of non-conservatism. . . . A clear distinction should be made between conservatism and downright concealment." They argue vigorously against this objection:

> Ignoring the appreciation of unsold assets which results in an understatement of assets and a corresponding misstatement of equities—is simply another method of building up secret reserves; and it is essentially as misleading a practice as the charging of capital outlays to expense. . . .
>
> To insist that inventories in certain cases must be taken at a figure far below the actual values in order to prevent a general overstatement of assets is from the accountant an admission of incompetence.

Paton and Stevenson were willing to devise modes of presentation in order to meet part-way the defenders of historical cost. Appreciation "need not obscure cost figures" and "might [even] be kept out of the operating accounts." Supplementary statements might be used to maintain the record of appreciation. But the authors persisted in the belief that "accounts and statements which take into account *all* value changes would surely seem to be of more practical use to all parties concerned than records prepared on any other basis."[26]

Paton and Stevenson continue to defend the practice of crediting currently accrued appreciation to net income, although they confess at one point that "in general it is desirable to use the Surplus account to reflect all speculative changes in the equities."[27]

Finally worth noting: the recommendation in the 1916 and 1917 versions of *Principles* that appreciation not be recorded on most short-term assets, except when significant and over long periods, appears not to be repeated in the 1918 edition.

This third version of *Principles* was, as Hatfield later suggested, a bold argument for the "consistent treatment of fluctuations in

25. Paton and Stevenson, *Principles of Accounting* (1918), pp. 243, 467.
26. *Ibid.*, pp. 467, 469.
27. *Ibid.*, pp. 108, 238–42.

value."[28] In all of Paton's writings, it was his most inspired defense of current-cost accounting.

"Depreciation, Appreciation and Productive Capacity" (1920)

In a 1920 article entitled "Depreciation, Appreciation and Productive Capacity," Paton abruptly revises his stance on current-cost accounting.[29] No longer does he unreservedly favor crediting appreciation to net income. Indeed, his entire position on the booking of appreciation is less than clear, for he fails to reply to criticisms which he had calmly brushed aside in 1918. The tenor of this article is in stark contrast to his earlier writings. While his 1918 book with Stevenson brims with self-confidence and idealism, the 1920 article is tainted with doubt and pragmatic skepticism.

The excuse for the article is a reply to Bauer and Rastall,[30] chiefly to argue that replacement-cost depreciation should not be charged to operations unless the gross appreciation in the depreciable assets is also accorded accounting recognition. Paton's evident retreat from the view that appreciation credits should be made to net income seems to be explained, at least in part, by the persistent inflation of 1914–20, during which the consumer price index doubled. Paton writes,

> Is the proprietary credit, which should be made when a fixed asset is charged with the increment necessary to bring the book value up to the effective current cost, in any sense an index of income? So far as its expressing improved economic condition is concerned this depends . . . upon whether the price change in any particular instance involved is more or less acute than the general movement. In the average case it would no doubt be true that such appreciation would represent pretty largely not income but the application of the new measuring unit to the proprietary accounts.[31]

His discussion of the general price-level implications for accounting is more fully developed than in 1918. He again refers to Middleditch and cites a recent article by Scovill, and while he concludes that "it

28. Henry Rand Hatfield, "Book Reviews," *Journal of Accountancy* (Nov. 1925), p. 390.

29. W.A. Paton, "Depreciation, Appreciation and Productive Capacity," *Journal of Accountancy* (July 1920), pp. 1–11.

30. John Bauer, "Renewal Costs and Business Profits in Relation to Rising Prices," *Journal of Accountancy* (Dec. 1919), pp. 413–19; Ernest A. Rastall, "Depreciation Reserves and Rising Prices," *Journal of Accountancy* (Feb. 1920), pp. 123–26.

31. Paton, "Depreciation," p. 10.

is perhaps not unreasonable to argue that the accountant should prepare supplementary statements at the end of each period designed to show—by making proper allowances for the change in the value of money—the true comparative economic status of the enterprise," in the end he reaffirms his conclusion of 1918 that accounting should have regard to changes in specific prices, not general prices.[32]

But the principal point of interest in this article is Paton's less ardent support, expressed in the final two pages, of the accounting recognition of appreciation in any form. When Paton is sure of his ground, he does not fail to reply energetically to opposing arguments. Here he leaves them unanswered. In a remarkable modification of his 1918 stand, perhaps induced by the cumulative effect of an apparently unrelenting inflation coupled with the postwar economic uncertainty of 1919–20, Paton gives credence to arguments which he had enthusiastically rejected two years earlier:

> At any rate [an appreciation] credit in a practical case would not measure an amount which could conveniently or safely be turned over to the stockholders. . . .

> In view . . . of the conjectural character of asset values at best and the consequent importance of conservatism [sic], the difficulties in the way of determining effective replacement costs in the case of complex assets, the constant fluctuation of such costs and the fact that having once made an investment the management is often thereby committed to a policy for a considerable period regardless of the movement of prices, probably most accountants would feel that original cost is the best basis upon which to value fixed assets.[33]

Does Paton include himself among "most accountants"? Is he abandoning entirely the accounting recognition of appreciation, or is he limiting this reply to Bauer and Rastall to the points raised in their articles? However one might interpret this article, something has taken the wind out of Paton's sails.

A comparison of the 1918 and 1920 positions vividly demonstrates how much Paton was affected by the swirl of economic events. For all of his life, he has been a firm believer in the market system; it was, in effect, the text from which he read.

Evidently Paton's article had an impact. More than forty years later, Sweeney wrote,

32. *Ibid.*, p. 4.
33. *Ibid.*, pp. 10–11.

That excellent article, far in advance of its time, entitled "Depreciation, Appreciation and Productive Capacity" . . . was the first exposition I had seen of how accounting figures, representing depreciation, could be revised to show the changing purchasing power of money. It stimulated and encouraged me to try to develop all the great possibilities that this new subject in the United States seemed to offer.[34]

ACCOUNTING THEORY (1922)

Paton's celebrated *Accounting Theory—With Special Reference to the Corporate Enterprise*, published in 1922, reaffirms his position on fixed assets as set out in the 1920 article and discloses his qualified approval of showing appreciation on current assets.[35] *Accounting Theory* has erroneously been said to be the publication of Paton's doctoral dissertation.[36] In fact, *Accounting Theory* is four times the length of the dissertation, and while Chapters I through VII and X through XI of *Accounting Theory* largely correspond to material in the dissertation, the remaining chapters (including four which, Paton reported, were adapted in part from previously published articles) either did not appear in the dissertation or were lightly treated there.

Of particular importance is Paton's major change in posture on appreciation between the 1917 dissertation and *Accounting Theory*, published five years later. Where he concluded in the dissertation that it would be inexpedient to record appreciation in most instances on current assets, in *Accounting Theory* (as, apparently, in the 1918 version of *Principles of Accounting*) he actually espouses the normal booking of appreciation on certain kinds of current assets, and he would even credit such accruals to income.[37] Where, in the dissertation, he would credit the currently accrued appreciation of

34. Henry W. Sweeney, "Forty Years After: Or Stabilized Accounting Revisited," in the reissue of his *Stabilized Accounting* (New York: Holt, Rinehart and Winston, Inc., 1964), p. xx.

35. William Andrew Paton, *Accounting Theory—With Special Reference to the Corporate Enterprise* (New York: Ronald Press, 1922). Reprinted in 1962 by A.S.P. Accounting Studies Press, Ltd., Chicago, and in 1973 by Scholars Book Co., Houston.

36. This writer is among those who have erred. In the publisher's preface to the 1962 reprint of *Accounting Theory*, signed by this writer and three others, it is said that *Accounting Theory* "was [Paton's] doctoral dissertation at the University of Michigan." In many respects, *Accounting Theory* was based on the dissertation, but it went beyond the dissertation and departed from it in significant points (chiefly in the treatment of appreciation).

37. Paton, *Accounting Theory*, pp. 466–68.

fixed assets, notably land, to "net revenue," in *Accounting Theory*, following the inconclusive discussion in the 1920 article, Paton reviews the pros and cons, and appears to conclude that the appreciation on fixed assets is best not even entered in the accounts. If such appreciation is recorded, however, he is exceedingly reluctant to classify it as income. On one point he is decisive: the portion of recorded appreciation which coincides with the general movement of prices should be credited to capital.[38]

In *Accounting Theory*, not all current assets would qualify for the booking of appreciation. "The consistent valuation of standard materials and marketable securities on the basis of replacement cost," he counsels, "is a thoroughly sound procedure. . . . Goods in process and finished stock furnish a more dubious case." Moreover: "With respect to plant and equipment and other classes of fixed assets the propriety of cost-of-replacement valuations is still more questionable . . . " As in the dissertation, where he recommended that the appreciation credit on fixed assets be classified as "net revenue" from other than operations, in *Accounting Theory* he denominates the appreciation credit on eligible current assets as "non-operating income." Paton's mild support for crediting income with the currently accrued appreciation of current assets evaporated by the 1930s, and he has never again argued for the inclusion in income of appreciation accruals. In *Accounting Theory* he continues to argue, as did Paton and Stevenson in 1918, that recorded appreciation should not be based on the selling prices of merchandise, because its inclusion in income "may mean the [improper] recognition of a fraction of the normal income margin in advance of sale."[39]

Paton's principal reason for rejecting the inclusion in income of appreciation of fixed assets may be traced to his desire, first given expression in the 1920 article, to assist management in maintaining its physical capital. To achieve this end, depreciation should be based on appreciation, but the appreciation accrual itself should not be credited to income. "To revalue assets and base depreciation upon replacement costs," he writes, "would be an entirely futile policy unless the appreciation credit were excluded from the income account—at least as far as disposable income is concerned."[40] Beginning with his 1920 article, therefore, Paton left the ranks of those who would endeavor to approximate economic income in the

38. *Ibid.*, pp. 441–42.
39. *Ibid.*, pp. 466–68.
40. *Ibid.*, p. 441.

income statement, and became a member of what I have called the "disposable income school."[41]

Paton's discussion of the accounting effects of general price movements is more extensive in *Accounting Theory* than in his previous writings. In somewhat more than seven pages, he concludes that accountants should be interested primarily in "*specific* price and value changes," not "*general* price movements"; yet he grudgingly concedes:

> It would perhaps not be unreasonable to urge that the accountant should be held responsible for the preparation of supplementary statements at the end of each period designed to show—by making proper allowance for the change in the value of money—the true relation between the current statement and the one immediately preceding (or a series of earlier statements).[42]

This suggestion was also contained in the 1920 article, expressed in the same cautious language.[43]

He also proposes (in more positive terms) that the accountant prepare supplementary statements which reflect *individual* price movements—in the event, one supposes, that appreciation is not deemed proper for inclusion in the formal financial statements.

Accounting Theory is characterized by indecision and contradiction, as Paton was evidently passing through a period of profound reassessment of the theories which he had propounded so confidently in 1917–18.

ACCOUNTING (1924)

Paton's first textbook, *Accounting,* after the publication in 1918 of the third version of *Principles of Accounting* invites comparisons between the two.[44] The differences are instantly noticeable. Nowhere in *Accounting* does one find the idealistic formulations about the valuation of assets in relation to income that are evident in *Principles.* In this respect, *Accounting* is the more pragmatic and down-to-earth of the two volumes.

After persuasively arguing that appreciation of readily marketable securities has a strong claim as a credit to income, and offering the generalization that "wherever appreciation consists in a bona fide

41. See Stephen A. Zeff, "Replacement Cost: Member of the Family, Welcome Guest, or Intruder?" *Accounting Review* (Oct. 1962), pp. 617–20.
42. Paton, *Accounting Theory*, pp. 428–29.
43. Paton, "Depreciation," p. 4.
44. W.A. Paton, *Accounting* (New York: Macmillan Co., 1924).

increase in value in reasonably liquid assets there is ground for urging that such appreciation is quite as substantial a basis for the recognition of income as an increase in value brought about through the sale of original assets," Paton hastens to point out that since the Treasury Department "does not permit the ordinary investor in securities to treat appreciation as taxable income . . . it is probably advisable in most cases for the investor not to set up appreciated values in his regular accounts."[45] Thus enters the Law, which plays a major role in Paton's writings in the 1930s.

The appreciation of plant assets is of "dubious significance as far as the asset accounts are concerned, and is of still more doubtful character as an income determinant," and only with respect to land which is highly marketable does "genuine appreciation [have] some significance as true income."[46]

Elsewhere Paton mentions several objections to crediting appreciation to income:

> . . . appreciation is not in general viewed as income from the legal point of view, . . . enhancement does not measure liquid assets which may be disbursed as dividends, and . . . appraisal values may be used illegitimately to conceal operating deficits and other losses.[47]

He does not undertake to dispute these objections—which are, in company with similar statements in his 1920 article and *Accounting Theory*, difficult to associate with the Paton of 1917–18.

Paton is still willing to countenance the upward revaluation of fixed assets and inventories so long as the credit is made to Surplus, not income.[48] But his support for the practice falls well short of advocacy, and when objections and limitations are raised, they are seldom rebutted.

In *Accounting*, Paton does not discuss the accounting effects of changing general prices. Nor does he make an issue of the preservation of physical capacity during periods of advancing prices, which was a pivotal concern in his 1920 article and *Accounting Theory*. Allowing for the fact that *Accounting* is an introductory text and *Accounting Theory* is a major treatise, the tenor of Paton's remarks on appreciation is in most respects similar in both. Perhaps the noteworthy difference is the somewhat greater attention accorded to legal prescriptions in *Accounting* than in *Accounting Theory*. The

45. *Ibid.*, pp. 624–25.
46. *Ibid.*, p. 625.
47. *Ibid.*, p. 367.
48. *Ibid.*, pp. 352–53, 368, 373–74.

differences between *Accounting* and the 1917–18 *Principles of Accounting* are, of course, graphic.

Four Articles and the AAA Statement in the Early to Mid-1930s

By the 1930s, Paton's enthusiasm for replacement cost accounting had diminished still further, and he began to warm to the recommendation that supplementary disclosures should report the effect of changing prices on the firm. The reasons were several. One, he was disturbed by the haphazard and unsubstantiated upward revaluations in the 1920s and downward revaluations in the early 1930s. He writes in 1934,

> One of the things which tends to discourage hopes of the possibility of improving accounting via the route of revaluation of fixed assets is observation of the way in which revaluations are handled in actual practice. The revaluations downward in recent years, for example, have in most cases been entirely unscientific and often arbitrary in the extreme.[49]

In 1932 he writes,

> And it is equally apparent that the [write-down] procedures being followed [in the early 1930s] are in many cases just as unsystematic and improper as were the procedures followed in many of the earlier write-ups.[50]

Also in the early 1930s, Paton began to be preoccupied with the legal boundaries within which the formal accounting system must operate. Paton's awareness of the growing importance of the federal income tax law coupled with the intense interest being shown during the Depression years in the legal definitions of income, capital, surplus, and dividends may have contributed to this concern.[51] The relative interests of different classes of investors in troubled corporations appear to have been a live issue in the early 1930s. Paton may also have been thinking of references to accounting figures in bond contracts. He reserved some of his most picturesque writing to describe the heavy hand of the law:

49. William A. Paton, "Aspects of Asset Valuations," *Accounting Review* (June 1934), p. 127.

50. W.A. Paton, "Accounting Problems of the Depression," *Accounting Review* (Dec. 1932), p. 264.

51. The attention being given to such questions may be discerned from reading issues of the *Accounting Review* during the early and middle 1930s.

It must also not be forgotten that our legal institutions care nothing for purchasing power and treat all dollars, regardless of changing price levels, as equivalents. And the accountant, called upon to report and trace the effects of a maze of specific legal relationships and contracts, cannot ignore the legal structure, and hence is circumscribed and harassed in his efforts to become a statistical economist.[52]

In a 1931 article, Paton reveals the philosophical underpinning for the use of current costs in financial statements. He argues that

to be an effective cost a cost factor must be significant in the competitive price-making process, or, to put the matter more definitely from the standpoint of accounting valuation, to constitute a legitimate asset in the balance sheet an element of cost incurred must be of such a character that the presence of the factor or condition represented by such cost makes it possible for the enterprise to avoid incurring another similar cost which would otherwise be required in the production of revenue.[53]

He concludes that by "effective cost" the economist means "the potential cost of replacement."[54] (In this period, Paton's references to replacement cost were to eventual replacement, not to simulated immediate replacement.) And "It is only in the case of a continuous flow of standard units that replacement cost can be held to have any marked influence on value."[55] The same article is one of the relatively few places in Paton's writings where he discusses in some depth a combination of replacement costs and general price-level changes, the change in the former in relation to the latter yielding the "real" (or "true") enhancement or decrement in economic status.[56]

But experiences during the Depression convinced Paton that this philosophy did not deal adequately with the times. By the end of 1932, he writes,

In fact in a time [of overcapacity, replacement cost] has been temporarily eclipsed as a price-determining factor, for the individual concern or for business in general. . . .

In the first place cost of replacement means very little if anything in the case of obsolete or semi-obsolete property which is not being reproduced in the form of a constant flow of new plants and new machines. Second, the complex plant property of modern times is so specialized

---

52. Paton, "Aspects," p. 126.

53. W.A. Paton, "Economic Theory in Relation to Accounting Valuations," *Accounting Review* (June 1931), p. 91. Compare the later article, David Green, Jr., "Moral to the Direct Costing Controversy?" *Journal of Business* (July 1960), pp. 218–26.

54. Paton, "Economic Theory," p. 94.

55. *Ibid.,* p. 95.

56. *Ibid.*

that much of it, even in the case of the newest and best types, will never be reproduced in precisely the same form.[57]

In 1934, he seemed to question the principle still further:

> Nevertheless it must be remembered, first that the operating expenses of the particular concern in which the accountant is interested will not as a rule be the focal point in price determination, and, second, that the influence of the depreciation charge upon price is obscure and not susceptible of statistical isolation.[58]

Only in the long run, or in periods of capacity operation, apparently, might the depreciation charge be price-determining, and Paton did not believe that the prospect of such a remote future effect was worth recording in the accounts.[59]

Paton was deeply troubled throughout the period. On the one hand, he wanted to argue on principle that historical costs constitute obsolete information, but on the other hand he felt constrained by institutional and economic considerations. It must have been painful for him to admit in 1934 that "barring exceptional circumstances the cost basis of valuation, with all its limitations, is not seriously defective for accounting purposes."[60] But then he adds his clarion call of the 1930s:

> These days of monetary tinkering, however, may be the "exceptional circumstances" which justify our giving more attention to devices and methods designed to *supplement*, in a useful way, our present types of records.[61]

He favored supplementary disclosures of the effects of changes in both replacement costs and general price levels,[62] and in a second 1934 article, he criticized accountants for being so "sluggish" in following the lead of Sweeney and others toward the preparation of supplementary analyses of the impact of inflation on enterprise affairs.[63]

By 1936, therefore, when he joined such arch historical costers as Eric L. Kohler, A.C. Littleton, and Howard C. Greer in the drafting of an accounting principles statement on behalf of the newly

57. Paton, "Depression," p. 266.

58. Paton, "Aspects," p. 126.

59. *Ibid.* See also p. 123.

60. *Ibid.*, p. 128.

61. *Ibid.* Emphasis added.

62. *Ibid.*

63. William A. Paton, "Shortcomings of Present-Day Financial Statements," *Journal of Accountancy* (Feb. 1934), p. 130.

reorganized American Accounting Association, Paton could fairly be said to be a historical coster himself in the basic financial statements. Nonetheless, the committee's assertion that "accounting is thus not essentially a process of valuation, but the allocation of historical costs and revenues to the current and succeeding fiscal periods" may not have been a genuine reflection of Paton's fundamental view of accounting.[64]

The committee's statement was a thoroughgoing paean to historical costs, although it conceded that "interpretation [of financial statements] is often impossible without extensive supplemental data, including the provision of common denominators through which comparisons may be effected."[65]

Elsewhere in the statement, the committee writes, "An extreme change in the value of money might vitiate the usefulness of cost records but there seems to be no sound reason for repeated adjustments of asset values for the ordinary changes in price levels commonly experienced from one generation to another."[66] This assertion is in line with Paton's separate writings on the desirability of preserving the record of cost in the accounts. Finally, the committee criticizes the "uncoordinated" appraisals of fixed assets in language that could well have been Paton's.[67]

Thus, by the middle of the 1930s, Paton had transformed his radical call for financial-statement reform of 1917–18 to a recommendation that corporations supplement their financial statements with informative disclosures. The questionable booking of write-ups in the 1920s and write-downs in the 1930s, the special problems wrought by the economic stagnation of the Great Depression, and his growing concern over the legal constraints within which accounting must be performed, collectively persuaded Paton that the formal accounting records and resulting financial statements were better kept on a cost footing than on a replacement-cost basis. When reporting to managers, Paton continued to prefer revaluations based on replacement cost to restatements in line with changing general price levels—a position from which he has never

64. "A Tentative Statement of Accounting Principles Affecting Corporate Reports," *Accounting Review* (June 1936), p. 188. Under the title, "A Tentative Statement of Accounting Principles Underlying Corporate Financial Statements," it was widely distributed as a reprint.

65. *Ibid.*

66. *Ibid.*, p. 189.

67. *Ibid.*

wavered.[68] Indeed, while he has recommended at different times that replacement costs might be reflected in the accounts and in the financial statements, he has never proposed that the effects of changes in general price levels be shown anywhere but in supplementary presentations. But in the 1930s, when economic conditions failed to substantiate the belief that replacement costs were price-influencing, Paton declined even to recommend that replacement costs be entered in the accounts. His conclusion during that era was that either replacement costs or general price-level effects should be displayed in supplementary disclosures.

ESSENTIALS OF ACCOUNTING (1938)

Essentials of Accounting was Paton's first textbook after *Accounting* (1924). In *Essentials,* Paton continues to espouse a cautious policy toward valuations other than historical cost. In the majority of instances, the financial statements should be based on historical cost, but Paton encourages supplementary disclosures to inform management of the impact of price fluctuations.[69] Nonetheless, in "periods of sharply changing prices," a departure from cost valuation of inventory "has some merit where the period of production is sufficiently long, and the selling market is sufficiently sensitive, to make possible modifications of policy based on observation of the changing costs of goods on hand." Paton adds, however, without rebutting the point, "The most common objection offered to the consistent use of replacement cost in pricing inventory is that such valuation will result in effect in the recognition of unrealized profit where replacement cost is higher than actual cost."[70]

In *Principles of Accounting* (1918), Paton and Stevenson were opposed to the inclusion in income of the margin between the net realizable value and replacement cost of merchandise inventories. In *Accounting,* published in 1924, Paton objected to crediting income with the spread between the replacement cost and historical cost of plant assets, but he seemed to countenance the inclusion in income of this spread in regard to "reasonably liquid assets," which excluded merchandise inventories. In 1938, he reaffirmed this position.

---

68. Paton, "Aspects," p. 126.
69. W.A. Paton, *Essentials of Accounting* (New York: Macmillan Co., 1938), pp. 482, 813.
70. *Ibid.,* pp. 482–83.

By 1938, Paton was prepared to consider a formal recognition in the accounts of the replacement cost of fixed assets. It is in *Essentials* that he reveals his new tactic. After stipulating that "the cost of replacement is truly significant [for business managements] only in the case of standard plant units which will presumably be replaced upon retirement substantially in kind," Paton recites "numerous difficulties in the way of achieving results which are worthwhile by attempting to shift the measure of depreciation from cost to replacement cost":

> Continuous revaluation is a costly process; appraisal results at the best are estimates; current costs of a particular date are not likely to measure the actual cost of replacement upon retirement; depreciation is only one cost and a modification of this element will not change the operating picture materially except where the movement of costs has been very sharp; [and] in general replacement cost is not recognized as a basis of depreciation for income-tax purposes or in other legal connections.[71]

If revaluations are nonetheless entered in the accounts, the "recorded cost figures [should not be] obscured." The gross revaluation of plant should be shown in a "distinct" account, the corresponding credit should be "segregated" from the ordinary capital and proprietary accounts, and as subsequent depreciation accruals are recorded on the basis of the revalued assets, a transfer should be made from the proprietorship account originally credited with the revaluation "to the income or [earned] surplus account as a correction." Thus, Earned Surplus, if not Net Income, would be shown as if the revaluations had not been recorded. "It is universally agreed," Paton asserts, incorrectly, "that no part of the unrealized appreciation or declination should be reflected in the income statement."[72] His recommended treatment of plant revaluations, including the "washout" of subsequent depreciation accruals in the income statement, was later labeled by Paton a "compromise procedure."

71. *Ibid.*, pp. 542–43.

72. *Ibid.*, p. 543. In 1939, Kenneth MacNeal published his controversial *Truth in Accounting* (Philadelphia: University of Pennsylvania Press) in which he advocated the inclusion of unrealized appreciation or declination of fixed assets in the income statement, but said these amounts should be carried to Capital Surplus, not Earned Surplus. He would, however, transfer the unrealized price appreciations and declinations on inventory to Earned Surplus (see chap. XIV). Sweeney recommended that each year's installment of real unrealized appreciation (the amount of unrealized appreciation which remains after allowing for changes in the general price level) be shown in the income statement as "unrealized net income," which would be transferred to "Unrealized Surplus," rather than the Retained Earnings-like account, "Realized Surplus." Henry W. Sweeney, *Stabilized Accounting* (1936), pp. 18–19, 50–52.

Finally, although *Essentials* was an introductory textbook, Paton devotes the last six pages to the impact of inflation on the accounts. He returns to earlier arguments:

> In attempting to deal with this problem the accountant is embarrassed by the fact that the law in general entirely fails to acknowledge the phenomenon of a variable unit of monetary measure. The accountant, in other words, is coerced in some measure by the framework of contracts and legal institutions by which the business enterprise—his immediate field of activity—is surrounded and sustained; he must report contractual earnings, amount subject to income tax, amount available for dividends, capital stock, accumulated surplus, etc., in the first instance at any rate, in accordance with impinging legal requirements. At the same time the accountant is coming to be depended upon more and more as an interpreter of the essential economic conditions of the enterprise for the purposes in particular of assisting in advising investors and framing managerial policies. And in these connections it is plain that he cannot fulfill his function adequately and remain blind to the limitations of the conventional accounts and reports in the face of a varying dollar. [73]

He discusses the impact of inflation on an enterprise's working capital and long-term liabilities, and illustrates in numerical format (for the first time) the conversion of a comparative balance sheet into dollars of a common index. "What is needed in most situations is a special report supplementing the periodic statements, [but] except in periods where the change in dollar value is sharp and prolonged as a result of emergency conditions and accompanying monetary tinkering the case for giving explicit attention to the problem is not very strong." [74] Here he uses, for the first time, the expression "common-dollar basis" to describe the method employed. [75] *Essentials* may well have been the first American accounting textbook to discuss and numerically illustrate general price-level accounting.

"Recent and Prospective Developments in Accounting Theory" (1940)

In April, 1940, Paton delivered the third Dickinson Lecture at the Harvard Graduate School of Business Administration. [76] Entitled "Recent and Prospective Developments in Accounting Theory," it

73. Paton, *Essentials*, p. 813.
74. *Ibid.*
75. *Ibid.*, p. 817.
76. *Dickinson Lectures in Accounting* (Cambridge, Mass.: Harvard University Press, 1943), pp. 85–131.

contains only a few pages on the effects of changing prices on accounting. Paton observes that the trends of specific and general prices "are regularly in the same direction," following which he offers a sly dictum which he became fond of repeating in later years,

> It is this fact which affords some justification for the paradoxical statement that "the proponents of replacement cost valuations are in effect defending adherence to the original cost basis." Interpreting cost incurred in the sense of economic power committed to the enterprise, there is a measure of truth in this observation.[77]

Whatever the validity of this statement, it was undeniably a clever debating tactic.

He continues to argue that the replacement-cost approach is more useful than the purchasing-power approach to managers and owners of enterprise. In a statement which is prophetic of the American accounting literature of the 1960s and 1970s, Paton writes, "Business management is concerned in some degree with the maintenance of the integrity of investment measured in purchasing power but is perhaps even more devoted to the protection of productive capacity and scope of activity."[78]

He nonetheless persists in his opposition to any role for plant valuations in the determination of income. Among the reasons given, he contends that the use of replacement cost is "of marked significance only in the case of standard, up-to-date facilities, which will presumably be replaced substantially in kind." Returning to a theme in his "Aspects" (1932) and "Depression" (1934) articles, Paton adds, "Neither the original cost nor the replacement cost of facilities of an obsolescent character are potent factors in the economic process." Another reason given, which elaborates on a point made briefly in *Essentials of Accounting* two years before, is Paton's belief that depreciation is in most cases a relatively small fraction of total operating costs, and thus the effect of a change from original cost to replacement cost would be of little practical consequence. Following World War II, however, Paton cited the size of depreciation in relation to *net income* as justification for a change in the basis of depreciation accounting.

In Paton's view, the most important argument against the use of replacement costs in the determination of net income is its "conflict with the legal point of view." In language reminiscent of his

77. *Ibid.*, p. 126.
78. *Ibid.*, pp. 126–27.

"Aspects" (1934) article and *Essentials,* he writes that "the accountant is inevitably coerced in considerable measure by the legal framework, and in his search for ways of improving the reporting of operating data for managerial purposes he should not lose sight of the legal criteria of the general income statement."[79]

The legal impediments to changing the way in which net income is determined have continued to be an influential factor in Paton's thinking. In his Dickinson Lecture, Paton unveils his adaptation of the quasi-reorganization to deal with *under*valued fixed assets, an accounting adjustment which he urged on numerous occasions in the 1940s and 1950s as a means of supplanting historical cost records by infrequent upward revaluations of nonmonetary assets.[80] That quasi-reorganizations were acceptable under certain conditions for downward revaluations persuaded Paton that, by analogous reasoning, the same accounting device could be extended to upward revaluations. Even if upward quasi-reorganizations were not available to a company, it might, according to Paton, book replacement costs without obscuring recorded costs, with the proviso that the subsequent depreciation based on the appraisal increments would appear in the income statement as information only, without reducing the reported net income below what would have been shown by the use of historical cost. This is the same method that he introduced and discussed in *Essentials.*

An Introduction to Corporate Accounting Standards (1940)

Paton's posture on the accounting response to changing prices was faithfully reflected in his celebrated 1940 monograph with A.C. Littleton, *An Introduction to Corporate Accounting Standards.*[81] The monograph was an outgrowth of the tentative "Statement of Accounting Principles Underlying Corporate Financial Statements," issued by the executive committee (of which Paton was a member) of the American Accounting Association in 1936.

At several places in the monograph, the authors draw attention to the importance of legal considerations, thus obliging the accountant to employ traditional historical costs in the reckoning of income.[82]

79. *Ibid.,* pp. 127–29.

80. *Ibid.,* p. 129.

81. W.A. Paton and A.C. Littleton, *An Introduction to Corporate Accounting Standards* (Chicago: American Accounting Association, 1940).

82. *Ibid.,* pp. 4, 9, 62, 123, 135, 136, and 141; but see pp. 10–11.

Indeed, they categorically exclude appreciation on nonmonetary assets from income:

> Appreciation, in general, does not reflect or measure the progress of operating activity; appreciation is not the result of any transaction or any act of conversion; appreciation makes available no additional liquid resources which may be used to meet obligations or make disbursements to investors; appreciation has little or no legal standing as income.[83]

A monograph in which "verifiable, objective evidence" is proposed as a basic concept is not a place where one would expect to find an argument for replacement costs in the principal financial statements.[84] Paton and Littleton acknowledge that managers should be made aware of the impact of changing replacement costs where such costs might affect business decisions, but they suggest that this information can be made available to management without altering the accounts. They enumerate several limitations of the replacement-cost approach, all of which would have been well known to readers of Paton's previous writings.[85] The set of entries by which historical-cost measurements of plant cost and depreciation would be accompanied by appraisal increments or decrements, but without altering the historical-cost net income, is discussed at length (the same approach was proposed in *Essentials of Accounting* and in the Dickinson Lecture). Paton's increasing interest in Sweeney's "stabilized accounting" is further evident in the monograph, where extensive discussion is devoted to a means by which recorded costs might be converted to "common dollars."[86] In regard to both replacement costs and common-dollar accounting, the authors conclude that supplementary disclosures would suffice to adapt the formal accounts to conditions of changing prices. It would appear that the imperative of "verifiable, objective evidence" together with the authors' pervasive preoccupation with legal considerations serves to defeat any argument which might displace historical costs in the formal financial statements. Replacement costs would perhaps be allowed in the financial statements only as bits of information, so long as they do not affect the measurement of net income.

Of interest, however, is the authors' reference (doubtless a Patonian initiative) to the possibility, albeit mildly suggested, that the

83. *Ibid.*, p. 62.
84. *Ibid.*, pp. 18–21.
85. *Ibid.*, pp. 131–34.
86. *Ibid.*, pp. 139–41.

difference between the incurred cost and book value of a corporation's reacquired shares might serve as a basis for the revaluation of
the corporate assets.[87] The suggestion is mentioned in the most
inoffensive terms, and the authors seem content not to carry out its
implications.

ADVANCED ACCOUNTING (1941)

Advanced Accounting was Paton's first textbook designed for students above the introductory level. It may be distinguished from
most other intermediate and advanced texts by Paton's determination to discuss and debate virtually all of the controversial issues
of the day. *Advanced Accounting* was hardly a compendium of
mechanics.

For inventories, Paton peremptorily rejects valuation at net selling
prices and shows little enthusiasm even for the use of replacement
costs.[88] Both of these alternatives to historical cost, he argues,
would give rise to the recognition of unrealized profit. He does not
discuss the alternative of crediting stockholders' equity instead of
income for the amount of any such appreciation, perhaps because
"for most trading concerns, it is fair to say, there is little to be
gained [in the income statement] in the way of useful reporting by a
shift from recorded cost to current buying price, particularly when
cost is estimated by the first-in, first-out method." Moreover, "replacement cost as an independent valuation base is not generally
approved by the income-tax authorities, and is viewed as noncon-
servative by many accountants, bankers, and business managers."
When he is not disposed to criticize extant practice, Paton takes
refuge in the word of other authorities.

In regard to the valuation of plant, Paton rejects valuation based
on a discounting of the prospective earning power of the assets.[89]
Two principal reasons are that such estimates "are none too dependable under the most favorable conditions" and that the income
streams are not uniquely linked to particular assets, but to a compo-
site of assets. In discussing valuation at replacement cost, Paton
argues once again that "the influential costs in the economic process are those that are reflected in the immediate level of prices."

87. *Ibid.*, p. 116.
88. W.A. Paton, *Advanced Accounting* (New York: Macmillan Co., 1941), pp. 151–
52, 160–61.
89. *Ibid.*, pp. 323–24.

But he cautions that the adoption of this view does not lead inexorably to "a continuous process of plant appraisal and a continuous revision of plant accounts." It would be "inexpedient" to embark on such a "systematic program" in the absence of a "major and persistent change" in prices. Furthermore,

> it must not be forgotten . . . that the price system is not uniformly sensitive throughout, and that for considerable periods selling prices may not move in harmony with changing costs of production. Selling prices, moreover, are not in general fixed by cost to the particular concern—whatever the basis on which such cost may be computed.

Finally (as in the 1940 monograph), he suggests that business management can take into consideration such price movements without necessarily "revamping the plant accounts." He concludes by striking a familiar chord:

> Particularly in view of income-tax regulations and other aspects of the legal framework within which a business enterprise must operate, the original cost of plant and the depreciation charges based on such cost are data which the accountant must continue to make available. From an accounting standpoint, that is, replacement costs are not a substitute for recorded costs, although they may represent significant supplementary facts.

Later in the same chapter, he claims that the failure of recorded cost to reflect replacement cost "is not the most serious weakness of the cost basis." Of greater consequence is that "the original dollar cost [of nonmonetary assets] is not a dependable expression of actual cost in the sense of economic sacrifice or committed purchasing power." Paton argues forcefully for an accounting recognition of changes in the value of the monetary unit and blames "the legal framework within which business transactions are conducted" for the lack of progress in this direction.[90] An entire chapter is devoted to "Common-Dollar Reporting," constituting (up to that time) the most extensive discussion of general price-level accounting in any American accounting textbook. In this 18-page chapter, he illustrates the conversion of the balance sheet and income statement and discusses the accounting treatment to be given to purchasing power gains and losses. Like Sweeney, Paton contends that the gains and losses on monetary items are unrealized so long as the monetary assets are held or the monetary liabilities are unpaid.[91] By 1955,

90. *Ibid.*, p. 329.
91. Sweeney, *Stabilized Accounting*, pp. 20–22, 33; Paton, *Advanced Accounting*, pp. 739, 748.

Paton modified this stance in regard to current monetary assets and liabilities.

Paton illustrates alternative accounting treatments for booked appreciation or "declination." His preference is to credit a special stockholders' equity account for the amount of the net appreciation (i.e., after allowing for accumulated depreciation on the appreciation) and then to "reserve" an amount of Surplus (Retained Earnings in today's parlance) equal to the accumulated depreciation on the appreciation. The object of the latter transfer is to "provide" for the understated depreciation of prior years. When depreciation is later recorded on the appreciated plant, an amount equal to the depreciation on appreciation is transferred to the income statement from the special stockholders' equity account. In this manner, the net income is undisturbed by the revaluation of the plant. At the end of the year, an amount equal to the year's depreciation on appreciation is transferred from the Surplus account to a surplus reserve. The effect of these entries is to display the revaluation in the balance sheet (while not erasing the historical costs) and to confine the revaluation in the income statement to disclosure of the year's depreciation on appreciation without thereby affecting net income. The unreserved Surplus account is nonetheless reduced as if net income had been lower by the amount of the depreciation on appreciation. "Declinations" would be treated, in a similar manner but with opposite effects, as appreciations. In later years, Paton came to call this treatment "a compromise procedure," as it recognized revaluations without obscuring historical costs or affecting the amount of the net income.[92] Paton defended this compromise as follows:

> Adoption of a policy of charging appreciation to operations, with no accompanying adjustment of profit and surplus figures, [would result] in a record of earnings that fails to satisfy legal requirements and may cause misunderstanding and definite impairment of the rights of particular classes of investors.[93]

Paton also apportioned the appreciation as between the real unrealized gain and the nominal unrealized gain. The latter was treated as a restatement of the Capital and Surplus accounts, while the former (being the residue after reducing the aggregate change in cost by the movement in the general price level) was denominated

92. Paton, *Advanced Accounting*, pp. 343–47.
93. *Ibid.*, p. 349.

as unrealized gain—and was credited to the special stockholders' equity account.[94]

Paton likewise argued against the inclusion of land appreciation in income, "as the enhancement does not represent realized or disposable income."[95] Here the role of income as a dividend base intrudes.

In a discussion of "Appreciation and Income" in the chapter on "Income Determination—Revenue," Paton rehearses the general arguments against booking unrealized appreciation as income. He summarizes his position as follows:

> Many accountants agree that where enhancement in value is unmistakable and is present in large amount it is not objectionable to give recognition thereto in the accounts and statements, although there is no consensus of opinion as to the details of how this should be done. Very few, however, are willing to view unrealized appreciation as genuine business income, no matter how apparent and fully validated the increase in value may be.
>
> The legal attitude is of decided consequence, if not controlling. The accountant is under obligation to report income in a manner that is acceptable in the eyes of the law, although this obligation does not prevent the disclosure of other significant figures.[96]

In *Advanced Accounting*, Paton repeats a suggestion which first appeared in the 1940 monograph, that a reacquisition by a corporation of a significant slice of its outstanding stock at a price different from its book value might be an occasion for recognizing an implied undervaluation or overvaluation of the corporation's assets.[97] This procedure would be parallel to a recommendation routinely made in leading textbooks in regard to partnerships, when the ownership interest of one of the partners is purchased by the partnership at a price above or below its book value—justifying in some circumstances the accounting recognition of an increase or decrease in the partnership goodwill. Thus, if a corporation reacquires a portion of its outstanding stock at a price lower than its book value, rather than recognizing a "profit from retirement," it would make an entry to remove the implied overvaluation of the company's assets. If 10 percent of the company's stock were purchased for $10,000 less than its book value, the overvaluation of ten times the discrepancy, or $100,000, would be eradicated as follows:

94. *Ibid.*, pp. 332–33.
95. *Ibid.*, p. 377.
96. *Ibid.*, p. 452.
97. *Ibid.*, pp. 543–45.

Estimated Loss of Capital and Surplus $100,000
   Allowance for General Revaluation
      of Resources $100,000

Although individual asset accounts may be found to be overvalued, the Allowance account may be retained as "a blanket contra to resources."

Paton would confine such revaluations to reacquisitions "carried out on terms which are equally fair to both parties—the corporation representing the remaining stockholders on the one hand and the retiring stockholders on the other." Paton continues:

> Assuming good accounting and ignoring wild swings in security prices it may be said that the excess of the price of shares over book values rests primarily on two factors: one, the amount of goodwill and other intangibles which reflect the existence of superior earning power; two, appreciation of existing assets which have not been traced in the accounts. Similarly, where book value exceeds market price under the assumed conditions the difference may largely be explained by reference to lack of earning power and declinations in asset value due to price movements not covered by depreciation accruals and other offsets.

Notwithstanding the evident appeal of this revaluation procedure to one whose deeper sympathies were with the expression in the accounts of current prices, Paton, plagued by doubts so evident in his writings throughout the 1930s and early 1940s, recoiled from a recommendation that the idea actually be implemented:

> While [this revaluation of the stock equity] has intrinsic merit it can hardly be explicitly employed in accounting for stock retirements. Ignoring considerations of law and assuming that a practicable procedure could be worked out—without impairing the usefulness of accounts in other directions—the fact remains that the retirement of a portion of the outstanding stock could seldom be rated as a compelling reason for a complete revaluation of the equity. Certainly the acquisition of a few shares, at what may be a very temporary price, would not be controlling, and even the purchase of a substantial block at an established market or negotiated price would scarcely justify revaluation, particularly where the accounting of the corporation has been on an acceptable basis.

His reasons for declining to recommend the procedure, especially the vague reference to "an acceptable basis" of corporation accounting, seem reluctant and unconvincing.

Paton has advised me that this revaluation procedure occurred to him after reading Warner H. Hord's "The Flow of Property as a Basis of Internal Control" in the *Accounting Review* of September 1939.

Finally, Paton carries forward the upward quasi-reorganization, which he first exposed to view in his Dickinson Lecture a year earlier. Journal entries are proposed for the "fresh start," but Paton's support for the procedure is restrained, owing to the omnipresent legal factors:

> On the score of simplicity the procedure under consideration is all to the good. From the standpoint of adequate recognition of the cost basis and full disclosure of pertinent data, on the other hand, the immediate capitalization of appreciation is not satisfactory. Adoption of a policy of charging appreciation to operations, with no accompanying adjustment of profit and surplus figures, results in a record of earnings that fails to satisfy legal requirements and may cause misunderstanding and definite impairment of the rights of particular classes of investors. [98]

Advanced Accounting may be seen as the most important and complete statement of Paton's views on the impact of changing prices on accounting since the publication in 1924 of *Accounting*. It reflects, on the whole, a caution induced by Paton's continuing preoccupation with the legal confines of accounting. By 1941, he had developed several innovations by which changing prices might find their way into the accounts, but it was not until the postwar period that he became their full-throated advocate.

Response to the Postwar Inflation

Paton was a member of the Committee on Accounting Procedure of the American Institute of Accountants (as it was then known) between 1939, when it began issuing *Accounting Research Bulletins*, and 1950. In 1945, the Committee unanimously recommended that quasi-reorganizations be reflected when asset values were understated as well as overstated. Quasi-reorganizations had been accepted practice for many years when corporations were facing severe financial difficulties and their assets were significantly overvalued. But the Securities and Exchange Commission (SEC) firmly registered its opposition to write-ups under quasi-reorganizations, and the Institute's Committee declined to press the matter further. [99]

In 1947, the Committee issued *Accounting Research Bulletin No. 33*, in which it opposed the incipient practice of recording depreciation based on replacement cost. Paton did not vote on that bulletin, but in 1948, when the Committee issued a letter reaffirming *Bulletin No.*

98. *Ibid.*, p. 349.
99. Stephen A. Zeff, *Forging Accounting Principles in Five Countries: A History and an Analysis of Trends* (Champaign, Ill.: Stipes Publishing Co., 1972), p. 156.

33 in the face of criticism from within the profession, Paton dissented. It was reported that Paton and the three other dissenters

> believe . . . that inflation has proceeded to a point where original dollar costs have already lost their practical significance and that where depreciation is an important element of cost the advantages which would result from a basic change in accounting treatment outweigh the possible disadvantage against it.[100]

The postwar inflation convinced Paton that measures had to be taken—within the legal framework—to restore the financial statements as meaningful economic indicators.

In "Cost and Value in Accounting," a March 1946 article,[101] Paton briefly refers to the (two-way) quasi-reorganization as "the necessary safety valve in a structure of accounting generally based on cost. It furnishes a means under which a corporation may restate its accounts, and provide a new basis of income measurement, without undergoing an actual legal reorganization."[102] In the article, Paton emphasizes that historical costs are not to be treasured in themselves, but are merely the initial indications of value, later subject to revision as conditions change. He writes,

> In fact cost is significant primarily because it approximates fair value at date of acquisition. Cost is not of basic importance because it represents an amount paid; it is important as a measure of the value of what is acquired. . . . The problem in accounting is primarily the question of how cost figures should be dealt with, and when and how they should be revised in view of changing conditions.[103]

Here Paton begins to diverge from the Paton-Littleton devotion to the *fundamental* importance of price-aggregates in accounting reckonings.

In a March 1948 note entitled "What Is Actual Cost in Depreciation Accounting?" Paton criticizes *Bulletin No. 33* for discouraging efforts at dealing with the kinds of changed conditions to which he referred in his March 1946 article.[104] He proposes two possible reforms: (1)

100. "Institute Committee Rejects Change in Basis for Depreciation Charges," *Journal of Accountancy* (Nov. 1948), p. 381.

101. William A. Paton, "Cost and Value in Accounting," *Journal of Accountancy* (March 1946), pp. 192–99. An earlier, but similar, version of this article was drafted by Paton in 1944 for a possible accounting research bulletin to be issued by the Institute's Committee on Accounting Procedure. The proposed bulletin underwent revision within the Committee but did not survive final scrutiny.

102. *Ibid.*, p. 199.

103. *Ibid.*, p. 193.

104. W.A. Paton, "What Is Actual Cost in Depreciation Accounting?" *Journal of Accountancy* (March 1948), pp. 206–7.

supplementary disclosures to financial statements "designed to show the limitations of the conventional, legalistic presentation, in which—erroneously—all dollars are assumed to be homogeneous," and (2) a "fresh start" or quasi-reorganization which "should be defined in such terms as to permit application to all situations in which recorded cost data are so far from economic realities that the resulting reports are misleading, regardless of the arithmetical direction of the adjustment." Ever the skillful debater, Paton, who railed in the 1940s against the infamous "original cost" of the utility regulatory agencies and against federal income taxation based solely on unmodified historical cost, argues that "those who support replacement-cost depreciation are supporting *actual cost* more effectively than those who advocate continued adherence to depreciation based on the so-called 'actual cost.' " He and others hoped that an argument by analogy (a favorite Patonian ploy) would persuade accounting authorities, chiefly the SEC, that quasi-reorganizations could be extended to cover upward revaluations. In that endeavor the Institute's Committee on Accounting Procedure failed in 1945 and failed again in 1950.[105] From its inception in 1934 until the early 1970s, the SEC was an unyielding foe of departures from traditional historical cost in the measurement of income. Only the long-accepted use of downward quasi-reorganizations was countenanced by the SEC when corporations were in financial straits.

In "Accounting Procedures and Private Enterprise," an April 1948 article, Paton suggested three alternative approaches to dealing with the impact on accounting of changing prices:[106] (1) Supplementary disclosure of the pertinent data. (2) A "compromise procedure" for the booking of replacement cost of plant, the recording of depreciation based on the replacement cost, but determination of net income based on conventional, historical cost principles after the depreciation on appreciation was washed out against a stockholders' equity adjustment account. (This alternative was first exposed in *Essentials of Accounting* and was also discussed on pages 815–16 in the third edition of the *Accountants' Handbook*, which Paton edited and largely wrote in 1943.)[107] (3) A quasi-reorganization.[108] He insisted that any

105. Zeff, *Forging Accounting Principles*, pp. 156–57.

106. W.A. Paton, "Accounting Procedures and Private Enterprise," *Journal of Accountancy* (April 1948), pp. 278–91.

107. W.A. Paton, ed., *Accountants' Handbook* (3d ed.; New York: Ronald Press, 1943). It is evident from the editor's preface on p. x that Paton himself wrote the section on "Plant Appraisals," pp. 787–833.

108. Paton, "Accounting Procedures and Private Enterprise," pp. 289–90.

accounting adjustments should "be handled in an orderly, systematic manner and with complete disclosure. Arbitrary increasing or decreasing of the depreciation charge, with no concurrent revision of the basic figures on which depreciation is computed, cannot be supported by the accountant." Here he evidently refers to the efforts in the late 1940s of several large companies (notably United States Steel Corporation, E.I. du Pont de Nemours & Company, and Allied Chemical & Dye Corporation) to record replacement-cost depreciation in their published reports. In this respect, Paton reiterates the view he expressed in "Depreciation, Appreciation and Productive Capacity," published in 1920.

In urging accounting reform, Paton was alarmed by what he regarded as a growing trend toward socialism. American industry was being accused of profiteering and earning excessive rates of return, and Paton feared a crumbling away of the free enterprise system in the wake of such criticism. He foresaw "a great confiscation of private property if the state were to take over business concerns at present book values."[109] He was worried that accountants would concentrate their reform on the income statement, ignoring an understated balance sheet and the resulting overstated measures of earning power. He believed that sound accounting procedures were essential to a preservation of private enterprise. On several occasions, Paton criticized his brethren for playing into the hands of the socialists. In an address given in June 1949, he said,

> What is important is that the aggregate of the earnings of American stockholders are being seriously overstated at a time when private property—particularly venture capital in the corporate field—is under attack and undergoing inequitable treatment tax-wise, as features of a strong current in the direction of state socialism. This is certainly a bad time in which to be lending aid and succor to those who are trying to hamstring and destroy private enterprise and our market economy by means— among other things—of accounting records and reports that seriously overstate the actual earnings of venture capital. This is a sad state of affairs and accountants should hang their heads as a result of their part in the process of encouraging misunderstanding and the unwarranted attack on the stake that the millions of common stockholders have in American business.[110]

109. *Ibid.*, p. 290.
110. William A. Paton, "Measuring Profits under Inflation Conditions: A Serious Problem for Accountants," *Journal of Accountancy* (Jan. 1950), p. 21.

Paton's great concern over the impact of overstated profits on decisions involving dividends, wages, prices (including especially those determined by utility regulatory commissions on the basis of "original cost"), and income taxes, evidently convinced him that informative disclosures accompanying a reckoning based on unmodified historical cost were not an adequate solution in most instances.[111] The figures in the financial statements themselves would need to be modified—either by means of his "compromise procedure" or a full-fledged "fresh start."

Paton spoke out frequently during the late 1940s and early 1950s on the dire effects of overstating companies' reported profits.[112] Although he evidently favored the quasi-reorganization approach when current replacement costs differed significantly from historical costs, he also complained of the confusion wrought by changes in the general price level.[113] He attacked on two fronts: relative price changes and economy-wide inflation. The tactical advantage of a general price-level reform would have been its evident objectivity and the commonsense appreciation of the diminishing purchasing power of the dollar. In testimony before the Subcommittee on Profits of the Joint Committee (of the U.S. Congress) on the Economic Report, in late 1948, Paton suggested that "we might call the 1948 unit the zollar, and this would encourage clear thinking when we were comparing the present value of money with, say the 1940 dollar."[114] Paton believed that the illusion that different years' dollars could meaningfully be added or subtracted was fortified by a continuing use of the same term to describe the monetary unit. He was later fond of saying that while accountants would carefully allow for a spread of 2 or 3 percentage points between the American and Canadian dollars, they would ignore altogether changes of 5 and 10 percentage points in successive

111. For Paton's views on the controversy over "original cost," see William A. Paton, "Accounting Policies of the Federal Power Commission—A Critique," *Journal of Accountancy* (June 1944), pp. 432–60.

112. In *Shirtsleeve Economics: A Commonsense Survey* (New York: Appleton-Century-Crofts, Inc., 1952), Paton makes many of his points in nontechnical terms. See pp. 232–58.

113. See, for example, the address by W.A. Paton in *Accounting Problems Relating to the Reporting of Profits* (New Wilmington, Pa.: Economic and Business Foundation, 1949), pp. 10–11.

114. U.S., Congress, *Corporate Profits, Hearings* before the Sub-Committee on Profits of the Joint Committee on the Economic Report, 80th Cong., 2d sess., 1948, p. 62.

American dollars.[115] In pressing his general price-level case, Paton repeatedly cited Henry W. Sweeney's path-breaking 1936 book, *Stabilized Accounting.*

In his congressional testimony in December 1948, Paton also modified his view of the late 1930s that depreciation was, after all, but a relatively small fraction of total expenses—implying that an adjustment of depreciation would not have a material effect on net income. In 1948, he said, "It must not be forgotten that although in many industrial companies the reported depreciation cost figure is not a large fraction of total expenses it may be an important figure when compared with net income."[116]

The base against which materiality should be judged was now net income, not total expenses.

Paton was greatly disturbed over the misuse of accounting information. In his speeches, monographs, and testimony, he dealt in particular with the need to reform the tax base (he recommended replacement-cost depreciation) and to predicate wage increases on sound measures of profit.[117]

ESSENTIALS OF ACCOUNTING (1949)

In the discussion of the valuation of plant, the principal difference between this second edition of *Essentials* and its predecessor of 1938 is the inclusion in the former of a reference to the upward quasi-reorganization. In the two editions, the treatments of general price-level-adjusted financial statements are virtually identical. But in 1949 Paton includes for the first time in *Essentials* a "fresh start" revaluation of assets arising from the reacquisition by the corporation of a significant block of its own shares. Carrying forward his discussion in *Advanced Accounting* (1941) and a commentary in the third edition of the *Accountants' Handbook* (1943) (where, on page 1010, Paton discloses his debt to Hord), Paton writes in *Essentials:*

115. See, for example, William A. Paton, with the assistance of William A. Paton, Jr., *Corporation Accounts and Statements: An Advanced Course* (New York: Macmillan Co., 1955), p. 531.

116. U.S., Congress, *Corporate Profits,* p. 63.

117. Regarding the latter, see his testimony before the Presidential Steel Board, *In the Matter of the United Steelworkers of America—CIO and Republic Steel Corporation et al.* (Aug. 19, 1949) and before the Steel Panel of the Wage Stabilization Board, *In the Matter of the United Steelworkers of America—CIO and Various Steel and Iron Ore Companies* (Feb. 14, 1952).

> Assuming that corporation and stockholder are fully informed and acting intelligently on a commercial basis acquisition at a figure materially below book value implies that such value is overstated from the standpoint of going-concern value. . . . Similarly acquisition of shares at a figure materially above book value implies that the going-concern values of specific assets are in excess of book amounts or that unrecognized intangibles, reflecting superior earning power, are present.[118]

This view, which is compared above with a parallel procedure in partnership accounting, also may be shown to be analogous to the allocation of the excess of acquisition cost of a corporation's interest in a subsidiary over the underlying book values of the subsidiary's net assets. Paton's recommended revaluation of assets on the occasion of reacquisition of shares under certain conditions seems to have been generally ignored by his academic colleagues as well as by corporations and practicing accountants. I am aware of only a single comment by other writers on this Patonian innovation.[119] Nonetheless, Paton contends that this version of an accounting "fresh start" should serve to indicate the unreasonableness of the common assumption that a gain to the corporation emerges when shares are acquired at less than book value, or that a loss is suffered when shares are acquired at more than book value.[120]

It is curious that *Essentials* is largely devoid of the enthusiastic advocacy of accounting reform which typified Paton's every speech and article of the period. The reforms are indeed mentioned and in some instances illustrated in the book, but the passionate argument which one finds in Paton's other writings, including some of his later textbooks, is missing here.

ASSET ACCOUNTING (1952)

Asset Accounting was the first of two volumes (the other was *Corporation Accounts and Statements* [1955]) which collectively constituted the revision of *Advanced Accounting* (1941). Here one finds Paton the advocate and debater in full cry. Fresh from the battles of

---

118. William A. Paton, *Essentials of Accounting* (New York: Macmillan Co., 1949), pp. 710–11.

119. The lone comment appears in the finance literature. See Charles D. Ellis and Allan E. Young, *The Repurchase of Common Stock* (New York: Ronald Press Co., 1971), pp. 128–32. I am grateful to William A. Paton, Jr. for this reference.

120. *Ibid.*, p. 712.

the late 1940s and early 1950s, Paton carries the fight into this intermediate-level textbook.[121]

For internal managerial accounting, Paton recommends that all calculations be based on current prices, not historical costs.[122] In regard to published financial statements, Paton admits that it was "very discouraging" that corporations were doing so little to explain the limitations of conventional, unadjusted figures.

> Corporate earnings have been overstated by many billions in recent years, and such figures have been widely used to fan the fire of misrepresentation of the facts of business operation, but neither accountants nor business managements have done much of anything to put the figures being issued in proper perspective. Public accountants continue to certify financial statements, and insist that they fairly present the picture of earnings and financial position, when they are in fact downright misleading.[123]

This is a bold indictment to appear in a primer on financial accounting.

In a 25-page chapter on "Adjusting Plant Costs and Depreciation," Paton presents and illustrates his three alternative approaches to dealing with the impact of changing prices: supplementary statements showing plant cost, depreciation charges, and stockholders' equity on a current basis; the "compromise procedure"; and the "fresh start." For the first time, Paton illustrates the income statement which would result from adoption of the "compromise procedure" (although on page 816 of the *Accountants' Handbook* (1943) Paton suggests how the statement might appear). His two subtotals would seem to be parallel to Edwards' and Bell's "current operating profit" and "realized profit";[124] Paton, however, would credit Edwards' and Bell's "realizable gains" directly to stockholders' equity. Paton's "compromise procedure" income statement would appear as follows:[125]

---

121. William A. Paton, with the assistance of William A. Paton, Jr., *Asset Accounting: An Intermediate Course* (New York: Macmillan Co., 1952). Internal evidence strongly suggests, and correspondence with William A. Paton, Jr. confirms, that Paton the elder was the de facto author of this book and of *Corporation Accounts and Statements* (see below). Accordingly, Paton, Sr. will be cited as the author of these works.

122. Paton, *Asset Accounting*, pp. 333–34.

123. *Ibid.*, p. 334.

124. Edgar O. Edwards and Philip W. Bell, *The Theory and Measurement of Business Income* (Berkeley, Calif.: University of California Press, 1961), esp. chaps. 4–6.

125. Paton, *Asset Accounting*, p. 343.

Sales and other revenues	$500,000
Expenses, taxes, and other charges (including depreciation on a current cost basis, $12,500)	465,000
Net earnings [Edwards' and Bell's "current operating profit"]	$ 35,000
Increase in plant cost absorbed in year's expenses	7,500
Net earnings on unadjusted basis [Edwards' and Bell's "realized profit"]	$ 42,500

In the course of discussing the "compromise" and "fresh-start" procedures, Paton offers the following criterion for their use: "Only where a major change [in prices] has occurred, that bids fair to be quite persistent, should restatement be undertaken, and this happens only during periods of serious inflation and deflation."[126]

Asset Accounting is rich in colorful expression and is a vintage example of vigorous Patonian argument.[127] In this chapter alone, we are advised, for example, that the "fresh-start" procedure is "simpler than the compromise approach, which involves riding two horses at once."[128] The efforts by several large corporations in the late 1940s to record replacement-cost depreciation are derided as "not very well thought out," "incomplete," "somewhat slipshod," and "half-hearted tinkering with the income statement alone, with no systematic, well-grounded adjustment across the board."[129] The reader is informed that "in the depression days of the early '30s, for example, one of the favored indoor sports in financial management was that of writing down plant." Paton was unflinching in his criticism of those who would applaud writedowns in the early 1930s "no matter how sloppy the procedure and questionable the amount," but who would oppose postwar write-ups which were "carefully substantiated and well worked out on the procedural side."[130] Paton's thinly veiled denunciation

126. *Ibid.*, pp. 349–50.
127. Doubtless one of the more graphic characterizations in accounting textbooks of managerial misunderstanding of accounting information occurs in Paton's discussion of the interpretation sometimes placed on fully amortized fixed assets: "Of course the owner of the amortized facilities can shut his eyes to their economic significance, if he doesn't know any better, but so can the owner of similar assets recently purchased, if he is determined to make an ass of himself." *Ibid.*, p. 309.
128. *Ibid.*, p. 346.
129. *Ibid.*, p. 351.
130. *Ibid.*, p. 354.

of the SEC's undeviating opposition to departures from conventional practice leaps from the page:

> Here is a conspicuous example of the fatuous worship of "decrease" and the indiscriminate condemnation of "increase" long characteristic of many people in financial and accounting circles. It's a ridiculous attitude, with no redeeming savor of professional integrity or competence, and deserves thoroughgoing repudiation by all who are interested in accounting as a means of providing useful and valid compilations and interpretations of the facts of business operation.[131]

Paton declined to recommend any of the three alternative approaches as possessing the greatest merit, although he was already on record in favor of the "fresh-start" procedure.[132]

In a separate chapter, Paton discusses the problems which must be solved in the valuation of plant. For going-concern purposes, he prefers replacement cost to a capitalization of future earnings, as the latter is seldom practicable.[133]

Finally, Paton continues to espouse the accounting recognition of "marked appreciation" in the price of shares, although the reader is encouraged to infer that the credit would be to a special stockholders' equity account, and not to income or to Retained Earnings.[134] This position is unchanged from that in *Advanced Accounting* (1941).

On the whole, *Asset Accounting* shows a clear preference for modifying conventional accounting for plant costs and depreciation charges. Paton was greatly disturbed by allegedly misleading inferences being drawn from conventional financial reports, and he had launched a vigorous campaign for reform.

CORPORATION ACCOUNTS AND STATEMENTS (1955)

As the Patons observe in the preface of *Corporation Accounts and Statements*, "It would not have been altogether inappropriate to have adopted the title 'Equity Accounting' " for the book, as it deals with "the array of problems having to do with the rights of common stockholders, senior investors, and other interested parties.[135]

131. *Ibid.*
132. In addition to his remark in *Accounting Problems Relating to the Reporting of Profits* (see above), he took this position in "Measuring Profits Under Inflation Conditions," p. 25.
133. Paton, *Asset Accounting*, p. 360.
134. *Ibid.*, p. 130.
135. Paton, *Corporation Accounts and Statements*, p. v.

Paton's discussion of the accounting recognition of asset value appreciation or declination based on a divergence between the book value and acquisition price of treasury shares is treated more elaborately and with greater enthusiasm than in *Advanced Accounting* (1941). Such acquisitions are divided into two types: those based on an "uneven-deal" assumption and those supported by an "even-deal" assumption. Acquisitions of the uneven-deal type represent bargains or are otherwise "onesided and unfair" and would not yield sound inferences about undervalued or overvalued assets.[136] Where, however, "the terms of the acquisition transaction are fair to both parties"—the "even-deal" assumption, which Paton regards as the much more reasonable interpretation—a revaluation of assets could be defended and would be followed, Paton suggests, by a "fresh-start" accounting for any subsequent depreciation charges.[137] Paton's argument for a revaluation based on the "even-deal" interpretation is energetically advanced:

> Where . . . a substantial fraction of the outstanding shares is acquired (say 5% or more), and the amount paid has been carefully determined in the light of prevailing conditions, and, moreover, there is a substantial difference between book value and the determined market value, it can be urged that a restatement of recorded values, in harmony with the settlement made for the acquired shares, would be fully justified.[138]

Paton continues to oppose the inclusion in income of unrealized appreciation, although his reasoning has changed from that in *Advanced Accounting*. In both books, he cites six "usual arguments" against this practice. As recited in *Corporation Accounts and Statements*, they are:

1. Appreciation of existing assets does not bring about any increase in liquid funds and hence cannot be made a basis for dividend disbursements or payments for any other purpose.

2. An increase in the market value of property intended for sale may be offset by a later decline and hence may never be realized; an increase in the value of property held for use in the business, even if persistent, will be realized only through the process of consumption in production or unexpected liquidation.

3. Appreciation is based on estimate and hence the amount of the enhancement is uncertain.

4. Reporting of appreciation in the income statement, even if the item

136. *Ibid.*, p. 191.
137. *Ibid.*, pp. 198, 202.
138. *Ibid.*, p. 204.

were clearly labeled and excluded from operating results, would not be conservative practice.

5. Appreciation is likely to be largely a reflection of a change in the general level of prices, and thus represents an adjustment of capital rather than true income.

6. Appreciation has no legal standing as income.[139]

In both books, Paton regards the first argument as "decisive" for fixed assets but possessing "less force" for current assets. Yet even in the case of current assets, Paton continues, the appreciation may not be in the form of disposable funds. Also in both books, the second point is said to have merit. "Obviously," he writes, "appreciation of asset value is not on a level with accounts receivable, resulting from delivery of product, as evidence of the presence of revenue. Aside from the possibility of failure to collect, usually of minor importance, revenue is conclusively and finally determined by sale of product, whereas realization of appreciation depends on future events." In both books, Paton views the third and fourth arguments as "less serious," since "no one has ever advocated booking appreciation except where the evidence is convincing [sic!]," and accountants have, in his opinion, placed undue reliance on conservatism.[140]

In regard to the fifth and sixth arguments, however, Paton takes different positions in the two books. In *Advanced Accounting*, Paton observes that the argument is "important" when the change in specific prices is matched by movements in the general level of prices, but this point "is offset somewhat by the fact that conventional earned income likewise may not represent an increase in effective purchasing power."[141] In the 1955 book, however, Paton says that the fifth argument "has special importance in view of the inflationary condition which has prevailed in recent years," but after repeating the countervailing point of 1941, he concludes that "it would not improve matters to adopt the policy of regarding nominal unrealized appreciation as a form of income."[142] By "matters," Paton could well be referring to the many misleading interpretations that he had been attributing to grossly overstated corporate profits. Thus, Paton's new stance on the fifth argument may be traced to changed economic conditions and especially to Paton's

139. *Ibid.*, p. 298.
140. *Ibid.*, pp. 298–99.
141. Paton, *Advanced Accounting*, p. 452.
142. Paton, *Corporation Accounts*, p. 299.

great concern over the consequences of overstated profits. His altered view of the sixth argument reflects a lesser preoccupation with legal arguments which tended to dominate his thinking in the 1930s and early 1940s. In *Advanced Accounting,* Paton writes, "The legal attitude is of decided consequence, if not controlling."[143] Fourteen years later, in *Corporation Accounts and Statements,* he says, "The legal attitude . . . is of consequence, although not necessarily controlling."[144]

Finally, Paton devotes an entire chapter to what he now calls "Uniform-Dollar Accounting." It is by far his most extensive treatment, in textbooks or articles, of general price-level accounting, and is twice the length of the comparable chapter in *Advanced Accounting.* He again exhibits his desire not to be confined to what the law requires. He writes:

> There is more involved [in accounting] than prevailing legal rules and concepts. More and more the accounting process is being relied upon as the major means of compiling and interpreting the economic data of business enterprise, for operating management, for current and prospective investors, for legislative bodies interested in basic problems of policy, and in other connections. And accounting cannot possibly fulfill its obligations in these directions by remaining blind to the limitations of raw accounting data in the face of a major and sustained decline in the purchasing power of the dollar. Moreover, there is no reason why accounting should not lead the way to changes in the legal structure as it relates to business enterprise in so far as new conditions provide a valid basis for such changes.[145]

Paton's chapter on "uniform-dollar reporting" is not a neutral, bland presentation. It is vigorous, undiluted advocacy, drawing on Paton's considerable skills as a debater. All of the color found in the best examples of Patonian rhetoric is present here in abundance. He marshals arguments of diverse kinds—from intrinsic deficiencies in accounting measurement to the necessity of replying effectively to "the enemies of private enterprise"—in order to fortify the conclusion that unconverted historical costs, in periods of significant inflation, yield misleading information.[146] Paton concedes that figures expressed in specific current costs would be more useful to internal management than historical costs which are expressed in converted dollars. But as a "year-by-year appraisal of all the assets of the

143. Paton, *Advanced Accounting,* p. 452.
144. Paton, *Corporation Accounts,* p. 299.
145. *Ibid.,* pp. 526–27.
146. *Ibid.,* p. 540.

enterprise [is] ordinarily impracticable," converted historical cost "can be strongly defended."[147] Since his first utterances on the impact of changing prices in *Principles of Accounting* (1916), Paton has preferred the specific cost solution. For tactical and pragmatic reasons, however, he has often proposed the conversion of historical cost into dollars of current purchasing power, but only in supplementary statements. But there was another argument for "uniform-dollar reporting": to place multi-earnings summaries and other inter-year financial presentations on a comparable basis. As corporations began to point to trends in earnings and other financial statistics, Paton believed that the "raw figures of the successive years are literally not comparable, and showing them in juxtaposition without explanation [or conversion] is almost sure to lead to misinterpretation."[148]

In *Corporation Accounts and Statements*, Paton abandons his support of Sweeney's view that the gains and losses on monetary items should be treated as realized only to the extent that the monetary assets are utilized or the monetary liabilities are settled. Paton now regards the gains and losses on *current* monetary items as being realized when the relevant index changes, but the gain or loss on long-term debt is still unrealized until it is paid. His logic is as follows:

> The recognition of a current liability has long been regarded as having substantially the same force as an expenditure, and the current receivables have long been regarded as providing an adequate foundation for the booking of revenue. And when it comes to cash on hand—purchasing power as such—it is hard to see justification for the contention that a change in value is not realized until there is an actual disbursement.[149]

One finds, therefore, that Paton incorporated in *Asset Accounting* and *Corporation Accounts and Statements* the essence and full force of the arguments he made during the late 1940s and early 1950s in speeches, congressional testimony, submissions to government panels, and articles. Both books are faithful to the view that positive action must be taken to accommodate accounting to an environment of changing prices. In a sense, Paton came full circle from his undiluted idealism of 1917–18, through a long period of doubt and reassessment of his position in the face of changing economic conditions, to a renewed call for accounting reform. To be sure, the

147. *Ibid.*, p. 537.
148. *Ibid.*, p. 554.
149. *Ibid.*, p. 550.

latter-day Paton was much influenced by his fundamental belief in the efficacy of the free enterprise system and in the role which he believed that accounting must play to counter the misguided critics of private enterprise. This is not to suggest that Paton's specific policy recommendations of the late 1940s and 1950s were identical to those of the 1910s. They were not. Following the 1910s, he never again embraced the general proposition that income should be credited with unrealized appreciation. Furthermore, the Paton of the 1940s and 1950s was more alive to the tactics of devising a *form* of revised accounting that might appeal to the authorities and the accounting establishment. An apt example would be his tailoring of the quasi-reorganization, a device originally intended to deal exclusively with overvalued assets, to the circumstance of undervalued assets. Doubtless his twelve years of service on the Committee on Accounting Procedure heightened his sensitivity to the tactics of accounting reform. The Paton of the 1940s and 1950s was a more clever and resourceful advocate than was the idealist of the 1910s.

Conclusion

One is able to discern four periods in the evolution of Paton's writings on the impact of changing prices on accounting. The first period, 1916–18, is typified by youthful idealism. Paton is confident of his position and confidently dismisses most criticisms. He sees an integral role in the financial statements for replacement costs, but by the end of this period he only dimly perceives the possibilities of general price-level disclosures.

The years from 1920 to near the end of the 1930s were ones of reassessment and reconsideration of the place of replacement costs in financial accounting. At the outset of the period, he began to retreat from his earlier advocacy of crediting appreciation to income. By the mid-1930s, he seemed to conclude that replacement costs are better reported in supplementary disclosures than in the body of the financial statements. Concerns over the unscientific appraisals during the 1920s, the economic stagnation of the early 1930s, and the growing importance of legal considerations in business operation seem to have been influential. During this period, however, the possible role of general price-level disclosures appeared to grow in importance, and the publication in 1936 of Sweeney's *Stabilized Accounting* was doubtless a significant event.

From the late 1930s to the end of World War II, Paton devised a number of accounting stratagems by which replacement costs might find their way into the financial statements without doing violence to accounting conventions. That this period coincided with the first six years of Paton's service on the Institute's Committee on Accounting Procedure may not have been altogether an accident. He proposed upward quasi-reorganizations, revaluations based on the discrepancy between the book value and reacquisition price of large blocks of treasury shares, and a "compromise procedure" for booking replacement costs without passing their effects through net income. During the same period, his advocacy of the supplemental disclosure of general price-level effects accelerated, and by the end of the war, the positions which he had espoused in his famous 1940 monograph with A.C. Littleton, *An Introduction to Corporate Accounting Standards*, evidently were undergoing a change.

Following the war, his arguments in favor of an accounting recognition of replacement costs or of supplementary general price-level disclosures, or of a combination of the two, veritably reached the fever pitch of a campaign, and in his articles, speeches, and even textbooks, he passionately called for accounting reform. The postwar attack on the excessive profits of large American corporations, coupled with the trend which he detected toward socialism, galvanized his energies to defend the free enterprise system and to urge accountants, Congress, the SEC, and government wage tribunals to recognize that conventional accounting practices did not accurately reflect profits during inflationary times.

Through all of his active career, Paton has been highly attuned to the economic circumstances in which corporations find themselves. Although historical analysis does not admit of rigorously defensible interpretations of the factors which might have motivated a writer at different points in his career, the evidence adduced in this paper strongly suggests that some kind of accounting reform to deal with the effects of changing prices was never far from Paton's mind even in the 1930s. Prior to the post-World War II period, his was a lonely crusade, and his writings show that he was sensitive both to the problems wrought by changing economic times as well as to criticisms by others of a replacement-cost solution (e.g., that the questionable appraisals of the 1920s might reappear). Without sacrificing his basic belief that historical cost accounting per se does not deal adequately with changing prices, he retreated in the 1930s until he had devised procedures that could give effect to his beliefs while overcoming the earlier criticisms. In this light therefore, Paton's succession of changed positions on the accounting response to changing prices reflects more his attempt to develop defensible procedures to achieve his fundamental objectives than a rethinking or recanting of his objectives and basic beliefs.

March 1978

Relationships among Income Measurements

Norton M. Bedford

Consider the proposition that the base, the roots, the hidden core, the unobserved essence from which we have derived accounting income measures rests not in economics but rather in psychology and the physiology of the brain, with the consequence that prevailing measures of income do not fit well with pre-established economic constitutive definitions of income.[1] In the classical sense that a measurement is an assignment of a number to a "thing" such as income, the inference is that accounting income measures suffer from the prevalence of an ambiguous and ill-defined constitutive notion of economic income. The failure of efforts to articulate an

---

1. The notion of a "constitutive concept" refers to the existence of a physical or psychological phenomenon having the capacity to be observed or felt by a recipient. It differs from an "operational concept," which refers to a measurement or a process. For example, an increase in the wealth of an individual if observable or sensed would represent a constitutive thing, whereas a process of assigning a number to that thing would reflect an operation; and the operational measure may or may not be a perfect surrogate for the constitutive element of wealth. Given the possibility that constitutive concepts and operational concepts may diverge as the sophistication of the measurement process develops, it seems preferable that we distinguish between the thing (constitutive concept) and the process by which it is measured or attained (operational concept) if we are to improve the quality of accounting information. The definition of income as the amount a person can spend and be as well off at the end of a period as at the beginning of the period is a constitutive definition. The definition of income as the measure by which revenues exceed expenses, both defined in terms of recording procedures, would be an operational definition. See also Norton M. Bedford, *Income Determination Theory: An Accounting Framework* (Reading, Mass.: Addison-Wesley, 1965).

unambiguous description of the substance of income leads to the conclusion that the content (meaning) of an income measure depends upon the measurement operations involved in bringing it forth.

From this arises the alternative proposition that the base, the roots, from which accounting income measures derive must rest neither in psychology nor in economics but in a set of measurement rules. And from this alternative base of observable rules springs forth the practical operational view that accounting income measures—the observables—first arise, and that recipients of the accounting measure then infer a constitutive characteristic to the measure.

Given the existence and somewhat arbitrary use of alternative accounting principles for developing accounting income measures, the alternative base seems quite realistic. It is axiomatic that different measures cannot all be true representations of the same income. Different constitutive concepts of income are implied by the different measures, and the constitutive meaning of any income measure can only be determined by knowing the measurement processes used in producing the measure. The rise of the alternative base implies that while a nebulous constitutive notion of income may have initiated attempts to assign numbers to the constitutive "thing" known as income, the haziness of the notion has resulted in a variety of measures each purporting to be the correct measure of income. Empirical support for the alternative base exists in examinations of some of the income measures, for they reveal that different constitutive notions of income underlie the different income measurements. From this, intuitive logic brings forth the belief that the nature of accounting income depends upon the way it is measured, because accounting income is merely the result of the operations used by accountants to develop the measure.

This is not to say that constitutive income plays no role in modern society. On the contrary it is the motivating force that causes much of the activity in a society, for the bulk of man's endeavor is directed to the acquiring of income. Not only must this desire for constitutive income be prevalent in society if it is to develop a civilization, but it must prevail at all levels of society if that society is to progress. Unless the masses of a society aspire to some type of constitutive income, the accumulated evidence of history is that the society falls far short of those in which the income motivation is strongly embedded. Striving by an elite at the top is not enough.

The problem with constitutive notions of income is that there are so blessed many of them that one can seldom say which notion is entertained by a particular person at any particular time. All of this tends to preclude the measurement of constitutive income, and from this ambiguity the operational concept of income has emerged.

Operational income operates within limits, however, for it loses creditability if it produces accounting income measures that exceed the range of the constitutive concepts gathered together under the umbrella of a broad, nebulous, economic-based constitutive concept of income. Currently the variation among income measures that can be developed by the use of alternative accounting principles suggests that a wide range of constitutive meanings attaches to accounting measures of income.

The difference between the two bases—the constitutive versus the operational—for accounting income measures is fundamental. According to the first, income is a constitutive "thing" of substance, possibly an increase in wealth—whatever that is—and it is the task of accounting to assign symbols (including numbers) to that "thing" so that information about it can be communicated between various parties. The alternative operational base, on the contrary, assumes that constitutive income is a subjective phenomenon, an individual feeling, that can never be measured as a general concept. It is situation specific. Accounting measures of income measure nothing of substance. Rather they represent bits of information which must be interpreted to have substance; and, while common interpretations of the substance may be made by one group of users, the income measure precedes the interpretation or determination of a substance or constitutive notion of income.

On the basis of the foregoing underlying philosophical notions, it is worthwhile to examine the five extant operational views of appropriate accounting income measurement models: historical cost, price-level adjusted historical cost, current replacement cost, current exit value, and present value of expected cash flows. Such a survey reveals some unusual relationships among the five. Before examining these operational accounting income measurement models, however, further insight and a stronger base for analysis will be provided by a critical review of the constitutive concepts of income: psychic, real, and money income, along with extensions of each. Based on the works of Fisher and Hicks, the following framework of income concepts will reveal distinctions among concepts of income.

Figure 1 suggests that the three basic income concepts are functionally related to each other but that each is ambiguous in itself. Thus, psychic income may refer to the satisfaction an individual obtains by consuming means to satisfy human wants, or to the

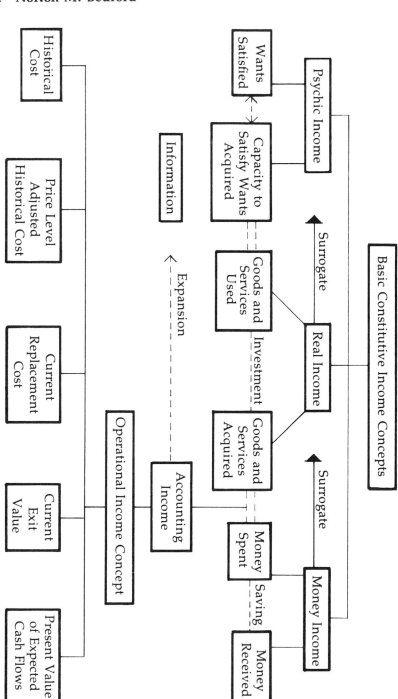

Fig. 1. Interrelationships among income concepts.

increase in an individual's capacity to satisfy wants. Since a substantial portion of such capacity to satisfy wants comes from goods and services used, a type of real income, a connection between real and psychic income is intuitively obvious. Real income, however, is also ambiguous, for among other distinctions it may refer to goods and services acquired or to those used. Presumably the difference between goods and services acquired and those used would represent "investments" or at least deferred consumption. Further, assuming that the lag due to credit extensions is constant, the amount of goods and services acquired will be related to money spent by an entity, a type of money income, and this ties real income to money income in some fashion. Because all money received without an obligation to repay in some way may be either saved or spent, the notion of money income is ambiguous to the extent that it varies between these two extremes.

From the foregoing basic income concepts, the notion of accounting income has been derived and used as an amount of measured income to motivate economic activity. As an accrual concept, without adjustment for price-level changes, it is closely associated with both increases in money income and with real income. To the extent that expenditures for capital goods are not treated as expense by accountants but depreciated over the life of the goods acquired, accounting income is associated with increases or decreases in real income. But to the extent that items such as research and development expenditures are treated as expense, or depreciation is expressed in terms of historical cost, accounting income is related to money income. Being neither "real" nor "money," accounting income serves as a general index of various constitutive notions of income, or as an information item that motivates economic activity.

The view that accounting income is merely a bit of information, or news of limited scope, has led to the proposition that the accounting concept of income should be replaced with the broader notion of "economic motivating information." The expansion of accounting income disclosures into accounting information disclosures that would motivate and direct the economic activity of a society has received little more than speculative attention in accounting theory, but the accounting income concept could well be expanded to include it in the future. Because accounting income is not a measure of any unambiguous constitutive notion of income, Figure 1 indicates that it represents operational income concepts and can be associated with at least five income measurement models.

Associated with the various notions and concepts of income are different criteria for classification, valuation, and recognition which have led to anomalies in economic constitutive concepts of income: situations where capital gains and losses have been excluded from the income concept at times and included at others, where holding gains have sometimes been distinguished from operating gains and sometimes combined, and where both price-level adjusted and unadjusted concepts of income have been advocated.

The problem with the constitutive economic distinctions is that they are based on a rather limited view of human psychological and physiological needs. This is a singular situation, for it is intuitively obvious, and empirically supported, that human wants and needs vary from person to person, from situation to situation, and from time to time; and they even conflict with each other in a single situation, at the same time, and for the same person. This being so, the economic income attributes of a thing or event must vary, just as individual human wants and needs vary. By inserting the collective wisdom of the market price into the income notion, it became possible to develop single-valued income measures; but just as any average seldom fits any particular need, so single-valued income measures represent a limited view of individual income.

Possibly awareness of this state of affairs contributed to Professor Kenneth Boulding's doubt as to whether or not economics should exist as a discipline. The confusion seems to have arisen because economists have dealt with concepts of constitutive income, an incoming of something of substance or constituting something real. Even in that sense, however, the economic analyses of income have never settled the question of whether income is the amount that can be consumed (spent) during a period without impairing capital (capital maintenance), or whether it is the amount that can be spent without impairing the ability to spend the same amount in future periods (spending power maintenance).

Given this variety of income concepts, it seems appropriate to clarify the relation between various aspects of the various constitutive income concepts that accountants have attempted to treat by using alternative accounting principles. The relation between the following income notions will be examined:

1. The nature of income—psychic versus real money income
2. The notion of periodic income—subjective versus realizable versus realized income
3. The elements of income—acquisition versus holding versus production versus distribution income

4. The recipients of income—entity versus equity holders' versus junior shareholders' income

5. The use of income measures—operating income versus variable income versus disposable income

Subsequently, to complete the topic under discussion, relations between the five operational income measurement models (historical cost, general price-level adjusted historical cost, current replacement cost, current exit values, and discounted cash flow) will be set forth.

The Nature of Income

The relation between psychic, real, and money income exists because they all flow from the basic concept of psychic income. Because psychic income is not easily measurable, the more objectively determinable notion of real physical income is substituted as a surrogate for psychic income. In this relationship, a measure of real income is held to be an index of psychic income. Because measures of real physical income do not provide for an income evaluation of the net effect of a decrease in one physical real income item and an increase in another, money income is used as a homogenizing attribute common to all real income items in such a fashion that gains and losses are additive.

In this function money income is a surrogate for real income. Since the accounting measures the falls between real and money income, operationally accounting income is a surrogate for a surrogate (real income) for the basic psychic income concept. While this relation between the three basic income concepts may be questioned, it seems obvious that unless income is assumed to be related to psychic income it can hardly claim to play a significant role as a meaningful motivational force in society. The surrogate relationship must hold, but it holds loosely and it varies. If the surrogate relationship were constant and a 10 percent increase in accounting income always meant an 8 percent increase in real income, and in turn a 5 percent increase in psychic income, constitutive interpretations of accounting income would be enhanced. But when the surrogate relation among the income concepts varies, given the tendency for functional fixation to develop among users of accounting income measures, lags occur in the functioning of the relations between the three constitutive income concepts. In the large and in the main, however, the surrogates do reflect the relation between the three constitutive concepts of income, and this relationship holds for group as well as individual income measures.

The Notion of Periodic Income

The relation between subjective, realizable, and realized income is a relation between periodic income concepts. Whether psychic, real, accounting, or money income is being measured, the question of the proper amount to allocate to a particular period depends upon whether subjective, realizable, or realized income is to be measured. In the ultimate sense, over the entire life of an entity, all three concepts should result in the same total income; but for any one period, significant variations in the income measure would be expected.

This relation between the periodic income concepts derives from the level of objectivity or degree of confidence that the measured income will ultimately be realized. Thus realized income is the ultimate test that income exists, leaving subjective and realizable income as predictions of the amount of realized income that will result from the activities of an entity in a given period. While the management of an entity may believe that the "value" of the entity has increased substantially in a given period (subjective income), this belief may not be the opinion of willing buyers and sellers in the market place who establish market price. Because market price, as a realizable price, reflects the opinion of several, it is considered more objective than the subjective opinion of one evaluator. If this difference between realizable value (market value) and subjective value is defined as subjective goodwill, the relation between subjective income and realizable income is that realizable income (I_m) is equal to subjective income (I_s) plus or minus the changes in subjective goodwill $(_cG_s)$ during the period of time:

$$I_m = I_s \pm {}_cG_s.$$

But market price constantly changes, and the use of it to measure the amount of income that has been created in a period of time and will ultimately be realized is always somewhat suspect as a measure of periodic income. While it may be contended that the realizable income concept allocates income more accurately to the period in which it is created than realized income does, it must also be recognized that income created by mere fluctuations in prices would be more volatile over time periods (as a review of changes in stock market prices reveals) than realized income would.

Some will contend that these very volatile changes in value should be reflected in income to reveal or suggest the risk associated with the activities and thus achieve a full and complete disclosure with a minimum allowance for the right to offset a gain against a loss. In answer one can only suggest that the frictions (commissions, purchasing and selling costs, freight, idle employees, and so on) that would result if all market value changes were realized by the entity through a sale would far exceed the income gain that could be realized if management were to confine its function to the trading of its assets in the market rather than creating new values by using the assets in the production and distribution process.

From this it follows that realized income will tend to be more stable and will serve to motivate economic activity toward the production and distribution of goods and services rather than toward the making of trading gains and losses. Realized income does suffer from a lesser ability to associate periodic income with the time period in which the income is created. Hence the relation between realizable income (I_m) and realized income (I_R) is that the latter includes income created and realizable in previous periods ($_pI_m$) and excludes realizable income created in the current period ($_cI_m$):

$$I_R = I_m - {_cI_m} + {_pI_m}.$$

Overall the relation between subjective income and realized income is

$$I_R = I_s \pm {_cG_s} - {_c(I_s \pm {_cG_s})} + p(I_s \pm {_cG_s}).$$

The Elements of Income

The relation between various kinds of income—acquisition, holding, production, and distribution (I_A, I_H, I_P, I_D)—is that of a partitioned set of periodic income (any combination of psychic, real, accounting, or money, and subjective, realizable, or realized). In this sense, the emphasis is on the conceptual independence of these income measures and the lack of a relation between them. They do have the common feature of being elements of total periodic income (I_T) and are thus additive

$$I_A + I_H + I_P + I_D = I_T.$$

The operational concept on which the partitioning of total periodic income is based is the notion of business functions. All income-producing activities of a business entity are attributed to the four operations of buying (acquisition gain or loss), holding resources (holding gain or loss), producing a good or service (production gain or loss), and distributing a good or service (distribution gain or loss). These income measures are based on the operations of a business entity and differ from income measures based on the accounting operations of assigning numbers to the business operations. These two notions of operational income must be distinguished, for only the accounting operations can provide unambiguous measures of income.

The Recipients of Income

The problem of whose income to report for a given period arises from the existence of multiple interests in an enterprise. To an economic entity, independent of its suppliers of labor and capital, income is the total increase in resources produced by the entity (I_E). Because creditors and employees claim part of the entity income, the residual equity holders' income (I_{SH}) is smaller than the total periodic entity income. Further, to the extent that senior shareholders (holders of preferred stock) have a prior claim on the equity holders' income, the junior shareholders' income (I_J) is still less a reflection of the economic contribution made by the economic entity in terms of value added. If all claims to entity income having priority over shareholders' income (I_C)—wages, income taxes, interest charges—are treated as distributions of income, and preferred dividend rights (I_{PR}) as nonincome items to junior shareholders, the relation among these income measures is:

$$I_E - I_C = I_{SH}$$

$$I_J = I_{SH} - I_{PR}$$

$$I_E - I_C - I_{PR} = I_J.$$

These foregoing categories of income recipients are, of course, a gross oversimplification because the priority of rights to entity income could be specified in some detail, if reason to do so existed, to permit disclosure of the income of multiple types of groups. Also excluded from the discussion is the transfer of rights of one type of income recipient to another type. For example, the "gain" arising from the retirement of bonds payable below carrying value would not represent an increase in entity income. Rather it would represent a gain accruing to shareholders because of the loss by the bondholders. It does seem fair to suggest that the classification of income recipients and the measurement of income according to income recipients have received far too little attention in accounting literature. Typically the problem is discarded with the suggestion that "different income measures are needed by different users."

The Usage of Income Measures

The relation between operating income, variable income, and disposable income is based on different constitutive concepts of income. Whether or not operating income should be categorized into "regular" and "extraordinary" items is not of concern. Rather, the distinction between operating and variable income relates to the costs or expenses to be deducted from revenue in measuring income, while disposable income relates both to the liquidity of the revenue items acquired and the cash flow requirements of the costs or expenses. Defining sunk, extraordinary, and nonrecurring items as E_I, and distinguishing between revenue and expense recognized on the accrual basis and revenue and expense recognized on a near cash basis, the relation between these income concepts is:

Operating income (I_o) less the sunk, extraordinary, and nonrecurring items (E_I) is equal to variable income (I_V) or $I_o - E_I = I_V$; and

If we then deduct from variable income the accrual and nondisposable elements in income (I_M), we have disposable income (I_D) and $I_V - I_M = I_D$.

From this the relation between operating income and disposable income is as follows: $I_o - E_I - I_M = I_D$.

Assuming that the foregoing relation between the five-segment framework of income concepts is valid, the complete structure of the income concepts will be provided if the relation between the five constitutive income concepts implied by the framework is set forth. In general, as Figure 2 shows, this relation lies in the fact that the nature of income (Framework I) is the overriding notion of income, so that periodic income (Framework II) refers to the portion of income, as predetermined in Framework I, that should be allocated to specific periods. Framework III deals with the components or elements of income as prescribed in Framework II, while Framework IV separates the periodic income prescribed in Framework II according to claimants to that income. It should be noted that a relation seldom exists between Framework III and Framework IV, though there are instances where the rights of income recipients or claimants are dependent upon the existence of specific kinds or elements of periodic income. Finally, the need to advise users of periodic income as to its availability for use requires consideration of Framework V.

Framework I represented by (a, b, c, d) is the set of income components (nature of income). Framework II represented by (e, f, c, g) is the subset of income components assigned to one period of time (periodic income). The four subsets (e, s, x, v), (v, x, u, g), (s, f, t, x),

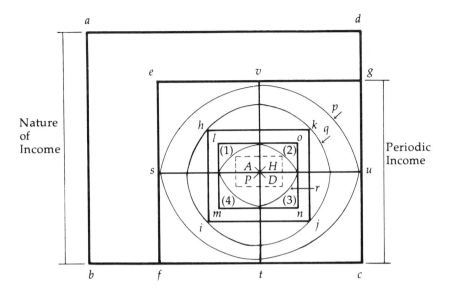

Fig. 2. Relation among frameworks of income characteristics.

and (x, t, c, u) are respectively acquisition, holding, production, and distribution income (the third framework of income elements). The fourth framework refers to the subsets enclosed in the circles q and r, which identify entity, equity, and junior shareholder income (income recipients). Framework V refers to the partitioning of periodic income (e, f, c, g) by items outside (h, i, j, k), items between (h, i, j, k) and (l, m, n, o), and items within the set $[(1), (2), (3), (4)]$. It indicates operating, variable, and disposable income measures for different uses (income usage).

Turning from the relation between constitutive concepts of income, and dealing with relations between measured income concepts in the area of practical affairs, the following relations are proposed between the historical cost, price-level adjusted historical cost, current replacement cost, current exit value, and present value of future cash flows income measurement models.

Common to all five of these operational income measures is the view that the periodic income of the shareholder group is the closest notion of constitutive income associated with all five of the income measurement models. But from this somewhat ambiguous base divergences exist.

The historical cost model is based on the matching concept and is oriented toward the accountability role of accounting. According to this model the income statement and the balance sheet articulate— the balance sheet being an instantaneous status picture between two income statements. The income statement aims to reflect the effectiveness and efficiency of the entity, whether managerially induced or due to the fortunes of change. As a measure of effectiveness and efficiency, the results of this model do not purport to depict the change in the economic wealth of an economic entity in any one period. Rather, the results reflect the ability of an entity to acquire resources and dispose of them in the same or a transformed form. Income reflects the periodic success of the entity, and over a longer period this success indicator would be reflected in an increase in wealth. Periodic income, according to this model, is a surrogate for the wealth-creating ability of the entity. Its relation to income measures produced by the other models is similar to that of a relativity index or surrogate for the long-range average increase in economic wealth. Conceptually, the historical cost model would reflect an assumption that there is no reality to notions of economic wealth and that the only reality is the relativity-based operational measure of input-output comparisons. But this assumption is seldom proposed in accounting literature, and the more pedestrian view prevails that the notion of increases in economic wealth is real and that measures of income based on historical cost are indicative of the extent of that increase. Some feel that variations in the purchasing power of money diminish the functional relation between historical cost income measures and increases in wealth, and they propose that the historical cost model be adjusted.

Theoretically the price-level adjusted income measurement model may be used in conjunction with all the other income measurement models. It is, however, typically associated with the historical cost model and represents an adaptation of it. Effectively, it adjusts historical cost data for changes in the general purchasing power of money, and thus removes from income as a measure of efficiency and effectiveness those historical cost "gains" or "losses" due solely to changes in the monetary measuring unit. Because the general purchasing power of money changes, particularly in times of inflation, the unadjusted monetary unit is not a stable measuring unit. By applying an index of changes in the purchasing power of money to historical cost data, the accounting measuring unit can be stabilized.

While it might seem that the relation between income based on historical cost and that based on historical cost adjusted to reflect purchasing power is merely the variation in the purchasing power of money, actually the relationship is much more complex. An additional element of income may arise, for gains and losses may occur if the entity has monetary debts or receivables that can be paid in cheaper money. Currently our monetary-based legal contracts are expressed in terms of the unadjusted monetary unit. Until this lag in legal custom is corrected, the gains and losses due to the monetary position held by a firm will go unrecognized unless price-level adjusted accounting is applied. Whether or not the accounting adjustment is made, the "real" gain or loss arising from the holding of a debit or credit net monetary position will continue to misdirect managerial efforts until the legal profession adjusts the wording of monetary-based contracts to a uniform monetary unit. The old basis of expressing monetary obligation in terms of gold is no longer available, and there is a social need for an alternative method of expressing such obligations. Until this is accomplished, accounting can help solve the problem by revealing the extent of the monetary gain or loss in the hope that disclosure will ultimately result in corrective action.

The price-level adjusted income measurement model is related to the historical cost model in the following manner: "gains or losses" due to changes in the purchasing power of money are separated into "fictional" and "real" component parts. The price-level adjusted income measurement model does not require a change in the revenue recognition point from that used for the historical cost model. Typically it too is based on the matching of revenues and expenses and serves to measure the efficiency and effectiveness of managerially controlled operations.

The current replacement cost income measurement model, which must be distinguished sharply from the price-level adjusted model, may be viewed as a moving forward of the revenue recognition point from the point of sale date to the balance sheet date, while the price-level adjusted model may or may not make the shift. The excess or deficiency of current cost over historical cost on unsold or unused assets is included as income (holding gain) along with other income items arising from the production and sale of goods and services. When current replacement cost refers not to the cost of replacing previously acquired economic resources, but rather to the current replacement cost of the service equivalent, the gain or loss involved may arise not only from a change in the revenue recognition point but also from a change in the values in the balance sheet. Income under this latter concept is the result of the difference in two balance sheets. Revenue is the increases in assets or decreases in liabilities, and expenses are the decreases in assets or increases in liabilities, both assets and liabilities being valued in terms of what it would cost to replace the services or obligations at a balance sheet date. It may be well to go over this distinction again, for it is not commonly discussed in the accounting literature.

In those situations where the only change from historical cost is that all assets are restated to current replacement cost, any difference between historical cost and current replacement cost would be merely a lag between the time a value increase had occurred and its recognition in the accounting records, because both would be revalued to the same amount at the date of sale.

As a consequence, the primary difference between historical cost income and current replacement cost income is the time the gain or loss is recognized, though increases or decreases in current replacement cost that are later offset by decreases or increases in current replacement cost before the point of sale would be reflected under the current replacement cost income model, but not under the historical cost income model. In the long run, total income under the historical cost model and the current replacement cost model would be the same. Both would include all "gains or losses" due to changes in the general price level as income.

When current replacement cost refers to the current replacement cost of service equivalent, and service equivalent is defined in terms of units of output, there is the possibility that technological change will introduce a significant decrease in the auxiliary costs of the productive capacity for each dollar cost investment. The resulting increase or decrease in current replacement cost may not result in a change in sales prices of outputs, and the operating efficiency of the management will not be reflected by matching revenues with the current replacement cost. That is, if income is defined as sales price (R) less depreciation (D) and less auxiliary costs of labor and overhead (A), an increase in D due to an increase in current replacement cost, caused by the opportunity to reduce auxiliary costs, could be offset by a decrease in A to such an extent that the sales price R would remain unchanged. But the decrease in A occurs only for physically replaced productive assets. For assets continued in use at replacement cost, the advantages of the lower auxiliary cost would not be available to the continuing management and a matching of the higher depreciation D against the unchanged selling price R would not reveal managerial efficiency. Only if replacement did in fact occur would income under the matching concept reflect managerial efficiency. The option is to abandon matching under the effort-accomplishment (input-output index) concept and adopt a noneffectiveness notion of income. In this way the comparative balance sheets approach for measuring income becomes appropriate.

The current exit value model reflects a somewhat more conservative concept of income. It tends to be associated with the constitutive concept of disposable income. Depending upon how it is measured (immediate liquidation, orderly liquidation in a systematic manner, and expected regular sales price), it indicates the cash that could be available for reinvestment (immediately, near term, or in the ordinary course of business) if the entity wished to reinvest. To the extent that the three alternative measurement methods yield the same measure of total assets-liabilities net, the entity possesses the capacity to adapt and change the type of economic activities in which it engages. In the instance of immediate cash liquidation, the measured income is the amount that the entity can spend and have the same amount available for investment as existed at the beginning of the period. The current exit model may well be appropriate for a society under a high degree of uncertainty and rapid change where the second-best alternative use value of a resource is significant as an indicator of the entity's ability to avoid the risk associated with the great uncertainty and rapid change. In a situation where it is not expected that resources will be sold for their second-best use, but will be used for the productive purpose for which they were acquired—the best use—realism would indicate that the current replacement cost income model would be indicative of the entity's success.

Thus the relevance of the current exit value income model to most notions of constitutive income is limited, not only because it is ambiguous but also because it is not in accord with the expected future. In a pure and perfectly competitive market, with no market frictions, the difference between the current exit value model and the current replacement cost model would be negligible. The relationship between the two is therefore founded on the extent of the frictions, risk, and imperfect competition of the market.

While the current exit value model assumes the sale of assets in their current form, the present value of the future cash flows income measurement model assumes the opposite: that the assets will be used according to management plans. The assumption is that a discount rate can adjust expected future cash flows for risk and for waiting and that the firm itself, knowing how its resources will be used, is in the best position to estimate future cash flows, whose present value is the most realistic value of the firm's resources and obligations. The resulting valuation of the entity at a point in time is rather subjective; and, while in a world of certainty the present value model would provide an ideal measure of income, the world is uncertain, and periodic income measures based on it might prove highly unstable over time as management expectations changed.

Given the foregoing basic relationships among income measurement models, opportunities arise to develop specific relations between them. Such is beyond the scope of this paper, but the following list of income measurement issues suggests the types of specific relationships in need of development.

1. What is the relation between income measured as the difference between the value of the assets and liabilities at the beginning and end of the accounting period and income as the difference between the matching of revenue and expense of the period?

2. What is the relation between articulated and unarticulated income statements and balance sheets (in the sense that all activities reflected in the income statement are also reflected in the balance sheet)?

3. What is the relation between assets defined as cash or cash equivalent and assets defined as means to future economic benefits?

4. What is the relation between liabilities defined as legally binding obligations and liabilities defined as obligations of all types?

This paper closes with the proposition that it is far more important for accountants to investigate the relation between income measures than to determine which income measure is "right," for there is no universal right. Disclosure of these relationships will enhance the understanding and usefulness of accounting income measures.

January 1977

Cost Accounting Principles for External Reporting
A Conceptual Framework

Gordon Shillinglaw

Unlike most of the other contributors to this volume I have never met William Paton. I haven't emerged untouched by the Paton presence, however. Most accounting texts when I started through were mainly descriptive, but when Frank Smith took a small group of us in hand at the University of Rochester in 1947 he gave us Paton's *Advanced Accounting* (Macmillan, 1947). Now that was a book of a different color! It challenged us, tested us, made us think. Even in print, Paton made us feel the force of his intellect.

My second exposure to Professor Paton came two years later, when I taught a section of the only accounting course offered to the undergraduates of Harvard College. The coordinator of the course was Edwin Frickey, a senior professor in the Harvard economics department. He had persuaded the Macmillan Company to keep enough copies of Paton's *Accounting,* originally published in 1923, in stock to service the Harvard course. No other text would do. And he was right. The writing was just as fresh in 1950 as it had been a generation earlier.

Paton's 1923 text was written long before we had official bodies to codify accounting standards. I'd like to think my contribution to this volume comes from the same tradition. Cost accounting, like financial accounting, has developed primarily because practical people have needed answers to questions arising in the course of their daily work. A body of concepts, principles, and practices has evolved over the years, gradually becoming what might be referred

157

to as generally accepted cost accounting principles. These principles are reflected in textbook descriptions and in the systems designed and used by practitioners, but they have never been codified by any authoritative body. The purpose of this paper is to outline a conceptual framework to serve as a foundation for such a code.

The Reasons for a Cost Accounting Code

A codification of generally accepted cost accounting principles certainly isn't indispensable for managerial accounting. Each management is free to perceive its needs in its own way and to adopt a set of measurement principles that seem to meet those needs. Textbook descriptions can provide the necessary conceptual foundation for systems of this sort.[1]

Pressures for codification, if any, arise from the needs of people outside the organization, those who must deal with information emerging from many different organizations at the same time. These users of information are investors, tax collectors, and purchasers of goods and services, through cost-based contracts, as well as regulatory bodies and even private individuals who interest themselves in the social aspects of business organizations. All of these groups have one element in common: they are interested in that part of cost accounting that determines how much cost is to be assigned to each of the goods and services the organization has produced or sold. This is the field of product costing, and it is here that the framework developed in the present paper is to apply.

Even in this field codification has had little appeal in the past. Authoritative financial accounting bodies have limited themselves to broad statements such as, "[T]he exclusion of all overheads from inventory costs does not constitute an accepted accounting procedure."[2] The Internal Revenue Service hasn't been much more specific, and even the Armed Services Procurement Regulations have provided only the broadest of guidelines to govern the use of cost accounting for contract-costing purposes.

The establishment of the Cost Accounting Standards Board in 1972 created a new situation. Although the pronouncements of the board

---

1. One of the better pronouncements on cost accounting was issued some twenty years ago by the Cost Committee, American Accounting Association, "Tentative Statement of Cost Concepts Underlying Reports for Management Purposes," *Accounting Review* (April 1956), pp. 182–93.

2. *Professional Accounting Standards*, vol. I (New York: Commerce Clearing House, Inc., 1977), sec. 5121.05.

have only a limited direct applicability, many observers are convinced they will have a far greater indirect influence. A conceptual framework therefore becomes essential, as a basis for evaluating whether the board's standards should be extended to other areas. It may also influence the board's own standard-setting process.

The Conceptual Framework

The conceptual framework outlined in this paper will emerge full-blown as an integrated set of relationships among six groups of elements: concepts, principles, constraints, criteria, standards, and methods:

1. A *concept* is an understood abstraction of a class of relationships, a trait, or a characteristic (e.g., *cost* is a concept describing a relation between a sacrifice of a resource and a result of that sacrifice).

2. A *principle* is a normative statement of how a concept or concepts should be applied.

3. A *constraint* is a boundary of the zone within which principles are allowed to govern.

4. A *criterion* is a test to be applied to alternative principles or alternative methods to help an interested party choose among these alternatives. Criteria are designed to reflect the objectives of the people applying them, or of the organizations these people represent, or of the purposes to be served. (E.g., in choosing between a full cost principle and a partial cost principle, the cost accountant should consider the purpose for which the measurement is intended.)

5. A *standard* is a prescription specifying the principles to be followed and the ways in which they are to be applied.

6. A *method* is a set of instructions and procedures by which the organization's personnel will assemble cost data to meet the needs of users of these data. Methods should be consistent with principles appropriate to these needs and with the standards embodying these principles.

The relationships among these elements can be summarized in a simple diagram:

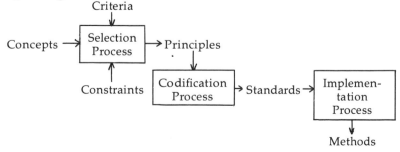

This paper will examine the relationships among concepts, constraints, criteria, and principles, with only passing reference to the codification process. Generous use will be made of materials published by the Cost Accounting Standards Board, but no attempt will be made to evaluate the standards issued so far by the board.

Basic Concepts

Concepts are essentially definitions of useful terms. As such, they form no structure in themselves; only when reflected in criteria and principles do they have an impact on the system. The following twelve concepts are the most important and must be described:

1. Cost objective
2. Cost
3. Causality
4. Traceability
5. Variability
6. Service generation
7. Capacity occupancy
8. Interchangeability
9. Interdependence
10. Homogeneity
11. Attributability
12. Jointness of cost

A number of other concepts, such as accuracy, verifiability, and materiality are more generally familiar and will be introduced only in connection with the discussion of the principles in which they are embodied.

Cost Objective

A cost objective in an organization is a result of the use of resources in that organization. Some results are productive—that is, useful products or services emerge from the use of resources. Other results are unproductive, meaning that the resources have been wasted. Costing systems for some purposes may recognize both productive and nonproductive results; systems for other purposes may recognize only productive results.

The terminology is slightly unfortunate here. Only productive results can be truly regarded as *objectives* of the use of resources.

Waste is never an objective. (Lighting a cigar with a $100 bill is wasteful, but the objective is to demonstrate affluence, not to create waste.) The term is widely used, however, and creating a new term would only compound the confusion.

Cost objectives are of two kinds: final cost objectives and intermediate cost objectives. A *final cost objective* is a specific end result or output of the application of resources in a given period, contributing to no other final cost objective during that period. An *intermediate cost objective* is any result of the use of resources in a given period that contributes to or supports two or more other cost objectives in that period.[3]

An intermediate cost objective may be the activity of an individual responsibility unit, or even a cost center within a responsibility unit. It may also be a group of similar activities carried out by many different responsibility units. Because intermediate cost objective is an awkward term, the terms cost center and cost pool may be used instead. A *cost center* is defined for this purpose as a unit in the organization structure serving as an intermediate cost objective; a *cost pool* can be any kind of intermediate cost objective, but generally the term designates one that is not also a cost center.

The structure of intermediate cost objectives may be very simple or very complex. In the simplest situation each intermediate cost objective serves or supports only final cost objectives. In complex situations long chains of intermediate cost objectives may be necessary to link the use of resources to the final cost objectives.

Cost

It was necessary to define cost objective before defining the more basic term, cost, because cost is always the cost of something. The structure of cost objectives must be built before costing can take place. Given that, cost can be defined as the amount of physical resources used to achieve a cost objective.

Since statements of physical resource consumption are difficult to use, physical quantities are usually multiplied by unit prices. Cost, therefore, can be defined further as a monetary measure of the sacrifice accompanying the use of resources to achieve a specified cost objective. (Notice that this definition can encompass historical

3. These definitions and a few others were developed jointly with Robert N. Anthony in connection with a joint submission to the staff of the Cost Accounting Standards Board. Some words have been changed; in any case Professor Anthony bears no responsibility for the ways these terms are used or interpreted in this paper.

cost, opportunity cost, or even estimated future cost, depending on the purpose of the system and the constraints within which it must operate.)

Causality

Causality is one of the most important concepts underlying cost accounting, and may be the least understood. According to one dictionary, causality is "the relationship between cause and effect."[4] In the present context, causality is a relation between a cost and a cost objective whose nature is such that the cost must be or must have been incurred if the cost objective is to be achieved. If such a relation exists, it can be said that the cost objective "causes" the cost.

Traceability

Traceability is an attribute of a cost that permits the resources represented by the cost to be identified in their entirety with a specified cost objective on the basis of verifiable transactions records.

Variability

Variability is the responsiveness of total cost in a period to variations in total operating volume during that period.

Service Generation

Service generation is not an attribute of a cost or even of cost behavior. Instead, it identifies a relation between the activities of a specific cost center or group of cost centers (the "supplying cost centers") and two or more other cost objectives. It signifies the existence of a quantifiable measure of the amount of work done by the supplying cost center to serve each of the cost objectives receiving the service.

Service for this purpose may be either tangible (physical goods) or intangible (personal advice or assistance). Consumption of services can be measured either by the quantity of resources used by the supplying cost center to provide the services (input basis) or by the number of units of service provided (output basis).

4. William Morris (ed.), *The American Heritage Dictionary of the English Language* (New York: American Heritage Publishing Company, 1969), p. 214.

Capacity Occupancy

Capacity is an attribute of a group of assets or an organizational entity, measured by the demand for service the asset group or entity is capable of meeting in a given period. Capacity occupancy is a measure of the demand for capacity imposed by the achievement of a particular cost objective.

The costs of resources that are consumed to give an organization the capacity to carry out its activities are referred to as capacity costs. A capacity cost is incurred, in other words, to provide the support necessary to achieve the cost objectives carried out within the limits of that capacity.

Interchangeability

Interchangeability is an attribute of any two or more resources that can be substituted for each other without affecting the costs of the other resources that are required to carry out the activities to which the interchangeable resources are devoted. Quantities of electric power obtained from two different generating plants and deliverable to the same consumption point are examples of interchangeable resources.

Interdependence

Interdependence is a relation between cost objectives which occurs when the use of resources to achieve one cost objective will affect the amount of resources required to achieve other cost objectives of the same level. For example, a manufacturer opening new production facilities may transfer experienced workers from existing operations to provide a nucleus for an efficient work force at the new location. The existence of interdependence is demonstrated by the consequent increase in the average cost of the final cost objectives achieved at the old location.

Homogeneity

Homogeneity is an attribute of any group of costs which are all governed by the same set of determinants and in an identical manner.

Attributability

Attributability is the responsiveness of cost to decisions to provide and use the capacity to support individual cost objectives. The attributable cost of a final cost objective is the sum of the variable costs of meeting that objective, plus any other costs that would not have been incurred if the organization had not provided the needed capacity for achieving that cost objective, all other things being equal.

Jointness of Cost

Some resources are used to achieve two or more cost objectives simultaneously. The costs of such resources are referred to as joint costs. The various cost objectives achieved immediately with the aid of these joint costs are known as joint products. Allocation of joint costs among the joint products is the most difficult conceptual problem in cost accounting.

System Constraints

Every system is constrained by requirements implicit in the context in which it operates. Cost measurement for external financial reporting appears to be subject to at least seven constraints:

1. Objectivity
2. Accuracy
3. Consistency
4. Verifiability
5. Measurability
6. Materiality
7. Articulation

Objectivity

Objectivity is an inescapable requirement of professional work of any kind. The objectivity constraint is simple: the costs assigned to any cost objective should not be influenced by biases arising from the personal or pecuniary interests of those measuring or relying on the costs to be assigned to that cost objective.

The meaning of this principle was set forth succinctly some years ago:

> One way of achieving objectivity is to eliminate the use of judgment entirely; quantities measurable without the exercise of the measurer's personal judgment are always objective. This solution may be incompatible with other [principles], however, and in such cases the choice of a

cost standard will have to be a compromise, accepting some application of judgment to achieve a greater degree of something else.[5]

Accuracy

Accuracy is an attribute of the costs assigned to a cost objective. The accuracy of a cost total is measured by its degree of fidelity to the cost concept that the cost total is intended to reflect. The users of cost information have the right to assume that the information provided them is accurate, subject to the levels imposed by the measurability and materiality constraints.

Consistency

It is unlikely that cost accounting standards will ever be so specific that only one measurement method will be possible in any given situation. This means that the amount of cost assigned to a cost objective will be affected to some extent by the methods chosen to implement the measurement principles. Accordingly, the user of cost information has a right to expect that costing methods will not be changed without good reason and due notification.

This notion is embodied in the consistency constraint, which others have phrased in the following terms:

> Cost measurement should be consistent from one period to another and even within an accounting period, unless there are significant reasons for changes. Changes in measurement methods should be made (a) to increase their accuracy materially . . . , (b) to attain an adequate degree of accuracy at a lower record-keeping cost, or (c) to comply with changes in standards.[6]

Verifiability

Accounting figures for different purposes are subject to differing verification requirements. A good definition of verifiability emerged from a committee of the American Accounting Association: "Verifiability is that attribute of information which allows qualified individuals working independently of one another to

---

5. Subcommittee on Basic Cost Concepts, National Association of Accountants, "Tentative Concepts for Cost-Type Contracts," *Management Accounting* (May 1971).

6. Management Accounting Practices Committee, National Association of Accountants, *Concepts for Contract Costing: Statement on Management Accounting Practices No. 1* (New York: National Association of Accountants, 1971), p. 5.

develop essentially similar measures or conclusions from an examination of the same evidence, data or records."[7]

Verification is always important in external financial reporting because of the interests of outsiders in the results. In cost measurement, the question to be verified is whether the appropriate measurement principles have been followed. The verifiability constraint is that the amount of cost assigned to each cost objective should be verifiable by independent professional observers through examination of the assumptions, records, and procedures which led to the assignment of costs to that cost objective.

Measurability

Some relations between resources and cost objectives are easy to identify; others are very difficult. Measurability is an attribute of a relation between a cost and a cost objective which enables the accountant to measure that relationship at a reasonable cost. Cost measurement is not an end in itself, and the purposes of assembling cost data may be achieved in other ways than by expending the costs and effort required to implement the measurement principles without modification. The fifth constraint, therefore, is the measurability constraint: any measurement principle may be modified if the modification will reduce the cost of implementation sufficiently to justify the resulting decrease in the accuracy of cost measurement.

Acceptance of the measurability constraint is only the first step, of course, and probably the easiest one. It requires that the appropriate standard-setting bodies undertake to develop practical tests of measurability. This task is far from easy, but it is better to establish measurability as a requirement than to leave it to individual ad hoc decisions at the point of measurement.

Materiality

No conceptual framework in accounting would be complete without some reference to the concept of materiality. This constraint differs from the others in that it does not refer to the measure of cost itself or to a relation between cost and a cost objective, but rather to errors embodied in the measure of cost. Materiality refers to any error large enough that a user of cost information would be

7. American Accounting Association, *A Statement of Basic Accounting Theory* (Sarasota, Fla.: American Accounting Association, 1966), p. 7.

led to a different decision from the one which accurate information would lead to.

The materiality constraint is simply stated: departures from the measurement principles will be accepted as long as they do not lead to material changes in the amounts of cost assigned to individual cost objectives.

Articulation

The final constraint is a requirement that the financial statements articulate—that is, for any given measurement basis, such as historical cost, the total amount assignable to cost objectives in any given period is fixed. If a change in a cost assignment principle increases the amount of cost assigned to one cost objective, it must decrease the amount of cost assigned to one or more other cost objectives.

Articulation is not an essential feature of the structure outlined in this paper. The articulation requirement is so ingrained in professional accounting practice, however, that it must be taken as given. According to generally accepted financial accounting principles, for example, finished goods inventories and the cost of goods sold must not be measured in such a way that the total amount assigned to these two quantities exceeds the total historical cost of the goods available for sale during the period. Any product costing system today must operate within this constraint.

Criteria for System Choices

The central element in any conceptual framework is the criterion (or set of criteria) to be applied to system choices. Four possible criteria need to be examined:

1. Relevance
2. Causality
3. Benefit
4. Equity (fairness)

Relevance

It was considered a great coup some years ago when a committee of the American Accounting Association adopted the relevance criterion as a key element in its structure of accounting theory.[8]

8. American Accounting Association, *A Statement of Basic Accounting Theory.*

Relevance in this context means the capacity to improve the decisions made by users of the system.

While this is a valid attribute of any system, it is not a very useful criterion. Usefulness to the user depends on what the user wants the cost figures to mean. User surveys haven't addressed this issue, and it is doubtful whether they would throw much light on it in any case. The answer must come from an analysis of the implied meaning of cost information, a process that requires examination of other criteria.

Causality

The choice of an operational criterion to be used in selecting costing principles for any purpose depends on the quantity which the cost figure purports to measure. The main clue therefore rests in the definitions of cost and cost objective, the two key concepts embodied in any measure of cost. These definitions, it will be recalled, require measures of the relations between resource consumption and the results of resource consumption. Another way to express the same relations is to say that the costs assigned to any cost objective (the result) should be the costs that have led to the achievement of this cost objective.

This is an expression of a *causal* relation, in that cost objectives are achieved only as a result of a purposive application of resources. The primary costing criterion arising from this definition of cost therefore is the causality criterion: costs should be assigned to cost objectives on the basis of the underlying causal relations between the costs and the cost objectives.

Since this criterion emerges from an analysis of the definition of cost, it would seem to be incontrovertible, not to say tautological. It is challenged, however, as we shall see in a moment, and support from other sources will be helpful. The principal support derives from the interests which outsiders have in the cost figures. The interests of those associated with contract costing are the easiest to deal with. Cost is to be used to determine the amount of the direct benefit to the organization from achieving the final cost objectives associated with specific contracts. Since the size of the benefit is directly related to the size of the cost, the cost can be regarded as the cause of the beneficial result.

Fiscal authorities are required to take the same view. Income taxation is based on the notion of a surplus of resource inflows over resource outflows. The relevant outflows (costs) are those that were necessary to generate the inflows (revenues). Again a causal relation is presumed; if costs have been incurred to achieve future revenues, they are to be deferred to the tax returns of future periods.

Finally, investors are also likely to be concerned with causal relations, although the case for this position is not as clearly demonstrable as it is in taxation and contract costing. The rewards to investors arise mainly from spreads between resource inflows and the resource outflows necessary to achieve them. The wider the spread, the greater the incentive to invest, other things being equal.

The causal relation may also be looked at from the other side. The achievement of the final cost objective may be viewed as the cause and the use of resources as the result. Either way, the relation between cost and cost objective is inescapably a relation between cause and effect. The causality criterion is the only one reflecting this relationship.

Benefit

Causality is not universally accepted as the only criterion in selecting product costing principles. Another term that is widely used is benefit. Most cost accounting textbooks, for example, apply it in phrases such as, "Costs should be allocated to the cost centers benefiting from them." The Cost Accounting Standards Board uses the phrases, "benefiting cost objective" and "beneficial or causal relationship" repeatedly in its public pronouncements.[9] A benefit criterion would require that costs be assigned to cost objectives in proportion to the benefits derived from the costs.

Vatter dismissed this criterion in a single sentence a generation ago in a paper still worth studying: " 'Benefit,' unless measured in terms of the use or provision of facilities, is too vague a term to result in objective division of joint cost among departments or other costing units."[10]

The truth of this statement is apparent from the meaning of the term, benefit. One definition is: "Anything that promotes or enhances well-being; advantage."[11] The same dictionary defines the

---

9. Cost Accounting Standards Board, *Statement of Operating Policies and Procedures*, March, 1977, pp. 16-18. This statement is now being revised, but preliminary drafts of the revised version retain this same language.

10. William J. Vatter, "Limitations of Overhead Allocation," *Accounting Review* (April 1945), pp. 163–176, at p. 171. Vatter used the term joint cost to refer to all nontraceable costs, including the unit prices of interchangeable resources.

11. *American Heritage Dictionary*, p. 123.

related term, beneficial, in the following way: "Promoting a favorable result; enhancing well-being; advantageous." Unfortunately, cost objectives are inanimate and therefore don't have well-being. Furthermore, the "advantage" or "favorable result" that a cost objective receives from the use of resources is the present value of the future cash flows that result from achieving the cost objective. These cash flows are the joint result of all the resources used. Adopting a benefit criterion therefore would require costs to be assigned in proportion to present value, and all cost objectives would have equal cost-benefit ratios. This is a clearly nonsensical result.

How, then, is the extensive use of the term, benefit, in cost accounting to be explained? Part of the explanation is that it is simply a synonym for a causal relation that is relatively imprecise. A cost center "benefits" from the cost of providing it with floor space because that space, and therefore the cost, is indispensable if the center is to achieve its objectives. The amount of the benefit is neither measured nor even considered. Since the presence of a dependency relationship is the basis for a presumption of benefit received, inserting the term benefit adds nothing to the causality criterion.

Equity

The final criterion to be considered is equity or fairness. This has been suggested by Anthony[12] as a companion to causality and by Bedingfield[13] as an overriding criterion. Bedingfield reaches his conclusion by examining the rulings of the Armed Services Board of Contract Appeals in cases involving the interpretation of benefit. He concludes, following the decisions in a number of cases, that benefit is too nebulous a term for practical application. Since the judges on the board have fallen back on the equity criterion to resolve issues presented as questions of relative benefit, Bedingfield concludes that equity is the more basic criterion.

Equity unfortunately suffers from as much vagueness as the benefit criterion. Equity is defined as "the state, ideal, or quality of

12. Robert N. Anthony, "What Should 'Cost' Mean?" *Harvard Business Review* (May-June 1970), pp. 121–131, at p. 127.

13. James P. Bedingfield, "Equity: The Implicit Basis of Accounting," *Federal Accountant* (Sept. 1972), pp. 101–9; also Howard W. Wright and James P. Bedingfield, "Benefit as a Criterion for Indirect Cost Allocation," *Federal Accountant* (Sept. 1973), pp. 67–76.

being just, impartial, and fair."[14] The problem is that equity is a highly subjective concept. What appears just and fair to one party may seem grossly unjust and unfair to another. Courts of law exist to resolve differences of this sort, and the rulings of these courts provide practical definitions of what is just and fair in specific cases. This is exactly what the judges of the Armed Services Board of Contract Appeals were called upon to do in the cases cited by Bedingfield.

It is uneconomical, however, to resort to judicial proceedings every time a costing principle is established or a cost is assigned. Costing principles are designed to help answer recurring questions. These questions deal with economic relationships, relationships between inputs and outputs. Subjecting these to tests of equity makes no more sense than using equity tests to choose between two explanations of the origin of the solar system.

Anthony's argument is different. He reasons that the application of logical, cause-and-effect tests to cost data will leave a residual of unallocated costs, because no clear causal relation can be found. The point is well taken. No costing principle based on the causality criterion is up to the task of dividing the president's salary among the final cost objectives of the period. If this cost is to be divided, some noncausal formula must be used.

The ideal solution to this dilemma is to define it away. No method of allocating the president's salary will make the cost total assigned to a cost objective more meaningful or more useful than any other method. This being so, it is better to regard such allocations as outside the realm of cost accounting than to try to develop criteria for bringing them in.

These allocations may be desirable as part of the pricing process, or for public justification of actions that management has decided on (or outsiders wish to impose), but they don't reflect economic relationships. Cost accounting is intended to measure relationships between inputs and outputs, and its meaning becomes confused if it includes costs for which not even the haziest relationship can be identified. The next section will examine how far this conclusion can be pushed.

Measurement Principles

Once causality has been accepted as the primary criterion for product costing, the remaining question is how causality is to be

14. *American Heritage Dictionary,* p. 443.

reflected in the body of cost accounting principles. A principle was defined earlier as a normative statement of how a concept or concepts should be applied. The following basic principles should guide the accountant in deriving the costs of individual final cost objectives for use in external financial measurement and reporting:

1. Attributability
2. Traceability
3. Interchangeability
4. Interdependence
5. Variability
6. Capacity provided
7. Homogeneity
8. Reasonableness
9. Imputability

The Attributability Principle

The greatest single advance in cost accounting theory in this century was the recognition that cost data for management need not always be based on estimates of the full cost of individual goods and services. The phrase "different costs for different purposes" could be emblazoned on the cover of almost any cost accounting text now in print.

Some authorities have tried to take this development one step farther, suggesting that costs for external reporting might be based on concepts such as variable cost or "relevant" cost. Much ink has flowed in an effort to resolve the issues these authorities have raised, mainly the issue of whether costs for external financial reporting should be based on causality in the short run (costs caused by the use of capacity) or on causality in the long run (costs caused by the provision and use of capacity). This is not the place to add to this flow. It is very clear that the use of variable costs to measure the costs of final cost objectives will not be accepted for external financial reporting in the foreseeable future. Enough important issues remain to be discussed without dwelling on this one, which appears to be moot.

The assumption here, therefore, is that the first costing principle is the attributability principle: the costs of individual final cost objectives should reflect the full costs resulting from the provision and use of capacity to achieve those cost objectives. This calls for the use of the concept of attributability because the causality criterion will take us no farther.

Attributability is not a widely accepted principle, nor even one that is widely understood.[15] Most authorities would substitute "full cost" for "attributable cost" in the preceding paragraph. Interestingly enough, they probably would change nothing else except for stylistic reasons. The explanation of this apparent contradiction is that full cost is generally presumed to answer the attributability question: "What costs would not have been incurred if the organization had not provided and used the capacity to achieve this specific cost objective, other things being equal?"

Even so, some authorities have been willing to move toward attributability without admitting to a departure from full cost. Full cost for costing inventories of manufactured products, for example, is supposed to include a share of all manufacturing costs necessary to place the goods in a form and condition suitable for sale. Although general and administrative costs presumably support both manufacturing and nonmanufacturing activities, they are still to be excluded entirely from inventory costs "except for the portion of such expenses that may be *clearly related* to production."[16] In other words, the fact that no clear relation exists between characteristics of individual manufacturing cost objectives is reason enough to exclude these costs from measures purporting to represent full cost.

This means that if full cost figures are deemed appropriate for specific purposes, the costing principle must be based on some criterion or criteria other than causality. The final principle in this set, imputability, will deal with just that situation.

The Traceability Principle

The second costing principle is traceability: costs traceable to a cost objective should be included in the costs of that objective.

The argument for this principle is that, in most cases, traceability is prima facie evidence that a causal relation exists between the cost objective and the cost. If the cost objective had not been created, the costs traceable to that objective would not have been incurred. Because this is such an important principle, three examples will be useful:

15. For more on the concept of attributable cost, see Gordon Shillinglaw, "The Concept of Attributable Cost," *Journal of Accounting Research* (Spring 1963), pp. 73–85.
16. *Professional Accounting Standards*, sec. 5121.05 (italics added).

Example 1: Materials costs of $2,000 are traceable to a batch of manufactured products. These costs can clearly be said to have been caused by the manufacture of that batch of products.

Example 2: Property taxes of $80,000 levied on a factory building are traceable to that factory's activities, taken as a whole; the taxes can be avoided by disposing of the building. Ownership of the building is the immediate cause of the company's obligation to pay this tax; the factory's activities are the immediate cause of the company's ownership of the building; the tax is therefore caused by the factory's activities.

Example 3: A company issues an electric typewriter to the secretary of one of its product managers. Depreciation on that typewriter, amounting to $200 a year, is traceable to the manager's product line. In the absence of this product line the company would have needed one less typewriter; the product line therefore caused the company to incur the depreciation cost.

Two comments should be made on the traceability principle. First, a cost can be said to be traceable to a cost objective even if it represents only a part of a single resource. Depreciation on the typewriter was traceable to the product line even though the amount of the resource used each year was estimated rather than measured.

This application of the traceability principle is likely to be the most controversial. The question is where the line is to be drawn. If a piece of equipment is used for one day on a particular project, can it be said that one day's depreciation is traceable to that project? The answer must be yes, as long as depreciation is assumed to be proportional to elapsed time. If depreciation is identified with an annual time period on the basis of that year's proportionate share of the asset's total lifetime, there is no way of denying its traceability to segments of this annual period. The only difference is that the interval on which the calculation of depreciation is based is much shorter than a year. This argument extends even to the assignment of depreciation charges to cost objectives on the basis of those objectives' percentages of the total hourly use of the depreciating assets.

A second point on traceability is that causality is present whether an activity uses resources already in the organization's possession or resources purchased in the spot market for carrying out a specific activity. The materials in example 1 may have been bought and paid for in previous periods; the typewriter may have been used in another department before being transferred to the product manager's office.

Management's earlier decision to acquire the resources caused the resources to be present and usable. This decision was based on the assumption that a specific use or uses would be found later on, and on the recognition that spot purchases of resources after a specific use had been identified would be either unfeasible or uneconomical. The cause, in other words, lies in the anticipated activity and can be identified with the activity that actually materializes. To deny this relation is to deny causative status to any resource acquired prior to the initiation of the activity being costed.

The Interdependence Principle

Traceability sometimes has a real shortcoming as a costing principle. When two cost objectives are interdependent, the costs traceable to each may not be a good measure of the underlying causal relations. In the example cited to explain this concept earlier, a manufacturer opening new production facilities transferred experienced workers from existing operations to provide the nucleus of an efficient work force at the new location. The costs traceable to the activities at the new location did not include the added costs of maintaining the production volume formerly achieved at the old location.

The solution to this problem depends on the level of verification required. In making decisions, management cannot ignore the indirect effects of operations at the new location; the revenues must cover the indirect costs as well as those technically traceable to the new activity. For external financial reporting, however, a high level of verification will be necessary. If convincing statistical evidence can be presented to document the effect on the costs at the old location, the traceability principle should not be allowed to block the transfer of costs from the cost objectives at the old location to those in the new facilities. The interdependence principle should be followed: when two cost objectives are interdependent, the costs traceable to one but attributable to the other should be transferred to the latter if they can be appropriately verified. If adequate verification can't be found, however, the traceability criterion will have to govern.

The Interchangeability Criterion

Although traceability is prima facie evidence of causality, it is not conclusive. Interdependence is one cause of exceptions; another is the presence of interchangeability. A problem will arise if different interchangeable resources have different costs.

For example, building space is often at least partially interchangeable. One space may have been leased recently at an annual rental approximating current market rates; another space may be in a building the company has owned for several decades. If the two spaces are interchangeable, then the causality criterion would suggest measuring *each* at the *same* cost.

A strict interpretation of historical causality would require each space to be measured at the cost of the one most recently acquired. After all, the relevant question is, what costs would not have been incurred if the company hadn't provided the capacity to achieve the cost objective? The implication is that the newly leased space was acquired because management anticipated the need to meet not only the cost objectives made possible by using the older space but additional cost objectives as well. Since each of a group of cost objectives being achieved simultaneously can be regarded as the "additional" cost objective, each can be assigned the cost of the space it takes to achieve additional cost objectives. (The amount of capacity required in any given period is a function of the total production load, regardless of the sequence in which orders were received.)

Although this argument is virtually irrefutable, it fails to satisfy the articulation constraint, since this approach will either overdistribute or underdistribute the costs clearly attributable to the need to provide space for achieving all of the cost objectives combined. As a result, neither the Financial Accounting Standards Board nor the Cost Accounting Standards Board, nor the Securities and Exchange Commission, nor the Internal Revenue Service, nor any other authoritative body is likely to give this approach more than a disdainful glance.

That being the case, the interchangeability principle has to be stated in a modified form: if similar interchangeable resources are available for achieving a cost objective, and if they have different unit prices, the unit price used in calculating the cost to be assigned to individual cost objectives should be the average unit price of the entire group of interchangeable resources. (Notice once again that nothing in this statement precludes the use of average replacement price or average anticipated resource price, if the appropriate authoritative body agrees to depart from historical cost.)[17]

17. Stating the principle in this way rules out the use of methods such as LIFO and FIFO, unless the differences are immaterial. Otherwise the sequence in which cost objectives are achieved will influence their cost.

The implementation of this principle will depend on how clear the interchangeability is and how much verification is required. In a relatively easy case, two different workers who have identical skills and identical job classifications but different seniority probably should have identical charging rates. Little disagreement about seniority is likely to arise, and the recorded job ratings would probably be acceptable as verification of the interchangeability.

At the other extreme, the interchangeability of 100,000 square feet of space in a downtown office building with the same amount of space in a manufacturing plant in the country is not obvious on the surface. If the purpose of costing is to help management decide whether to discontinue an activity in one of these locations, a judgmental estimate with little verification is likely to be acceptable. If the purpose is to measure cost for contract costing, however, judgmental estimates of this sort are likely to be rejected for lack of adequate verification.

The Variability Principle

Not all of the resources consumed in achieving a particular cost objective are traceable to it, even in a superficial way. The consumption of some of these nontraceable resources in individual periods is likely to be roughly proportional to some characteristic of individual cost objectives in these periods. For example, the amount of labor used in moving materials from stockrooms to production locations is likely to be closely related to the amounts of material required by production.

In cases of this sort, a causal relation can be assumed between the cost objective and the cost. The third costing principle therefore is the variability principle: when costs not traceable to a cost objective vary in total with variations in some characteristic of that cost objective, they should be assigned to the cost objective on the basis of the estimated rate of variability.

The only conceptual problem likely to be encountered in applying this criterion arises whenever variability is demonstrably nonlinear. The clearest example of this is the variability of overtime premiums. Budgeted overtime premiums may be virtually zero through much of the customary volume range but rise steadily after volume exceeds a certain threshold level. A strict application of the variability principle would require the use of a zero variability rate for overtime premiums when operations are below the threshold level; at higher volumes the rate should be the rate of increase represented by the slope of the solid line in the diagram below.

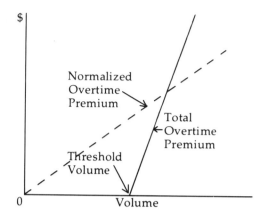

This solution creates the same problem that arose from the application of the interchangeability criterion. Use of the rate of increase will overdistribute overtime premiums because it represents a marginal cost rather than an average cost. As long as the financial statements must articulate—that is, a measurement change that affects a balance sheet figure must have a compensating income statement effect—overdistribution will be an unacceptable feature of a cost accounting system for external financial reporting.

The only acceptable alternative in such cases is to use an average rate of variability spanning the range of volume from zero to the outer limit of the range encountered—the cash line on the diagram. The argument to support this approach is that during an extended period overtime premiums will vary in this proportion rather than in the nonlinear fashion included in the short-term budget.

Notice that the rate of variability is to be expressed as a rate per unit of some characteristic of the cost objective to which the costs are to be assigned. This characteristic can be either an input measure (the total number of input units used to achieve the cost objective) or an output measure, indicating the amount of production arising from the achievement of the cost objective.

Notice also that this rule applies whether the cost objective is a final or an intermediate cost objective. If a production center receives service from a service center, for example, the "characteristic of the cost objective" can be a measure of either the amount of service provided or the amount of production achieved by the production center during the period. Input, in turn, can be measured by the number of units of service received from the service center or by the amounts of resources used by the service center to provide these services.

The Cost Accounting Standards Board, in Standard 403, recognized all three of these possibilities in establishing a hierarchy of bases for allocating the costs of home office service functions to individual segments of the organization.[18] These bases were prescribed for all costs, not just the variable costs, and the terminology was different, but all three were there, nevertheless, and are worth describing.

The board's first choice is to use "a measure of the activity of the organization performing the function." By this it means the number of labor hours or the amount of materials used by the service center to provide services to individual segments. This is like using a system of job order costing to account for the costs of the service center.[19]

The second basis in the board's hierarchy is "a measure of the output of the supporting function," meaning the number of units of service performed. Each unit of service is presumed to be like every other, and no effort is made to find out whether it has cost more to provide one than to provide any other. Here the analogy is to a process costing system of assigning the costs of the service center to the segments receiving the services.

The third basis in the board's hierarchy is a "surrogate" of some sort; generally these are "measures of the activity of the segments receiving the service." An example would be the number of labor hours in the segments themselves. If segment labor hours are used as a surrogate, the presumption is that variations in labor hours are highly correlated with the needs of the segment (cost objective) for services.

The Capacity-provided Principle

Many of the costs necessary to achieve a cost objective, but not traceable to it, are capacity costs. The causal relation between the cost objective and such costs is more indirect than in the case of the variable costs. The key phrase, however, is that they are necessary to the achievement of the cost objective. If they were not incurred, the cost objective could not be achieved. The various

---

18. Cost Accounting Standards Board, *Standards, Rules and Regulations* (Washington, D.C.: U.S. Government Printing Office, looseleaf service), pt. 403, para. 403.50(a), p. 132.

19. I am indebted to Nelson Shapiro of the board's staff for pointing out this analogy.

cost objectives supported by the costs of providing capacity are therefore the causes of those costs. The only question is what proportion of total capacity cost can be attributed to each of the supported cost objectives.

The answer to this question is embodied in the capacity-provided principle: the costs of providing capacity should be assigned to the cost objectives relying on that capacity in proportion to their relative occupancy of the capacity when it is used fully. In other words, if a cost objective uses capacity only at off-peak periods, it would not be charged a portion of capacity costs because it plays no role in causing the organization to incur any of its capacity costs.

This principle may not be strictly applied in practice, for any or all of three reasons. First, peak capacity occupancy may be too difficult to measure. The measurability constraint requires the use of average capacity occupancy in such cases.

Second, the principle of interchangeability may intervene, as it does in the case of some apparently traceable costs. If the cost objectives that are achieved at peak periods are interchangeable with those met at other periods, then causality has to be assigned equally to them all.

Third, the capacity-provided criterion may not be applied strictly because those doing the measuring believe it would lead to dividing costs "unfairly" among the various cost objectives. Instead, capacity costs are spread on the basis of the *average* use of capacity, rather than usage in the peak period.

This is not a legitimate reason for modifying the costing principle in such a way. The argument has already been made that fairness is either an ethical or a legal concept, and is not applicable to questions of economic consequences when adequate measures of causality are available. Equity may even be a political concept and thus even farther from the arena of objective economic measurement. When electrical power rates in the Northeast first began to rise sharply, people whose houses and apartments were heated by electricity demonstrated so loudly and persistently that the appointed regulatory officials assigned lower power rates to these users. The result, of course, was that other users had to pay a larger share of the costs of providing power capacity than their own capacity requirements justified. Because the users in this latter group were more numerous, the effects of the cost redistribution were spread over a much wider base and the cause-and-effect relation was not readily apparent. The political reaction of these users was therefore directed not at those who benefited from subsidized heating costs but at the average rates charged by the power-generating companies and at the regulatory commissions which approved those rates.

The main defect of the capacity-provided principle is its presumption that the long-run cost function is linear. If expansion or contraction of capacity will lead to a change in total capacity cost that is either greater or less than the proportionate change in capacity, then the average cost of a unit of capacity will be an inaccurate measure of the causal relation between capacity costs and the cost objective.

One sees here another example of the problems in applying the interchangeability and variability principles. Articulated accounting systems can't deal with nonlinear relationships. As long as articulation is a requirement, cost figures that are imperfect reflections of the causality criterion must be accepted.

The Homogeneity Principle

Cost objectives in any organization can be arranged logically in tiers, according to their distance from the final cost objectives and their degree of dependency on each other. The task of cost accounting may be to measure the cost attributable to cost objectives at any level. For external financial reporting, however, it is the costs of final cost objectives that matter.

Many costs are not traceable to final cost objectives, of course, but are needed to achieve those objectives. To assign these costs to final cost objectives, the accountant must use costing rates based on the variability and capacity-provided principles. Each costing rate applies to a particular group or pool of costs, and each pool consists of the costs of achieving an intermediate cost objective.

In structuring these pools, the cost accountant should follow the homogeneity principle: costs that are not traceable to individual cost objectives at a given level but are necessary to achieve those cost objectives should be grouped in pools, each of which is homogeneous. If the costs in a pool are homogeneous, a single variability rate and a single capacity rate will be appropriate. The application of the homogeneity principle usually means that costs will be assigned in stages, with many costs passing through two or more intermediate cost objectives before reaching the final cost objective.

The Reasonableness Principle

One final implication of the causality criterion is that the accountant can search for causes not only in what an organization accomplishes but also in what it doesn't accomplish. One set of causes of costs consists of events that lead to waste. Waste can be regarded as a form of cost objective. (Remember that the term cost objective was defined in terms of the *results* of the use of resources, and waste is a result in many cases.) From this conclusion one may arrive at a reasonableness principle: the costs of wasted resources should be excluded from the costs of productive final cost objectives.

Application of this principle requires judgment. It also requires a probabilistic approach to costing; a provision for "normal" waste because of factors inherent in a process should be included in the costs of productive final cost objectives because these costs are "reasonably necessary" to achieve those objectives. Abnormal and subnormal wastage on any particular final cost objective should be excluded from the calculation of the cost of that cost objective.

The Imputability Principle

Joint production is the only situation in which the causality criterion fails to provide a clear conceptual guide to cost assignment. Joint production is undertaken to obtain all of the joint products as a group; causality applies to the group as a whole, not to any one joint product.

The obvious solution is to recognize only one cost objective—the entire group of joint products. This will not be enough, however, if the joint products are inventoried in substantially different proportions or if different joint products are elements of different final cost objectives, at least one of which is a cost-based pricing contract.

The solution in the first of these two situations is to apply the imputability principle: the cost of each joint cost objective should be measured by the imputed opportunity cost of achieving this objective independently by other means, usually by open market purchases.

This principle has three weaknesses. First, it can't be applied in contract costing because the values of joint products used to meet final cost objectives embodied in cost-based pricing contracts are unknown. Second, it fails the articulation test in that its application will either underdistribute or overdistribute the total joint cost. Third, data on opportunity costs may be unavailable because no outside markets exist.

The second and third of these weaknesses can be overcome quite simply, either by reducing all of the opportunity cost figures proportionally to bring the total down to the total of the joint costs, or by using some variant of the net realization method. Both of these solutions finally bring the benefit criterion into the system, benefit being measured by the value of the joint products. As such, they are expedients and the resulting cost figures will lack economic meaning.

The first weakness of the imputability criterion is even more intractable. If cost is a determinant of value, value can't be used as a determinant of cost. Here at last may be a place to apply the equity criterion—that is, the principle should be that joint cost will be assigned in contract costing by a method negotiated by the parties in advance and therefore accepted by both as "just, impartial, and fair."

The Cost Accounting Standards Board or other authoritative body could shortcut this process by establishing a standard to govern situations of this sort. Any such standard would be arbitrary, substituting the board's definition of equity for the specific definitions that would emerge from bargaining between the contracting parties. This may not be too high a price to pay, however, to avoid lengthy, contentious bargaining on an issue with no "true" answer.

The exceptions to this final principle should serve to demonstrate that cost allocations of this kind, although probably an unavoidable part of the costing structure in some situations, have no firm roots in the theoretical foundations of cost accounting. They must of necessity rest on concepts drawn from other disciplines or, preferably, be left to the affected parties to resolve for themselves. Only when this is impractical, as in taxation or financial reporting to investors, should a standard solution be developed.

May 1977

Social Performance Accounting
An Unheeded Challenge to the Accounting Profession

R. Lee Brummet

Never has there been such a demand for individual and organizational accountability. Never has there been such a felt need by such large numbers of people for so much information. Never has there been such emphasis on integrity of information and credibility of sources. Never has the accounting profession enjoyed such visibility and notoriety, and never have the services of the accounting profession been in such demand by a society so willing to pay for them.

The challenge and the potential for the accounting profession are unmistakably greater than at any previous time in the history of the profession. Yet the response is uncertain, sometimes confused, usually defensive, and in my opinion far short of the mark to assure a bright future for the profession.

My purposes in this paper are twofold. The first is to consider the challenge to the accounting profession provided by demands for information on social performance and the profession's reluctance to be responsive to that challenge. The second is to encourage members of the profession to think more broadly of their role in the present environment—an environment which reflects a montage of social and economic cross-currents. More specifically, my purpose is to encourage members of the accounting profession to welcome the challenge by becoming active if not aggressive participants in developing and improving a technology for the measurement, communication, and attestation of social performance of organizations.

4. The substitution for financial accounting of both financial and human resources and social accounting[3]

This perception of a changing role for the business enterprise in our society has not been limited to those outside the real world of business. In 1973, C. Peter McColough, president of Xerox Corporation, was quoted in *News Front* as saying, "We do not see Xerox as solely a profit-making institution. I don't want to minimize profits . . . but I must emphasize that we regard Xerox as a social institution as well as a business institution."[4] This is indeed not at all an unusual statement.

Many private sector enterprises are responding, and in some instances they are taking leadership roles. While financial performance remains critical, many companies are planning, executing, and assessing their operations within a broader framework of responsibility to society. Some are well down the road to an emphasis on contribution to human welfare rather than simply profit maximization.

As our business leaders increasingly recognize this changed role of private sector enterprises and consider social performance as a clear objective, the need for information surely becomes obvious. Accountants could assist in articulating objectives, analyzing cost-benefit relationships, and providing information on performance to help monitor progress toward social objectives. Yet the accounting profession has not responded to any significant extent.

A Minimal Response from the Accounting Profession

While I believe that I am justified in charging the accounting profession with a lack of responsiveness, it would be unfair not to recognize some commendable responses of certain individuals and groups within the profession. In 1972, when Walter Oliphant was its president and Leonard Savoie was its executive vice-president, the American Institute of Certified Public Accountants (AICPA) sponsored a conference which brought together businessmen, political scientists, economists, sociologists, government officials, and accountants to discuss the broad areas of social measurement. In his opening remarks at this conference, Oliphant referred to the institute's description of the professional practice of accounting as "a discipline which provides financial and other information essential

3. Carl H. Madden, "Changing Roles of Government and Industry," *Evaluating Government Performance: Changes and Challenges for GAO* (Washington, D.C.: General Accounting Office, 1975), p. 136.

4. *News Front*, Jan.-Feb., 1973.

to the efficient conduct and evaluation of the activities of any organization."[5] Also at this meeting, Arthur Toan pointed out that

> the accountant's interest in social performance measurement evolves
> quite logically from the knowledge and experience he has accumulated
> over centuries of producing relevant financial information in an organi-
> zational setting for a variety of uses and users. . . . As soon as it became
> apparent that financial data would be understandable and more useful
> when coupled with non-financial information, the accountant was asked
> to obtain that information also and to integrate it into financial re-
> ports. . . . The trend toward blending both kinds of data continues; in
> fact, it continues at an accelerated pace.[6]

Within a few months after this conference President Oliphant asked
Arthur Toan to serve as chairman of a task force on measurement of
corporate social performance for the AICPA. Other accountants who
participated in the conference agreed to serve on this task force. After
some three years of study and deliberation, this group authored a
book, *The Measurement of Corporate Social Performance*, which has
now been published by the Institute. This work, while admittedly
only a preliminary coverage, represents a demonstrable indication of
the profession's interest in the area. In addition, a subcommittee of
the Management Advisory Services division of the AICPA is active
in the study of accounting professional services to be provided in
connection with ecology and the physical environment.

In 1973, Robert Beyer, then the incoming president of the National Association of Accountants, published his paper, "Pilots of
Social Progress," stating that "because of our [accountants'] unique
relationship with business and the public, we must become the
pilots of social progress, charting the course for business and government."[7] He then named a Committee on Corporate Social Performance Measurement for the NAA with I. Wayne Keller as its
chairman. During the following years this committee published an
outline for study and research in the area and sponsored and super-
vised several research projects whose results were reported in NAA
publications.

During the past five or six years the American Accounting Association has had several committees working on nonfinancial measures, environmental pollution, and social cost measures; and most

---

5. Walter Oliphant in *Social Measurement* (New York: American Institute of Certified Public Accountants, 1972), p. 2.

6. Arthur Toan in *Social Measurement*, p. 41.

7. Robert Beyer, "Pilots of Social Progress," *Management Accounting*, LIV (July,
1972), 11.

recently this association sponsored a project and published a report prepared by Professor Robert Jensen with the intriguing title of "Phantasmagoric Accounting."

Several accounting academicians have published materials on social measurement and accounting. Three of these noteworthy authors include Ralph Estes and Lee Seidler of Wichita State University and New York University, respectively, and Trevor Gambling of the University of Birmingham in England.

One of the more highly regarded publications with relevance to social accounting is the report of the Committee on Objectives of Financial Statements, chaired by the late Robert Trueblood. This committee included the following statement in its list of twelve items:

> An objective of financial statements is to report on those activities of the enterprise affecting society which can be determined and described or measured and which are important to the role of the enterprise in its social environment.[8]

Thus there are numerous indications of individuals and groups of individuals who favor the profession's participation in activities that measure social performance. Yet real involvement of the profession continues to be limited mainly to cost-benefit or cost-effectiveness analysis for public sector organizations and for some nonprofit entities, such as hospitals and educational institutions; and these services are provided by only a very small portion of the accounting profession.[9]

Even though the accounting profession is not greatly involved, many organizations are doing some social accounting. The most usual approach is to inventory those activities of the corporation that are socially motivated. This is at least a reasonable start, utilizing a process not totally unfamiliar to accountants.

Each year more corporations reflect their sensitivity to public interests by increasing the disclosure of their social performance in

8. Robert M. Trueblood in *Objectives of Financial Statements, Report of the Study Group on the Objectives of Financial Statements* (New York: American Institute of Certified Public Accountants, 1973), p. 66.

9. The General Accounting Office (GAO), which serves the Congress of the United States, has undoubtedly done more than any other group toward developing technology for measuring social performance, since such performance is usually the goal of government programs sponsored by our congressional bodies. At the conference on social measurement in 1972, referred to earlier in this article, Stuart McElyea of the GAO said, "It seems to me somewhat unrealistic to be discussing here whether social programs are to be measured. I think [such] measurement is inevitable."

annual reports. Dennis Beresford reports that 425 of the Fortune 500 companies made social responsibility disclosures in their 1975 annual reports, whereas only 239 did so in 1971.[10]

An Unjustified Reluctance of the Profession

A most compelling question in the minds of many accountants, as they consider their role in social measurement, relates to their belief in the free enterprise system and their uncertainty about the role of the private sector in our society. Should corporations in a "free society" accept conscious and substantive responsibility for social welfare, or should they rely on the "invisible hand" and strive within the limits of the law to maximize profits? If the answer to this question is the latter, then the reluctance of the profession is to some extent understandable. If the answer is the former, then the profession may well be derelict in its hesitancy.

Monolithic Accounting and the Objective of Business

Neatness of structure and orderliness have been ingrained in the business establishment and in accountants. This has caused a common bias among business managers and accountants in favor of the great simplicity represented by the single objective of profitability. The accountant feels a kinship with the business manager who strives to bring about satisfying profits, and the business manager feels a like kinship with the accountant who is expert in applying the measuring rod of success or failure in terms of this single dimension. Each contributes to the other's myopia concerning long-range perpetuation of the organization in a changing society by resisting a change to a more complicated system of multiple objectives and multiple areas for performance measurement.

Breaking out of these intersupportive attitudes is a difficult challenge—particularly when such views represent a school of thought led by Milton Friedman, the noted economist and recipient of a Nobel prize in 1976, who wrote in the *New York Times* in 1970, "There is only one social responsibility of business—to use resources and engage in activities designed to increase its profits."[11] Other similar statements of Professor Friedman could be noted. Yet

10. Dennis Beresford, *Social Responsibility Disclosures—1976 Survey of Fortune 500 Annual Reports* (Cleveland, Ohio: Ernst & Ernst, 1976), p. 4.
11. Milton Friedman, "The Social Responsibility of Business Is to Increase Profits," *New York Times Magazine*, Sept. 13, 1970.

Time magazine reported in 1975 that seven other Nobel prizewinners, including Gunnar Myrdal and Kenneth J. Arrow, signed a declaration condemning Western capitalism for bringing on a crisis by producing "primarily for corporate profits."[12] So we see the paradox of conflicting views on this most important issue of the role of business.

Yet I believe the direction of change in the value structures within society, the broadening of the public's expectations of how enterprises perform, and the increasing demands reflected in governmental legislation are clear, and that although the trend may vary in intensity from time to time, we may expect it to be unrelenting. Far from sounding the death knell of free enterprise—a possibility that some have bemoaned—the response of business enterprises to the many and varied pressures from the many different public interests is itself critical to the survival of that free enterprise system. Alfred C. Neal, president of the Committee on Economic Development, writes:

> The larger companies of necessity must be more concerned about their integration with the best of society, especially with those groups in society that constitute their most important constituencies. The view that business firms should concentrate only on their own profitability—behaving like mindless atoms reacting to the economic environment but unresponsive to the social environment—is, I hope, relegated to the archives, and to a few warlock economists who conjure up a world that never was. A few hundred large companies which account for the bulk of the nation's output largely determine the level of the economy and greatly influence the quality of our lives. Such companies cannot divorce themselves from their environment—be it physical, social, economic, or international.[13]

All of this does not mean that the profit objective is passé. It does mean that other objectives are also critical to an enterprise's success and survival. It does mean that a visible hand can and should supplement the invisible one. To the accountant it should mean that corporations need assistance in fulfilling a complex of objectives rather than only financial accounting assistance in monitoring profit performance.

Stewardship and Accountability

Stewardship and accountability relationships between people and organizations are among the most critical aspects of our society.

---

12. "Can Capitalism Survive?" *Time*, July 14, 1975, p. 50.

13. Alfred C. Neal, foreword to J. J. Corson and G. A. Steiner, *Measuring Business's Social Performance: The Corporate Social Audit* (New York: Committee for Economic Development, 1974).

There is strong support for the contention that the fundamental role of accounting is to facilitate this accountability function. Yuji Ijiri states, "Accounting . . . starts with the recording and reporting of activities and their consequences and ends with the discharging of accountability. . . . We may . . . say that accountability is what distinguishes accounting from other information systems in an organization or in a society."[14] This view is reflected significantly in early writings of William A. Paton and particularly in the 1940 Paton and Littleton monograph, which emphasizes the "need for developing standards of accounting to secure proper protection for the equities of corporate investors."[15]

Our economic, social, and political setting has changed significantly during the past forty years. There has clearly been a shift of emphasis to "performance" accountability in addition to asset stewardship, and this emphasis has extended to a number of objectives, including employee and community welfare, quality of products and services, and other social performance goals as well as profits for equity holders. Further, the Paton and Littleton monograph reflected primary concern for the relation between managers and owners. This continues today to be an important relationship, but we now must also consider relations between the organization and many other interested and involved constituencies in our society. Rosita Chen concludes succinctly from her study of the stewardship function of accounting that "management's performance should be evaluated in terms of both profit and the accomplishment of social objectives. The latter aspect has long been neglected by the accounting profession. It is the responsibility of the accountant, therefore, to measure, report, and audit management's social performance."[16]

With regard to possible dereliction, the profession may sometimes be naive about the impact of what it does or does not do. While recognizing that the accounting profession has made a great contribution to social and economic welfare, Norton Bedford states:

> Accounting is closely related to [some] social problems and opportunities and to an extent may be partly responsible for them. That is, performing a quantitative information function, accountants have measured and disclosed the private costs of consumer-selected choices and have ignored or

14. Yuji Ijiri, *Theory of Accounting Measurement*, Studies in Accounting Research #10 (Sarasota, Fla.: American Accounting Association, 1975), p. 32.

15. William A. Paton and A. C. Littleton, *An Introduction to Corporate Accounting Standards* (Chicago: American Accounting Association, 1940), p. 2.

16. Rosita Chen, "Social and Financial Stewardship," *Accounting Review*, L (July, 1975), 542.

discounted certain overall elements of social costs and benefits. As a result, accountants must bear some responsibility both for opportunities not realized and for any loss of dignity of human life that is due to overall misdirected economic activity or to the over-crowding, pollution, transportation failures, crime, and inadequate housing and education that may have resulted. It is becoming increasingly apparent that with changes in society, the conventional accounting disclosures cover a smaller proportion of those activities that affect the quality of human life. . . . An appropriate adjustment in the scope of accounting disclosures may now be the need of the land.[17]

Accountants are probably well advised to take part in economic, political, and social movements only as good and intelligent citizens and not as accounting professionals. Yet their work plays an important role in success or failure in these areas. We, as accountants, must view—with all the objectivity and intelligent perception we can muster—the changes taking place in our economic and social environment, and we must respond in the way that will contribute the most.

A Matter of Definition

Some of the reluctance of the profession to expand into new areas of social measurement and disclosure may relate to our self-imposed definition of accounting. We have repeatedly defined and explained our profession and its aims. For example:

> Accounting is the art of recording, classifying, and summarizing in a significant manner and in terms of money, transactions and events which are, at least in part, of a financial character, and interpreting the results thereof. (Terminology bulletins of the 1930s.)

> The purpose of accounting is to furnish financial data concerning a business enterprise, compiled and presented to meet the needs of management, investors, and the public. (Paton and Littleton, 1940.)

> Accounting is the process of identifying, measuring, and communicating economic information to permit informed judgments and decisions by users of the information. (*A Statement of Basic Accounting Theory*, American Accounting Association, 1966.)

> Accounting is a service activity. Its function is to provide quantitative information, primarily financial in nature, about economic entities that is intended to be useful in the making of reasoned choices among alternative courses of action. (Accounting Principles Board Opinion No. 4, 1970.)

17. Norton Bedford, *Extensions in Accounting Disclosure* (Englewood Cliffs, N.J.: Prentice-Hall, Inc., 1973), pp. 74, 75.

It is noteworthy that all these efforts to articulate the fundamental nature of accounting use such constraining words as economic, financial, and quantifiable; they reflect, it seems to me, a tendency to be conditioned by the boundaries of current practice.

Now definitions are of some importance. In this instance they enable accountants to perceive their role and to concentrate on developing a technical expertise within an identifiable body of knowledge. They provide some feelings of security. Further, they may help the users of accountants' services to know what to expect and thus to avail themselves of the profession's well-known stock in trade. Yet definitions of the societal role of the profession should not be only a reflection of the basic techniques—techniques that may for some period be fundamental to the services performed, but may outlive much of their usefulness. If what we do conditions our definition and our definition conditions what we do, our ability to adjust—to be imaginative and creative—is seriously limited.

Accounting should be defined in terms of its role in society. If the needs of society change, calling for new techniques to enable accounting to continue to fulfill its role, then the profession and its activities can and should change within the framework of the definition. I suggest that for the good of the accounting profession and for the good of us all, we adopt the following definition:

> Accounting is a systematic symbolic process which enables individuals, organizations, and society to articulate objectives, to provide projections and feedback information that assists in monitoring efforts to accomplish such objectives, and to provide reliable information regarding performance and condition accountability to legitimate constituencies.

This definition captures a most critical and eminent domain for the profession. It does not include constraints implied by adjectives such as economic, financial, or quantifiable, which may encourage or at least allow the use of tenacious caveats by accountants—caveats that may cause the profession to ignore the changing needs of society and relegate itself to performing only the more menial kinds of bookkeeping and reporting of less and less important data. It challenges members and prospective members of the profession to be creative in developing concepts and techniques which best serve this proclaimed role. The accounting profession, as currently practiced and perpetuated by our educational establishment, carries out this role in a very minimal way, and it will continue to serve only minimally or even come to serve less than minimally if the self-imposed constraints of the more usual definitions of accounting are not abandoned.

The proposed definition is general enough also to include national economic and social accounts and economic and social indicators—areas of concern that have not enjoyed adequate attention from accountants. The techniques and problems of measuring the success or performance of a country are of course somewhat different from those related to corporate organizations, but the role of objective articulation, performance monitoring, and accountability to constituencies is common to these settings, and accountants' concern for relevance, objectivity, and freedom from bias applies equally well.

Exchange Transactions and the Bookkeeping Equation

Another reason why the accounting profession is reluctant to respond to today's challenge relates to the assumption that its techniques must be limited to exchange transactions and "events" that are amenable to the use of the bookkeeping equation and entry into financial statements which the bookkeeping equation supports. Accountants are quick to point out the differences between bookkeeping and accounting, yet they allow the duality of the impact of exchange transactions and the neat fit of the entity-oriented bookkeeping equation to establish the limits of "financial reports," and virtually the limits of the role of accounting in society. This self-imposed constraint of the profession was not seriously objectionable a half-century ago, when there was not the perceived need to consider social costs, externalities, and enterprises' responsibility to broad constituencies. It is objectionable now.

Over forty years ago J.M. Clark asked:

> Does anyone really accept the scale of the competitive market? We shall have found such a man, when we have found one who honestly approves of existing conditions of poverty: not one who is resigned to them as an inevitable evil, but one who would not lessen them if he could. So long as this does not represent the prevailing sentiment, so long it will be impossible to say that market value measures "social value" in the sense of "value to society."[18]

Clark was writing as an economist four decades ago, but economists of today recognize the wisdom of his words. Such words also have special relevance to the social accountant of today. Executives of modern corporations must think in terms of generalized social

18. J.M. Clark, *A Preface to Social Economics;* Seidler and Seidler, *Social Accounting,* (Los Angeles: Melville Publishing Co., 1975), p. 33.

values as well as economic values to limited constituencies. Accountants of these modern corporations and accountants in the public arena could provide important assistance.

Accountants do, of course, deal with value concepts, but their techniques apply almost exclusively to economic value concepts as they relate to individual entities and as they are validated in the market place. Although the profession appears to sense great changes that it may champion in connection with "fair value" accounting, its self-imposed constraints continue to establish boundaries that seem almost inviolate. Referring to the possibility of accountants' stretching their domain of activity, Daniel Gray expresses first pessimism and then optimism as he writes:

> Because conventional accounting has been so useful to business, it is only natural to try to stretch it to cover social costs and benefits. . . . We have concluded that traditional corporation accounting is a derivative of, and is coterminous with, the theory of market economy. As such, it is concerned with transactions. Yet the social problems that disturb us most lie outside the realm of transactions. To some extent, they have become problems because they had to be excluded for our theory of a market economy to achieve closure. Accounting has the same kind of closure. It owes its rigor to what it excludes. To try to stretch it to measure all social costs and benefits is to violate its very foundations. Isn't it ironic that a theory that has encouraged us to neglect "externalities" is now embarrassed by its inability to measure "external" distress? It looks to us as though it is not "stretching" but innovation that is required if we are to have social accounting. Accounting has renovated itself in the past—most recently in the areas of national-income accounting and management accounting—and must now do so again.[19]

I suggest that our profession can maintain its rigor and enjoy the closure provided by our conventional approaches relating to the economics of our market system. But we can and should do more. We can develop new approaches to the measurement and communication of social welfare efforts and impacts. We can deal in a broader arena of performance assessment while continuing to improve our ability to perform our conventional role.

Credentials of the Accounting Profession

Since I am concerned both for the need for better information on social costs benefits and for the future of the accounting profession,

19. Daniel Gray, "Methodology: One Approach to the Corporate Social Audit," in Dow Votaw and S. Prakash Sethi, *The Corporate Dilemma: Traditional Values Versus Contemporary Problems* (Englewood Cliffs, N.J.: Prentice-Hall, Inc., 1973), pp. 93–94.

I am naturally led to a conclusion which favors significant involvement of accountants. Some may ask and some have asked, "Why
accountants?"

The conventional roles of accountants and the thrust of their
training have emphasized (1) the design and installation of information detection and measurement systems, (2) the administration
and operation of such systems in an organization, (3) the communication and interpretation of information systems outputs, and (4)
the verification and perhaps attestation of information provided by
such systems. The design of information detection and measurement systems in the social accounting area must rely substantially
on the expertise of social scientists other than accountants. Surely,
psychologists and sociologists must be involved, but involvement
or dependence on outside expertise is of course not at all new for
accountants.

When it comes to the administration and operation of the detection and measurement system and communication of results to appropriate decision points in organizations or in society, accountants
have much to offer. In most instances accountants have "the ear of
management," and increasingly they are becoming oriented toward
a wide-ranging set of users. They have the ability to speak the
language of users and thus affect decisions—the obvious goal of
social accounting.

In the area of attestation of information regarding social performance, accountants should play the primary role, although the development of measurement technology must precede the development of verification, audit, or attestation technology. The inherent
uncertainty related to social performance information may necessarily prevent the development of audit techniques to justify our usual
unqualified opinion, but some degree of assurance may be provided short of attestation. The Committee on Social Measurement
has suggested the concept of a "Redsa," an acronym for "review to
develop a suitable appraisal."[20]

Still another reason for accountants to be more involved in measuring social performance relates to the profession's primary com-
mitment to independence and objectivity and the old saw that "if
accountants don't do it some other group will." It is clear that some
other groups are already involved. For the most part, these groups

20. American Institute of Certified Public Accountants, Committee on Social Measurement, *The Measurement of Corporate Social Performance* (New York: American
Institute of Certified Public Accountants, 1977), p. 255.

such as the Council on Economic Priorities and the consumer advocates come into the field with a motivational bias that assumes or implies varying degrees of social irresponsibility in corporations. Clearly such a bias is contrary to the primary roles of objectivity and independence for important experts. Social activism and social accounting expertise do not mix well. The professional hallmarks of objectivity and freedom from bias in the information function clearly favor the involvement of accountants. Accountants, more than any other obvious group, can enter the field because their expertise is needed, and not because of any perception that corporations are more or less socially responsible than they should be.

We should recognize some of the potential pitfalls of the profession's involvement in social measurement, especially since this new area for accountants relates so directly to human welfare. Mildred Francis has reflected her concerns for our profession's activities in assessing performance of social programs—one aspect of social accounting—charging their lack of expertise, particularly in experimental design and statistical sampling theory. She points out:

> (1) Since the starting point in the development of accounting theory was a set of axioms or postulates, the systems he [the accountant] developed were classification systems which rearranged the facts already contained in the axioms; and (2) whatever system of checks and balances he developed to validate these rearrangements had, as its rationale for existence, the protection of moneys against fraudulent use. . . . Maybe the time has come for society to consider establishing an independent body to put its stamp of approval on statistics and statistical series of public importance. But nothing can be gained by delegating this responsibility to inexperienced people [accountants]—people who are not familiar with statistical theory and its problems, the data needs, and the data collection problems in the functional area of concern.[21]

These concerns are appropriate and perhaps understandable for a statistician with a very narrow view of accounting. And indeed the narrow view is not far from the mark if we consider the history of our profession up to the most recent decade. However the profession itself and the expertise of its members are changing. Axioms and postulates have been useful in implementing the double entry accounting model and "rearranging facts." But these axioms and postulates do not and certainly need not provide boundaries for the accountant's role. Accountants can work effectively—and some are doing so—using both inductive and deductive approaches to

21. M. E. Francis, "Accounting and the Evaluation of Social Programs: A Critical Comment," *Accounting Review*, XLVIII (Apr., 1973), 250—51.

understand and represent economic and social phenomena. "Protection of moneys against fraudulent use" is an important role of the accountant but certainly not the sole "rationale for existence." The suggestion of a new "independent body . . ." is also understandable but probably not a likely response. My view that the accounting profession should respond is made with full recognition of the mind-boggling complexity of this new area that we call social accounting. It is made, nevertheless, on the solid foundation of (1) the substance of the needs of society for social information, and (2) my faith in the capability of present and future members of the profession. While accountants do not all have currently the needed understanding of concepts and the tools of measurement needed for this new area, the profession is rich with perceptive men and women who are committed to serve the information needs of their constituencies—men and women who are capable and willing to develop and apply new paradigms in their activities, new concepts of organizational performance, and new techniques of measurement and communication.

Accounting has relied greatly in the past on measurement concepts of engineering and economics, and of course on algebraic and arithmetic notions. The field must now consider the concepts and possible measurement constructs that may be provided by statisticians, sociologists, psychologists, and perhaps anthropologists. A joining of the expertise of these groups with that of accountants would provide good justification for an optimistic forecast of progress in the new field of social accounting. The accounting profession should, with reasonable modesty, take a leadership role. Accountants should be aggressive participants in the development of social accounting without any thought of preempting any other groups. There are not, I think, too many groups clamoring for primacy in this area. I think, rather, there are probably too few trying to "light the candle" or "get on the learning curve."

Responsibility of Accounting Educators

Accounting education is the principal agent for change in our profession. Accounting educators have a critical responsibility if social accounting is to become a significant part of the activities of the profession. *First,* we, as educators, must instill in our students a view of the broad and honored role of the profession that they aspire to enter. *Second,* we must encourage our students to develop viewpoints and concepts which enable them to grasp the nature and significance of social performance and social well-being. *Third,* we must see that our students develop a firm grasp on the measurement techniques that are most likely to find application in this new area of interest. And *fourth* and finally, we must encourage our students to develop a kind of personal modesty regarding their capability in this field, recognizing the tentative nature of our knowledge in these early days of the development of the area and the dangers as well as the great potential for our profession's involvement.

The educational setting should be one in which optimality is not necessarily synonymous with profit maximization. Concepts of social good and welfare economics should be considered as critical as classical economics with its emphasis on marginalism, price theory, and rather elegant model building which generally ignores individual differences. Psychometrics should be considered as important as econometrics. The setting should be amenable to dealing with concepts of attitudes, judgments, and perceptions and thus with less elegant models that do consider individual differences. Accountants in such an environment should in time become almost as comfortable in dealing with "sensing" technology as they are today with "counting" activities.

These may seem to be almost revolutionary ideas. They should not be interpreted as a weakening of the accounting profession's role in the management of private sector, profit-making organizations or of its service in the maintenance of orderly and active capital markets. They are, rather, expansionistic, based on a conviction that our profession can in time expand its role and become stronger by serving society in a broader spectrum of ways.

Extending the Role of an "Embattled" Profession

Some accountants find entry into the field of social performance accounting particularly unacceptable to them at a time when the profession is experiencing more and more critical pressures from many directions. I suggest that some prodding is in order at this time, especially because of this special juncture in the history of the profession. The profession must resist understandable tendencies to find comfort in safe, continually more limited and less relevant areas. The future of the profession depends far more on its success in fulfilling the legitimate and deeply felt needs of society in the next decades than it does on the resolution of all of the controversial technical issues that it considers day after day, or on the success of its major firms in winning their day in court in connection with pending litigation.

John Lawler made the point very well when speaking to the
Council of AICPA in 1976:

> The mission of accounting is being dramatically redefined by public
> needs—summoning the profession not only to experiment with creative
> approaches to its traditional responsibilities, but to venture forth into
> new areas of service even though that entails the risks inherent in all
> pioneering efforts.
>
> The ogre of legal liability will remain a frightening presence; but the
> most grievous injury that this threat could inflict upon the profession is
> to instill a timidity which inhibits CPAs from achieving their full poten-
> tial in service to society.[22]

We must not claim to be able to do that which the state of the art
does not make possible, but we must not shrink from the effort and
opportunity to extend the state of our art. Measuring the unmeasurable is not possible today, but measuring that which previously
was unmeasurable is always a possibility. As Leo Herbert stated
several years ago:

> . . . to retain its present commanding role in the society and to play a
> more significant one in the future, the accounting profession must legiti-
> mately extend its boundaries and capabilities. It then will not only have
> to accept what changes the environment forces upon it but will be able to
> direct needed changes in social, economic, governmental, and other en-
> vironmental conditions.[23]

A great profession constantly does its research in an effort to prepare for the future. It reviews and anticipates its potential for service
to society. It continually retrains itself to serve in the fullest and most
relevant ways. At the same time, it is expert in highly specialized
areas of service and eclectic in its view of its role in society.

The accounting profession cannot claim such greatness. Accountants continue to cling tenaciously to practices that are crudely
based on the questionable assumption of "the economic man," and
to the double-entry balancing techniques so ingeniously devised in
Italy over five centuries ago.[24] The accounting profession needs to

22. John Lawler, Remarks before the AICPA Council, Boca Raton, Fla., May 3, 1976.
23. Leo Herbert, "A Perspective on Accounting," *Accounting Review,* XLVI (July
1971), 440.
24. This point comes through clearly in the work thus far on the Conceptual
Framework Project of the Financial Accounting Standards Board, where the role of
accounting is visualized as providing "investors" and "lenders" with information
useful in "assessing the risks and returns associated with an investment." Then,
further, it sets out to determine definitions of assets, liabilities, revenues, and expenses and to decide whether the first two or the second two elements should
dominate in keeping the books in balance.

define its role in society—not just to determine the purposes of financial statements. It needs to assess performance of organizations along many dimensions—not just to determine standards for financial accounting. An aggressive move to become involved in measurement and communication of social performance of corporations could contribute to the image and stature of the profession and go far to assure it a bright future.

April 1977

Bibliography

Comprehended within this bibliography are virtually all of Paton's major published writings. Every effort has been to make the list complete, although it is improbable that the compilation is wholly without errors or omissions. We have elected not to include translations into other languages of works originally published in English. Also excluded are reprintings, in anthologies and other collections, of articles already listed. Although we have endeavored to include book reviews and submissions to the federal government, we have made no attempt to cite all of the many occasions when Paton gave testimony before regulatory commissions in the several states.

BOOKS

Principles of Accounting. (Russell Alger Stevenson, co-author.) New York: The Macmillan Co., 1918.

The Economic Position of the United Kingdom: 1912–1918. Economic Studies of Countries during the War. Bureau of Foreign and Domestic Commerce, Misc. Series No. 96. Washington: Government Printing Office, 1919.

Studies prepared for the Bureau of Research and Statistics, War Trade Board, and published in 1919 by the Government Printing Office:
  Japanese Steel and Shipping Negotiations.
  Rationing Agreement with Norway.
  Rationing and Shipping Negotiations with Sweden.
  Requisitioning of Dutch Shipping.
  Trade and Shipping Negotiations with Denmark.
  Trade and Shipping Negotiations with Spain.

Accounting Theory, With Special Reference to the Corporate Enterprise. New York: The Ronald Press Co., 1922. Reprinted, Chicago: A.S.P. Accounting Studies Press, Ltd., 1962; Lawrence, Kan.: Scholars Book Co., 1973.

Accounting. New York: The Macmillan Co., 1924.

Editor, *Accountants' Handbook.* 2d ed. New York: The Ronald Press Co., 1932; 3d ed., 1943.

Corporate Profits as Shown by Audit Reports. New York: National Bureau of Economic Research, Inc., 1935.

Essentials of Accounting. New York: The Macmillan Co., 1938; 2d ed. revised, 1949.

An Introduction to Corporate Accounting Standards. (A. C. Littleton, co-author.) Chicago: American Accounting Association, 1940.

Recent and Prospective Developments in Accounting Theory. Boston: Bureau of Business Research, Graduate School of Business Administration, Harvard Univ., 1940. (Lectures delivered under the Arthur Lowes Dickinson Fund at the Harvard Graduate School of Business Administration in the spring of 1940.)

Advanced Accounting. New York: The Macmillan Co., 1941.

Statement of W. A. Paton Regarding Overstatement and Misinterpretation of Corporate Earnings under Current Conditions. New York: Republic Steel Corporation, 1949.

Asset Accounting. (With the assistance of William A. Paton, Jr.) New York: The Macmillan Co., 1952.

Shirtsleeve Economics: A Commonsense Survey. New York: Appleton-Century-Crofts, Inc., 1952.

Statement of W. A. Paton Regarding the Interpretation of Corporate Earnings and the Position of Stockholders under Current Conditions. New York: Republic Steel Corporation, 1952.

Corporation Accounts and Statements: An Advanced Course. (With the assistance of William A. Paton, Jr.) New York: The Macmillan Co., 1955.

Essentials of Accounting. (Robert L. Dixon, co-author.) New York: The Macmillan Co., 1958.

Make-or-Buy Decisions in Tooling for Mass Production. (Robert L. Dixon, co-author.) Michigan Business Reports, No. 35. Ann Arbor, Mich.: Bureau of Business Research, School of Business Administration, The Univ. of Michigan, 1961.

Corporate Profits: Measurement, Reporting, Distribution, Taxation; A Survey for Laymen and Accountants. Homewood, Ill.: Richard D. Irwin, Inc., 1965.

Assets—Accounting and Administration. (William A. Paton, Jr., co-author.) Warren, Mich.: Roberts & Roehl, Inc., 1971.

ARTICLES

"Severity of Trade Cycle in America," *Current Economic Problems*. Edited by Walton H. Hamilton. Chicago: University of Chicago Press, 1915, pp. 265-67.

"Theory of the Double-Entry System," *Journal of Accountancy*, XXIII (January, 1917), 7-26.

"Significance and Treatment of Appreciation in the Accounts," *Twentieth Annual Report, 1918*. Edited for the Michigan Academy of Science by G.H. Coons. Ann Arbor: Michigan Academy of Science, 1918, pp. 35-49.

"Some Phases of Capital Stock," *Journal of Accountancy*, XXVII (May, 1919), 321-35.

"Transactions between Partner and Firm," *Journal of Accountancy*, XXVIII (July, 1919), 33-38.

"Proprietors' Salaries," *Journal of Political Economy*, XXVIII (March, 1920), 240-56.

"Some Current Valuation Accounts," *Journal of Accountancy*, XXIX (May, 1920), 335-50.

"Depreciation, Appreciation and Productive Capacity," *Journal of Accountancy*, XXX (July, 1920), 1-11.

"The Drug Store's Overhead," *American Druggist*, LXVIII (September, 1920), 17-24.

"Interest during Construction," *Journal of Political Economy*, XXVIII (October, 1920), 680–95.

"Methods of Measuring Business Income," *Administration*, I (April, 1921), 509–26.

"Assumptions of the Accountant," *Administration*, I (June, 1921), 786–802.

"The Pro and Con of a Sales Tax," *Administration*, II (September, 1921), 367–72.

"The Valuation of Inventories," *Papers and Proceedings of the Fifth Annual Meeting*, American Association of University Instructors in Accounting. Chicago, 1921, pp. 66–77.

"Inventory Valuation," *Administration*, III (March, 1922), 291–302.

"The Relation of Accounting Training to Economics," *Commerce and Administration*, II (March, 1922), 110–12.

"Dividends in Securities," *Administration*, IV (October, 1922), 394–402.

"Valuation of Inventories," *Journal of Accountancy*, XXXIV (December, 1922), 432–50.

"The Educational Value of Training in Accounting," (President's Address) *Papers and Proceedings of the Seventh Annual Meeting*, American Association of University Instructors in Accounting. Chicago, 1922, pp. 66-73.

"Simplification of Federal Income Taxation," *Certified Public Accountant*, II (June, 1923), 141–43.

"Tendencies in Accounting Literature," *Papers and Proceedings of the Ninth Annual Meeting*, American Association of University Instructors in Accounting. Chicago, 1924, pp. 64–69.

"Shall Whole Matter of International Debt Settlements Be Re-opened?" *American Accountant*, XII (February, 1927), 17, 62.

"Accrued Depreciation on Seasoned Properties," *Certified Public Accountant*, VII (July, 1927), 206–10.

"Distribution Costs and Inventory Values," *Accounting Review*, II (September, 1927), 246–53.

"The Program in Accounting at Michigan," *Michigan Alumnus*, XXXIV (February, 1928), 167–68.

"Limitations of Financial and Operating Ratios," *Accounting Review*, III (September, 1928), 252–60.

"Special Applications of Discounting," *Journal of Accountancy*, XLVI (October, 1928), 270–82.

"How Michigan Trains Her Young Men for Accountancy Careers," *American Accountant*, XIV (September, 1929), 495–96.

"The Dividend Code," *Accounting Review*, IV (December, 1929), 218–20.

"Economic Theory in Relation to Accounting Valuation," *Accounting Review*, VI (June, 1931), 89–96.

"Working Capital in Public Utility Regulation," *Journal of Accountancy*, LIV (October, 1932), 287–99.

"Accounting Problems of the Depression," *Accounting Review*, VII (December, 1932), 258–67.

" 'Shoestring' Banking," *Certified Public Accountant*, XIII (June, 1933), 333–38.

"Public Ownership Unnecessary," *Public Service Magazine*, LVI (February, 1934), 41–42.

"Shortcomings of Present-Day Financial Statements," *Journal of Accountancy*, LVII (February, 1934), 108–32.

"Aspects of Asset Valuations," *Accounting Review*, IX (June, 1934), 122–29.

"Costs and Profits in Present-Day Accounting," *National Association of Cost Accountants Bulletin*, XVI (October 1, 1934), 123–39.

"Valuation of the Business Enterprise," *Accounting Review*, XI (March, 1936), 26–32.

"Presentation of Bond Discount," *Accounting Review*, XII (September, 1937), 285–90.

"Comments on *A Statement of Accounting Principles*," *Journal of Accountancy*, LXV (March, 1938), 196–207.

"Is It Desirable to Distinguish between the Various Kinds of Surplus," *Journal of Accountancy*, LXV (April, 1938), 285–89.

"The 'Gross Profit' Convention," *Accounting Forum*, IX (October, 1938), 19–20.

"Principles Related to 'Deferred Charges' and 'Prepaid Expenses,' " *Papers on Accounting Principles and Procedures*. New York: American Institute of Accountants, 1938, pp. 26–30.

"Recording Revenue on Other Bases Than Sales," *Accounting Ledger*, I (April, 1939), 22–24.

"Income and the Inventory Problem," *Proceedings of the Dedication of Vincent Hall*. Minneapolis: Univ. of Minnesota, 1939.

"Objectives of Accounting Research," *Papers on Auditing Procedure and Other Accounting Subjects*. New York: American Institute of Accountants, 1939, pp. 229–33.

"Last-In, First-Out," *Journal of Accountancy*, LXIX (May, 1940), 354–60.

"Analysis of Financial Statements," *Cost and Management*, XXII (September, 1940), 303–19.

"Basic Concepts in Property Accounting," *Edison Electric Institute Bulletin*, IX (March, 1941), 93–96. (Address at Fourth National Accounting Conference, Detroit, Michigan, December, 1940.)

"Accounting Reports," *Proceedings of the Third Annual Institute of Accounting*. Columbus: Ohio State Univ., 1940, pp. 5–12.

"The Cost Approach to Inventories," *Journal of Accountancy*, LXXII (October, 1941), 300–307.

"Comments on *The Cost Principle* by Walter A. Staub," *Accounting Review*, XVII (January, 1942), 10–19.

"Accounting," *Encyclopedia Americana*, Vol. I. New York: Americana Corporation, 1943—.

"Adaptation of the Income Statement to Present Conditions," *Journal of Accountancy*, LXXV (January, 1943), 8–15.

"Classification and Sequences in Financial Statements," *Accounting Problems in War Contract Termination, Taxes, and Postwar Planning*. New York: American Institute of Accountants, 1943, pp. 57–67.

"Simplification of Federal Tax Administration," *Accounting Review*, XIX (January, 1944), 11–19.

"Accounting Policies of the Federal Power Commission—A Critique," *Journal of Accountancy*, LXXVII (June, 1944), 432–60.

"Responsibilities of the Postwar Accountant," *Ohio Certified Public Accountant*, III (June, 1944), 1.

"Modern Reports to Stockholders," *Current Considerations for Controllers* (Annual Meeting Proceedings, No. 2). New York: Controllers Institute of America, 1944, pp. 116–24.

"Responsibilities and Training of the Postwar Accountant," *Proceedings of the Seventh Annual Institute on Accounting.* Columbus: Ohio State Univ., 1944, pp. 6–18.

"Transactions between Affiliates," *Accounting Review,* XX (July, 1945), 255–66.

"Current Economic Fallacies," *Commercial and Financial Chronicle,* CLXII (August 23, 1945), 825, 843.

"Balance Sheet," Chapter II of *Contemporary Accounting.* Edited by Thomas W. Leland. New York: American Institute of Accountants, 1945.

"Cost and Value in Accounting," *Journal of Accountancy,* LXXXI (March, 1946), 192–99.

"Accounting Policies and Management," *Proceedings of the Accounting Conference.* Chicago: Illinois Society of Certified Public Accountants, 1946, pp. 11–16.

"Restoration of Fixed Assets to the Balance Sheet—Second Affirmative." *Accounting Review,* XXII (April, 1947), 198–200.

"The Queue Society—Do We Want It?" *Michigan Alumnus Quarterly Review,* LIII (May, 1947), 185–91.

"The Accountant and Private Enterprise," *Journal of Accountancy,* LXXXV (January, 1948), 44–58.

"What Is Actual Cost in Depreciation Accounting?" *Journal of Accountancy,* LXXXV (March, 1948), 206–7.

"Accounting Procedures and Private Enterprise," *Journal of Accountancy,* LXXXV (April, 1948), 278–91.

"Depreciation and the Price Level—Second Affirmative," *Accounting Review,* XXIII (April, 1948), 118–23.

"Some Comments on Group and Sectional Interests," *Michigan Alumnus Quarterly Review,* LIV (May, 1948), 203–8.

"Analysis of Financial Statements," *Cost and Management,* XXII (September, 1948), 303–19.

"Why Corporate Profits Are Overstated," *Commercial and Financial Chronicle,* CLXVIII (December 16, 1948), 2, 33–35.

"Basis for Adequate Financial Reporting," *Organization Controls and Executive Compensation.* New York: American Management Association, 1948, pp. 34–44.

"1948 Revision of the American Accounting Association's Statement of Principles: Comments on Item 5, under 'Expense,' " *Accounting Review,* XXIV (January, 1949), 49–53.

"Profits Are *Not* Too High," *Credit and Financial Management,* LI (January, 1949), 15–17, 28–29.

"Financing Problems as Seen by the Accountant," *Credit and Financial Management,* LI (September, 1949), 18–20.

"Lack of Venture Capital," *National Savings and Loan Journal*, IV (September, 1949), 23–24.

"Semantics of Annual Reporting," *Annual Report Forum*. Ann Arbor: Detroit Trust Company in Co-operation with the School of Business Administration, Univ. of Michigan, 1949, pp. 4–11.

"Accounting Problems Relating to the Reporting of Profits," *Proceedings of a Public Forum*, with J. K. Lasser and Herbert E. Hetu. New Wilmington, Pa.: Economic and Business Foundation, 1949, pp. 8–23.

"Measuring Profits under Inflation Conditions: A Serious Problem for Accountants," *Journal of Accountancy*, LXXXIX (January, 1950), 16–27.

"Economic and Accounting Aspects of Pension Plans," *Michigan Certified Public Accountant*, II (September, 1950), 5–6.

"Use of Accounting Data in Economic Analysis," *Accounts and Taxes*. Kentucky Institute on Accounting and Tax Practitioners Forum Bulletin, No. 21. Lexington, Ky.: Bureau of Business Research, College of Commerce, Univ. of Kentucky, 1950, pp. 66–83.

"How Have Stockholders Been Faring?" *Michigan Business Review*, IV (May, 1952), 8–13.

"Should the SEC Continue to 'Study' Utility System Operation?" *Public Utilities Fortnightly*, L (October 9, 1952), 473–80.

"Common Sense—The Curb to Public Spending," *Tax Digest*, XXXI (March, 1953), 81–86.

"Utility Rates Must Recognize Dollar Depreciation," Howard C. Greer, co-author, *Public Utilities Fortnightly*, LI (March 12, 1953), 333–56.

"Unless We Have Courage—Spending Won't Be Cut Until 'Handout' Demands Stop," *Tax Outlook* (April, 1953), 9–11.

"The Curb to Public Spending—There's No Such Thing as a Free Lunch," *Public Service Magazine*, XCV (July, 1953), 4–8.

"Premature Revenue Recognition," *Journal of Accountancy*, XCVI (October, 1953), 432–37.

"The Depreciation Deduction—A Neglected Aspect," *Michigan Business Review*, V (November, 1953), 23–26.

"Effect of Inflation on Measurement of Cost and Income," *Underwear News* (August, 1959), pp. 4, 16–20.

"Depreciation—Concept and Measurement," *Journal of Accountancy*, CVIII (October, 1959), 38–43.

"Insufficient Depreciation: What It Does To The Economy," *Current Business Studies*, Nos. 32–33. New York: Society of Business Advisory Professions, Inc., 1959, pp. 26–40.

"Depreciation Deduction—LIFO Principle Should Be Extended to Cover Depreciable Plant," *Tax Revision Compendium*, II (1959), 877–90.

"Measuring the Depreciation Deduction," *Proceedings of the Conference of the Great Lakes Utility Commissioners.* Columbus, Ohio: Great Lakes Railroad and Utility Commissioners, 1960, pp. 59–65.

"More Squeeze on Earning Power Could Spell Trouble," *Credit and Financial Management,* LXIII (January, 1961), 11–12.

" 'Deferred Income'—A Misnomer," *Journal of Accountancy,* CXII (September, 1961), 38–40.

"Taxpayer Support for Higher Education in Michigan—Some Sidelights," *The Detroiter,* LII (September 25, 1961), 6–7.

"The Tale of the Little Red Hen," *The Freeman,* XXI (November, 1961), 18–19.

"On Going Underground," *Michigan Quarterly Review,* I (January, 1962), 19–26.

"The 'Cash Flow' Illusion," *Accounting Review,* XXXVIII (April, 1963), 243–51.

"Accounting and Utilization of Resources," *Journal of Accounting Research,* I (Spring, 1963), 44–72.

"Incredible Schlude Decision," *The Michigan CPA,* XV (July-August, 1963), 17–18.

"Comments on Stock Options," *Michigan Business Review,* XV (November, 1963), 21–26.

"The Beetle and the Centipede," *The Freeman,* XIII (October, 1963), 27–29.

"Middle-of-the-Roadism—A Questionable Stance," *Michigan Quarterly Review,* II (Winter, 1963), 22–26.

"Let's *First* Mend Tommy's Trousers," *The Freeman,* XV (January, 1965), 12–17.

"U.S.A.—Disaster Area," *The Freeman,* XVI (February, 1966), 16–20.

"Controlling HCL," *The Freeman,* XVII (January, 1967), 25–31.

"Some Reflections on Education and Professoring," *Accounting Review,* XLII (January, 1967), 7–23.

"Why Splits?" *Michigan Business Review,* XX (January, 1968), 16–19.

"Observations on Inflation from an Accounting Stance," *Journal of Accounting Research,* VI (Spring, 1968), 72–85.

"Comments" in *Accounting for Goodwill,* Accounting Research Study No. 10, by George R. Catlett and Norman O. Olson. New York: American Institute of Certified Public Accountants, 1968, 143–51.

"An Inquiry Concerning Inequality," *The Freeman,* XIX (January, 1969), 53–60.

"Postscript on 'Treasury Shares,' " *Accounting Review,* XLIV (April, 1969), 276–83.

"Funds, Flows, and Fancies," *U.S. Army Audit Agency Bulletin,* (Winter, 1969), 49–59.

"The E's Have It," *The Freeman*, XX (February, 1970), 108–21.

"The Protesters," *The Freeman*, XXI (January, 1971), 51–59.

"Earmarks of a Profession—And the APB," *Journal of Accountancy*, CXXXI (January, 1971), 37–45.

"Do Casualties Accrue?" *Michigan Business Review*, XXIII (November, 1971), 20–24.

"Accounting's Educational Eclipse," *Journal of Accountancy*, CXXXII (December, 1971), 35–37.

"Let's Recognize Depreciation in Government Operations," *GAO Review*, (Winter, 1971), pp. 38–44.

"Recollections Re a Kindred Spirit," in *Toward Liberty*, a collection of essays honoring the 90th birthday of Ludwig von Mises. Menlo Park, Calif.: Institute of Humane Studies, 1971, vol. II, pp. 249–67.

"Can We Sustain Prosperity?" *The Freeman*, XXII (January, 1972), 33–41.

"Who Is the Marginal Producer?" *The Freeman*, XXII (March, 1972), 160–63.

"5° Above Zero," *The Freeman*, XXII (October, 1972), 612–15.

"Inflation—Measurement, Impact, Culprits," *Financial Executive*, XL (November, 1972), 48–60; XL (December, 1972), 44–54.

"Back to Basics—Fable of the Berry Pickers," *The Freeman*, XXII (December, 1972), 707–14.

"Comments on the Role of Professional Accountants," *Michigan CPA*, XXIV (January-February, 1973), 11–13.

"What P-R-O-D-U-C-T-I-O-N Means," *Michigan Business Review*, XXV (March, 1973), 7–8.

"Financial Misrepresentation and Measurement," *Financial Executive*, XLI (April, 1973), 14–21.

"Competition—What and When?" *The Freeman*, XXIII (June, 1973), 353–65.

"The Gullible Society," *The Freeman*, XXIV (January, 1974), 3–9.

"Accounting Today—A Bird's-Eye View," *Michigan Business Review*, XXVI (January, 1974), 22–25.

"The 'Social Security' Mirage—Current Production Paramount," *The Freeman*, XXIV (March, 1974), 167–71.

"Facts and Fallacies in Business Finance," *Financial Executive*, XLII (June, 1974), 76–82.

"Opportunity for the Financial Accounting Standards Board," *Michigan CPA*, XXV (May-June, 1974), 27–30.

"Some Amendments to Interest and Profit Theory," *Michigan Business Review*, XXVI (September, 1974), 16–24, 33–35.

"Significance of Services—Hiring and Firing," *The Freeman*, XXV (January, 1975), 48–57.

"Sensitivity to Dollar Devaluation—Bane or Blessing?" *Michigan CPA*, XXVI (January-February, 1975), 9–11.

"An Ancient Fable Retold," *The Freeman*, XXVI (March, 1976), 150–54.

"Notes on Handicapping," *The Accounting Historian*, III (Spring, 1976), 4.

BOOK REVIEWS

Review of *Income in the United States: Its Amount and Distribution, 1909–1919* (New York: National Bureau of Economic Research, 1922), in *Journal of the American Statistical Association*, XVIII (June, 1923), 804–8.

Review of *Anthracite Accounting and Finance*, Statement to the United States Coal Commission by the Anthracite Representatives of the United Mine Workers of America, 1923, in *Journal of the American Statistical Association*, XVIII (December, 1923), 1071–73.

Review of *Studies in the Economics of Overhead Costs*, by J. Maurice Clark (Chicago: University of Chicago Press, 1923), in *Journal of the American Statistical Association*, XIX (June, 1924), 257–59.

Review of *Interest as a Cost*, by Clinton H. Scovell (New York: Ronald Press Co., 1924): in *American Economic Review*, XV (March, 1925), 321–26.

Review of *Managerial Accounting*, I, by J.O. McKinsey (Chicago: University of Chicago Press, 1924): in *Journal of Political Economy*, XXXIII (August, 1925), 470–72.

Review of *Theory of Accounts*, by D. R. Scott (New York: Henry Holt, 1925), in *Journal of the American Statistical Association*, XXI (March, 1926), 102–5.

Review of *Retail Accounting and Control*, by Albert C. Hodge (Chicago: University of Chicago Press, 1925), in *Journal of Political Economy*, XXXIV (December, 1926), 782–83.

Review of *Income in the Various States: Its Sources and Distribution, 1919, 1920, and 1921*, by Maurice Leven and Assistants (New York: National Bureau of Economic Research, 1925), in *Journal of the American Statistical Association*, XX (March, 1927), 116–18.

Review of *Survey Course in Accounting*, by Wesley James McCarty and L. Cleveland Amidon (New York: Prentice-Hall, Inc., 1926), in *Journal of Political Economy*, XXXVI (February, 1928), 174–76.

Review of *Accounting Method*, by C. Rufus Rorem (Chicago: University of Chicago Press, 1928), in *Accounting Review*, III (December, 1928), 411–13.

Review of *Consolidated Balance Sheets*, by George Hillis Newlove (New York: Ronald Press, 1926), in *Journal of the American Statistical Association*, XXIV (March, 1929), 96–97.

Review of *Economic Rhythm, A Theory of Business Cycles*, by Ernst Wagemann (New York: McGraw-Hill, 1930), in *Accounting Review*, VI (March, 1931), 75–76.

Review of *A Source-Book for the Study of Industrial Profits*, by R.C. Epstein and F.M.A. Clark (Washington, D.C.: Government Printing Office, 1932), in *American Economic Review*, XXIV (March, 1934), 172–73.

Review of *The Depreciation of Capital, Analytically Considered,* by R. F. Fowler (London: P. S. King, 1934), in *American Economic Review,* XXIV (December, 1934), 726–27.

Review of *Accounting,* by Charles H. Porter and Wyman P. Fiske (New York: Henry Holt, 1935), in *American Economic Review,* XXVI (March, 1936), 122–24.

Review of *Engineering Valuation,* by Anson Marston and Thomas R. Agg (New York: McGraw-Hill, 1936), in *American Economic Review,* XXVII (March, 1937), 155–57.

Review of *Studies in Income and Wealth,* I, Conference on Research in National Income and Wealth (New York: National Bureau of Economic Research, 1937), in *Journal of Accountancy,* LXVII (January, 1939), 63.

Review of *Depreciation: Principles and Application,* by Earl A. Saliers (New York: Ronald Press, 1939), in *Journal of Political Economy,* XLVII (October, 1939), 735–38.

Review of *Capital Consumption and Adjustment,* by Solomon Fabricant (New York: National Bureau of Economic Research, 1938), in *Journal of Accoun tancy,* LXVIII (November, 1939), 358–59.

Review of *Truth in Accounting,* by Kenneth MacNeal (Philadelphia: University of Pennsylvania Press, 1939), in *Journal of Political Economy,* XLVIII (April, 1940), 296–98.

Review of *The Taxation of Corporate Income,* by Charles John Gaa (Urbana, Ill.: University of Illinois Press, 1944), in *American Economic Review,* XXXV (December, 1945), 976–78.

Review of *Accounting: Administrative/Financial,* by George R. Husband (Philadelphia: Chilton Co., 1960), in *Accounting Review,* XXXV (July, 1960), 572–73.

Review of *Principles of Public Utility Rates,* by James C. Bonbright (New York: Columbia University Press, 1961), in *Accounting Review,* XXXVII (January, 1962), 166–69.

CORRESPONDENCE

"Some Phases of Capital Stock," *Journal of Accountancy,* XXVIII (August, 1919), 158–60.

"Some Phases of Capital Stock," *Journal of Accountancy,* XXVIII (November, 1919), 474–77. "A Statement of Accounting Principles," *Journal of Accountancy,* LXV (April, 1938), 328.

"A Question of Usage," *Journal of Accountancy,* CI (June, 1956), 24.

Reproduction of correspondence with Howard C. Greer, *Accounting Review,* XXI (January, 1946), 85–88.

"An Application of Replacement Value Theory," *Journal of Accountancy,* CX (September, 1960), 31–33.

"Tax Reform for Goodwill," *Tax Adviser,* II (May, 1971), 262.

"Pollution Cost," *Journal of Accountancy*, CXXXIII (June, 1972), 28, 30.

"Calendars and Time Zones," *Journal of Accountancy*, CXXXIII (June, 1972), 28.

The Accounting Historian, III (Winter, 1976), 4.

Submissions to the Federal Government

Revenue revision. Hearings before the Committee on Ways and Means, House of Representatives, 72d Congress, 1st Session, January 13, 1932 (Statement, pp. 366–71).

Corporate profits. Hearings before the Joint Committee on the Economic Report, U.S. Congress, 80th Congress, 2d Session, December 7, 1948 (Statement, pp. 53–77).

General revenue revision. Hearings before the Committee on Ways and Means, House of Representatives, 83d Congress, 1st Session, Part II, July 22, 1953 (Statement, pp. 699–704).

Financial policy for the Post Office Department. A statement by the Post Office Department, 1954 (letter on "nonapplication of 'incremental cost' principle to postal cost accounting," dated January 22, 1954, pp. 221–25).

Federal tax policy for economic growth and stability. Papers submitted by panelists appearing before the Subcommittee on Tax Policy, Joint Committee on the Economic Report, U.S. Congress, 84th Congress, 1st Session, November 9, 1955 ("Significance of Depreciation Accounting with Special Reference to Plant Replacement," pp. 528–38).

Federal tax policy for economic growth and stability. Hearings before the Subcommittee on Tax Policy, Joint Committee on the Economic Report, U.S. Congress, 84th Congress, 1st Session, December 13, 1955 (Panel discussion, pp. 417–56).

Postal rate revision. Hearings before the Committee on Post Office and Civil Service, House of Representatives, 84th Congress, 2d Session (Letter dated March 14, 1956, pp. 195–96).

Postal rate revision. Hearings before the Committee on Post Office and Civil Service, House of Representatives, 85th Congress, 1st Session (Letter dated March 15, 1957, p. 706).

General revenue revision. Hearings before the Committee on Ways and Means, House of Representatives, 85th Congress, 2d Session, Part II, January 30, 1958 (Statement, pp. 2402–25).

Tax revision compendium. Compendium of papers on broadening the tax base, submitted to the Committee on Ways and Means, House of Representatives, 86th Congress, 1st Session, Volume II ("The Depreciation Deduction—Lifo Principle Should be Extended to Cover Depreciable Plant," pp. 877–90).

Income tax revision. Panel discussion before the Committee on Ways and Means, House of Representatives, 86th Congress, 1st Session, November 30, 1959 (Statement, pp. 416–19).

Economic concentration. Hearings before the Subcommittee on Antitrust and Monopoly, Committee on the Judiciary, Senate, 89th Congress, 1st Session. Part IV, August-September, 1965 (Statement on make-or-buy decisions, pp. 1855–61.)

Statement regarding the overstatement and misinterpretation of corporate earnings under current conditions. In the matter of United Steelworkers of America—CIO and Republic Steel Corporation, et al., before the Presidential Steel Board, August 19, 1949.

Statement regarding the interpretation of corporate earnings and the position of stockholders under current conditions. In the matter of United Steelworkers of America—CIO and various steel and iron ore companies, before the steel panel, Wage Stabilization Board, February 14, 1952.

MISCELLANEOUS WRITINGS

Editorial Note, in Maurice Moonitz, *The Entity Theory of Consolidated Statements.* Bloomington, Ind.: American Accounting Association, 1944, pp. 52–53.

Foreword to the reissue of Henry W. Sweeney, *Stabilized Accounting.* New York: Holt, Rinehart and Winston, Inc., 1964, pp. xiii–xv.

Introduction, in Williard E. Stone (ed.), *Foundations of Accounting Theory.* Gainesville, Fla.: University of Florida Press, 1971, pp. ix–xi.

Foreword to the reissue of Charles E. Sprague, *The Philosophy of Accounts.* Lawrence, Kans.: Scholars Book Co., 1972, pp. iii–vii.

Response, in *Economic Calculation Under Inflation.* Indianapolis, Ind.: Liberty Fund, Inc., 1976, pp. 65–72.